LEADERSHIP
OF GIRL SCOUT TROOPS

LEADERSHIP

OF GIRL SCOUT TROOPS

CONCERNING THE INTERMEDIATE PROGRAM
FOR GIRL SCOUTS TEN THROUGH THIRTEEN

ILLUSTRATED BY CATHARINE C. LEWIS

PROGRAM DEPARTMENT
GIRL SCOUTS OF THE UNITED STATES OF AMERICA
155 EAST 44TH STREET, NEW YORK 17, N. Y.

Catalog No. 20-115, 75 cents

Contents

Dear Leader

WHEN THIS BOOK comes into your hands for the first time, we hope that you will give it a fair chance to fulfill its chief purpose—to help make your job as a leader of an Intermediate Girl Scout troop an interesting and rewarding job.

You can help us correct its faults in some later edition, if you will. Certainly without the direct assistance of many leaders like yourself it would not be in your hands today.

This is a handbook, of course, for reference and study, though at times we trust it will engross your attention and stimulate your imagination somewhat as indicated by our symbolic reader at the beginning of each chapter.

The illustrations and charts are an intrinsic part of the handbook itself, and will repay your study of them. We owe a special debt to our artist, Miss Catharine C. Lewis, for using her skill and keen observation to our great advantage.

This book was first written and published during a World War that touched all nations and affected, directly or indirectly, all youth. We have learned during these past years that the fundamental needs of young people do not change, but that certain ones are highlighted and receive special attention as conditions in a country change.

One great fact of national importance has been called forcibly to our attention—we cannot and must not neglect the right kind of adult guidance and leadership for youth, the kind of guidance that helps develop democratic attitudes, acceptable social behavior, the practice of useful skills, and a zest for life. The fundamentals of good leadership for youth groups are the same—in war or peace.

The Girl Scout program with its flexible plan and its definite suggestions has stood the test of time. It has proved capable of adaptation to national emergencies and local differences. Suggestions for all the things that our country has asked of girls may be found within the covers of the *Girl Scout Handbook*. Physical fitness, service suggestions, conservation of food and other resources, morale-building activities, and democratic ways of work are an integral part of the Girl Scout program. You, as a leader, need only current suggestions on how to use the wealth of Girl Scout program material in relation to today's needs. With the suggestions included in this book on program planning, on knowing girls, and on working with one's community, you can feel confident that your troop program can be both timely and significant.

Nearly forty years of experience in working with girls have given the Girl Scout organization a great reservoir of information on what girls like to do and on what leaders need to know. We are grateful to all the leaders of Girl Scout troops who have contributed to this reservoir. We wish to thank the committee members and staff members all over the United States who read the manuscript of this book in preparation and gave us constructive suggestions and the benefit of their practical experience. The material from the leaders' *Correspondence Course* will be found incorporated in chapters five through ten. Records and troop experiences contributed by leaders will be found in these pages.

Sit down, now, with this book, but take it in small doses. Mark the sections you will want to go back to and indicate those that seem inadequate or unclear. A careful use of the Index should aid you in finding answers to most of your questions.

We have enjoyed preparing your book; we hope you will find it useful and, at times, entertaining.

EDITH W. CONANT

MARTHA JANE SMITH

A Code for Citizenship

THE GIRL SCOUT PROMISE

On my honor I will try:
To do my duty to God and my country,
To help other people at all times,
To obey the Girl Scout Laws.

THE GIRL SCOUT LAWS

I. A Girl Scout's honor is to be trusted.
II. A Girl Scout is loyal.
III. A Girl Scout's duty is to be useful
    and to help others.
IV. A Girl Scout is a friend to all and a sister
    to every other Girl Scout.
V. A Girl Scout is courteous.
VI. A Girl Scout is a friend to animals.
VII. A Girl Scout obeys orders.
VIII. A Girl Scout is cheerful.
IX. A Girl Scout is thrifty.
X. A Girl Scout is clean in thought, word,
    and deed.

Chapter One

Leadership of Youth

You WHO ARE READING this book are interested in children, or you would not have this volume in your hand. Perhaps you are going to take over the leadership of a group of girls and are wondering what it will mean to you and to them. This chapter aims to give you a picture of the part Girl Scouting can play in citizenship training, and to show you why adult leadership in a youth program is a significant piece of community service.

The material includes:

What girls want and need.
The place of Girl Scouting in a modern community.
What girls get from membership in a Girl Scout troop.
The importance of the volunteer leader.

IN YOUTH LIES THE FUTURE

DEEP INTEREST in the growing up of young people is as old as history. Every tribe, community, or nation has realized that youth was a valuable asset for its own future. Parents, religious leaders, and the community were all concerned—whether the youth was coming of age in Samoa, preparing for life in a Spartan state, or growing up in a community that is feeling its way toward world citizenship.

Whatever methods were used to educate and develop the character of boys and girls, there were certain common elements, such as:

The desire to hand on to the next generation what the wise men had found to be true.

Skills that were necessary for survival.

The feeling of pride in and loyalty to one's own clan, state, or nation.

Those of us living in this twentieth century have recent evidence of how the education of young people in one country can affect the entire world. We do not need an excursion into ancient history to understand that what happens to youth in one nation can influence all nations; that what happens to youth in one community can become nation-wide. Everything we plan these days must fit into a world picture frame.

Therefore, it seems essential that each of us has a share in seeing that the boys and girls of our community get the kind of citizenship training that will make a better world for all youth.

GIRLS ARE IMPORTANT

There was once a time when the current educational theory for girls was based on the fact that woman's place was in the home; her education and abilities were carefully centered around present and future homemaking activities. This was probably never quite as true as the fathers, brothers, and husbands thought it to be, but still it did limit a girl's opportunities. Home is still of vital importance to a woman, but now homemaking is one of many responsibilities. Even our mothers and grandmothers, who worked for equal educational opportunities and the right to vote, had little conception of the enormous responsibilities that face the women of tomorrow. Probably few of them envisioned women in the Army and Navy, women riveting and welding, women engineers, women in every trade and occupation that seemed to demand masculine stamina and brains. For better or worse, boys and girls are growing up into a world that concedes the potential equality of the mental, physical, and spiritual power of men and women.

This puts a grave responsibility on those who are bringing up girls—as new privileges and freedoms lie ahead. The trial and error casualties may be great, unless wise guidance and a sense of responsibility accompany the growing up of this important new citizen. For there is one thing that woman still retains, an influence for good or bad that is peculiarly her own. As long as she bears the children and influences their early years, as long as the children and men of her family love and respect her, she is a most potent force in developing the kind of world and the kind of community in which we wish to live.

What Girls Want and Need

A girl growing up these days needs a variety of things. She needs friends of her own age and the feeling that they like and accept her for what she is. She wants to feel important and useful as an individual by knowing how to do some things well. She wants information on all sorts of subjects—some of which she does not get in school or at home. She wants plenty of activity that is lively, fun, adventurous. She must have ideals and a religious faith. She wants an older, understanding friend to whom she can talk. The trust and affection of older people, both within and without her family circle, are very important to her—although often one would never suspect it.

She needs all of these things to satisfy her zest for life and to help her grow up into a mature woman ready to take a responsible place in the home and community. For it is only as we grow older that we realize that happiness is a subtle thing—depending on satisfying work, right human relationships, and spiritual maturity. Girls need to see the problems of ethics, group living, and democracy worked out in a girl-sized setting they can understand. A community that cares for its own future will see that girls have this opportunity.

[4]

THE MODERN COMMUNITY

The complex life of a modern community, large or small, and the widening of our citizenship horizons make two vital facts stand out today. Communities must contain people who can work together and organizations that will cooperate. We need citizens of character, with public as well as private integrity. Unless our young people learn how to plan together, to understand and accept racial and religious differences, and to apply a socially acceptable code to their own activities, the cause of democracy is lost. Lip service is not enough.

There is a nation-wide need for more citizens who know more about governing themselves, and who are strong enough and resourceful enough to put into action the things they know should be done. If more Americans were aware of the importance of training youth for responsibilities as well as privileges, and for practical cooperation as well as good intentions, then millions, instead of thousands, of girls would be prepared to take their place not only in the home but in community and national affairs. America can work for the conditions that maintain peace only if its women, as well as its men, are trained to make democracy work.

This training starts in the home with family life. Ideals are inculcated in the religious teachings of the church. Schools add knowledge and practice for democratic citizenship. Yet, we all know that no action or attitude becomes an integral part of us until we have practiced it over a period of time and found that it works to our satisfaction. The ideal practice and proving ground for working with others is in a group that is chosen by the individual when compulsion is removed.

Standards that seem important are set by one's own crowd, and great effort is made to live up to them. Discipline is received best when applied by a chosen group of friends. That is why leisure-time activities become so significant, why clubs that children join of their own free will have so much influence in character development.

In all schools, no matter how good, there is an element of compulsion: the children must go to school; the teacher must do what is expected of her; her pupils must, if it is humanly possible, make the grade, pass examinations—or whatever is the ideal of that particular school. In leisure-time clubs, on the other hand, both leaders and girls

[5]

Constructive leisure-time activities develop resourceful and responsible young citizens.

Free time with nothing interesting to do leads to boredom, mischief, or unhappiness.

are there because they want to be; they have chosen just this relationship, hence there is a potential freedom for creative thought and action that is not often found elsewhere. Learning takes place best when the learner is having a good time.

So potent a force for education and character training have these groups become that our modern communities support and finance organizations, such as the Girl Scouts, that undertake to select and train group leaders for this contribution to community life. A local Girl Scout council representing various aspects of community life guides the work of the organization in the larger towns and cities. In small towns a committee of civic-minded men and women takes the responsibility for backing individual troops. Group work is a vocation to some, an avocation to others—but it is service for all.

It is essential that all organizations concerned with the welfare of young people should work together harmoniously in a community of any size. In no other way can our boys and girls be given the all-round training they need. Home, church, school, and group work organizations have a common goal—to develop a well adjusted individual capable of taking a constructive place in society. If these organizations can cooperate to this end, each individual will have a richer personality and will have learned, by experience, that cooperation works. The welfare of youth in a modern community can cause many different groups to decide on common aims, to respect each other's differences, and to give a practical demonstration that democracy must begin in neighborhoods if it is to prove worthy of spreading over the world.

THE AIMS AND OBJECTIVES OF GIRL SCOUTING

From its earliest beginnings the Girl Scout movement has been recognized as a way of developing good citizens. The original troop in Savannah, Georgia, was started in 1912 by Juliette Low, a friend of the Founder of the entire Scout movement for boys and girls, Lord Baden-Powell. Girl Scout troops have always been planned as small, democratic working groups in which girls elect their own officers, delegate authority, make their own arrangements, and accept responsibility for carrying them out. Girl Scouting is non-sectarian;

[7]

its membership, regardless of race, creed, and color, provides an ideal framework in which to learn and practice democracy, for it understands and respects the rights and beliefs of others.

Its appeal to youth is through the fun and adventures shared by its members; its methods aim to develop each girl to her fullest capacity through a group experience. Girl Scouting aims to show a girl how to use in a practical way what she has already learned, to encourage her to develop new abilities and appreciation, and, most of all, to help her develop a healthy attitude toward life and a set of true values.

When a girl accepts the Girl Scout Promise and Laws, has a real share in accomplishment and fun with her own group, and is given an opportunity to render service that is of actual value to her community, the Girl Scout organization believes that she will learn to assume the responsibilities as well as accept the privileges of citizenship.

SERVICE TO OTHERS

Emphasis on service has always been an important part of Girl Scouting. Long before America entered the Second World War, Girl Scouts were reporting tree planting and conservation activities, helping in a day nursery, managing a shadowgraph and record library for shut-ins, equipping baby trays for clinic use, planning and broadcasting a Fun-at-Home program for infantile paralysis epidemic areas, operating back yard playgrounds, mending books at the library. These were peacetime jobs of young citizens getting acquainted with the work the community must do. These were also war jobs for the maintenance of civilian morale. Girl Scout cooperation with the aims of public-spirited citizens has been as varied as the needs of a nation, region, or neighborhood.

Fun for All

The program has been designed to meet the needs of three different age groups. Brownie Scouts—girls from seven through nine or in second to fifth grade in school; Girl Scouts from ten through thirteen or in fifth to ninth grade in school; and Senior Girl Scouts, fourteen through seventeen or in ninth through twelfth grade in school. Each age level has its own activities, but all are bound together by the organization's basic philosophy and methods. The activities cover the same program fields, each of which represents a present or potential interest of girls: Agriculture, Arts and Crafts, Community Life, Health and Safety, Homemaking, International Friendship, Literature and Dramatics, Music and Dancing, Nature, Out-of-Doors, Sports and Games. Camping plays a prominent part in the program, and camps of all sizes and types throughout the United States are eagerly attended by girls of all ages. The combination of troop and camp life builds health, resourcefulness, courage—qualities that have made America great.

International Aspects

The national Girl Scout organization is a member of the World Association of Girl Guides and Girl Scouts. Branches of the movement are to be found in every continent, all linked by a common Promise and by a desire to create better international understanding and friendship. The World Bureau has its headquarters in London, and there is a special Western Hemisphere committee concerned particularly with the growth of the movement in North, Central, and South America.

THE INTERMEDIATE GIRL SCOUT PROGRAM

The ten- to fourteen-year-old Girl Scout belongs to a troop that uses the Intermediate program. The activities are arranged in the form of ranks and badges that provide progression and stimulation for this age girl. Since this book is written especially for the leader, it might be well to consider briefly the impulses that draw the girl into a troop.

[9]

What a Girl Gets from Membership in a Girl Scout Troop

I. FRIENDS AND FELLOW WORKERS:

This age girl has her strongest enthusiasm and greatest loyalties centered in the crowd or "gang" of friends. She has cast off as childish the dependence on older folk. She is a young person of great activity; violent likes and dislikes; hidden, yet budding, idealism; sensitive to the vocabulary and customs set by her own crowd. She is often a cause of great despair to her parents and teachers, since she seems to concentrate on her own thoughts and acts at the moment they are most anxious for her attentions. She accepts responsibility gravely one minute and "forgets" the next. Her most dependable method for communicating her thoughts and feelings takes the form of giggling, whispering, and talking when quiet would be appreciated; being tongue-tied when something obviously should be said. But her very loyalties to her own group and her ardent desire for activity and new experiences make this very period in her life an ideal one to learn to work, to think, and to play with other people. While struggling to express her own individuality, she honors and respects a group code. In the very demand for activity she will delve into and try out without too much self-consciousness all kinds of new interests and activities. Manual skills and intellectual appreciation become her own if the group also approves and participates. The give-and-take of group discipline becomes a kind of self-discipline, because she chose to expose herself to it. The Girl Scout who is shy and lonely becomes an interesting person just because other Scouts show confidence in her; the bossy girl, or the show-off, tones down her solo act because the group will not stand for it but offers instead many opportunities to demonstrate real leadership and honest ability.

No democracy can survive without these qualities being developed in its young citizens. Each girl learns what the group chooses to learn because they all enjoy doing it together. She has her opportunity to practice leadership and to earn the respect of her peers. If the guiding influence of the group is right, she is emerging as a young citizen capable of taking a respected place in a modern community.

[10]

Brownie Scouts, Girl Scouts, and Senior Girl Scouts with their
adult leaders stretch clear across the United States of America and,
with their world sisters, encircle the globe.

2. THINGS TO DO:

There are all sorts of things that would appeal to any girl of any age living in any community. There are cook-outs, treasure hunts, and nature trails for the Girl Scout who is outdoor minded; troop dramatics, gay songs, crafts of every kind, and the latest dance steps for those who wish them. There is exploration through town, country, the world of books, and international friendship for those who wish to expand their ideas, their appreciations, and their service to mankind. And homemaking activities make everything, from necessary routine tasks to the art of being a gracious hostess, seem delightfully simple and easy. All of these are offered in the many badges that are suggested in the Girl Scout program. A plan for progression and advancement that a girl selects for herself offers another opportunity to develop a sense of personal adequacy for which the young adolescent is busily seeking. Interesting things to do are eagerly sought after by any youngster, but their value is doubled if she feels they are "getting her some place." Adventure for its own sake is fun; adventure that leads to more adventure is even better.

The place of new skills, hobbies, and healthy recreation is so important in the life of every man, woman, and child in this country today that it need not be amplified here. But, how many of you have thought, or know people who have said, "I wish I had started that [swimming, skiing, sketching, singing, camping, et cetera, ad infinitum] when I was younger."

3. A CODE TO GO BY:

The Girl Scout Laws and Promise are accepted by Girl Scouts the world over, and thus offer a sense of security and of belonging to something big and worth while. Duty to God and one's country, honesty, and thoughtfulness for other people suggest a code of behavior for citizens of any age. Young people respond to the Girl Scout Promise and try to incorporate the Laws in their daily life through discussion and practice. The democratic form of self-government that each Girl Scout troop uses, and the activities chosen and carried out according to a recognized standard, serve to make each girl feel she has a significant contribution to make. The desire to help is one of

[12]

the most beautiful and universal traits of young people and of children. Through knowledge of community needs and resources, Girl Scouts turn this trait into the performance of vital services.

4. UNDERSTANDING ADULT LEADERSHIP:

The common purpose that drew young and old together in establishing this country or in opening up new frontiers was partly responsible for the success of the undertaking. The enthusiasm, energy, restlessness, and idealism of the young combined with the experience, knowledge, and faith of those who have known life make a potent combination. During the past decades youth and maturity have been apt to go their separate paths, because their work, their pleasures, and their civic responsibilities, if any, were in different places. Our country, and every country in the world, is now confronted with a mighty task—that of attempting to educate citizens to maintain peace. It needs the best efforts of all people, young and old, united again in a common purpose. Each of us in our own community can make an immediate contribution by thinking in terms of youth, of the world they are growing up into, and of what we can do together.

The effectiveness of Girl Scouting, as of any other youth program, has depended on the wisdom and guidance of its adult leaders. Girls want older friends who understand them, who expect the best of them but not the impossible. A person who has a long view because she has been over the path herself helps maintain stability and direction to any program selected by young people. This working together of youth and maturity—with the exchange of ideas, attitudes, and activities—will develop a happier community for all.

The Impetus for Starting a Troop

The actual impetus for starting a troop may come from one of many sources. The more enthusiasm behind the idea, the more successful it is liable to be. Few good troops have been developed from a mere sense of duty or lukewarm interest. The surest place to find the spark of enthusiasm is in a group of girls about the same age

[13]

who know each other or who have similar enough interests to enjoy doing things together. Often the girls themselves who know about Girl Scouting will try to persuade some older person to be their leader.

Churches, schools, and civic organizations encourage this formation of troops because they believe in this Girl Scout program and want it for their own young people. They usually provide leadership and sponsorship.

Parents who want the influence of Girl Scouting for their daughters may locate leadership and be anxious to get a troop started.

The local Girl Scout council may see a need in a certain part of town and initiate the formation of new troops.

A teacher, a former Girl Scout leader, or a person interested in girls may offer her services in the neighborhood.

Frequently those on the waiting list of an already established troop may get tired of waiting and want action in the form of a new "younger sister" troop.

In all of these ways the need for new troops and new leaders comes constantly forward. The next chapter in this book explains the steps that need to be taken and the qualifications for leadership.

THE VOLUNTEER LEADER

Eloquent testimony to the service that women render by volunteering to lead Girl Scout troops lies in the multitude of girls who are, or who are clamoring to be, Girl Scouts. The organization has now over a million members. It will have double this number when more women understand that girls have a right to the fun, the creative activities, and the citizenship training that the Girl Scout program offers. It will grow as more women understand youth leadership as an important civic service.

Eloquent testimony of the satisfaction that women as well as girls receive from this joint enterprise lies in the thousands of troop leaders and other adults who are developing Girl Scouting in their communities.

[14]

Who Is This Leader?

She is homemaker, teacher, professional or business woman. No one is too busy. She likes girls; she enjoys doing things with them and learning with them the things they want to do. She has a few skills or abilities of her own that she is able to share. She is interested in the welfare of her community and in working toward a peaceful world. She believes that a happy experience in democratic living right now in home, school, and club groups by persons of all ages is the best preparation for life in a democracy. Many leaders are former Girl Scouts or women who have had experience in other organizations for girls.

What Does This Leader Do?

She undertakes with some qualms the great adventure of leading a group of girls, possibly fifteen or twenty of them, in the neighborhood. An outline of what she does with these girls will be found in the table of contents of this book.

She puts aside one afternoon a week for the Girl Scout troop meeting and an occasional Saturday for expeditions or special events. The troop meetings usually last from an hour and a half to two hours, but extra time will be needed for making plans.

She opens up her mind to the fact that she will spend some time learning things she never knew before, and considerable time doing things she never thought she could do. She may take a training course in Girl Scouting, and many are available; she may go in for self-training; she will certainly learn from her girls.

She will use her executive ability not only in helping the troop plan its program and manage its finances but also in working with other adults. Troops have assistant leaders and a troop committee who are anxious to assist but do not always know how. She will make an effort to become acquainted with the parents of her girls. Thus she makes sure she does not stand unaided or alone.

She will have certain responsibilities to the local and national Girl Scout organization that share with her an interest in what is happening to the girls in her troop.

[15]

WHAT SATISFACTION DOES THIS LEADER GET?

She gains many new friends—young and old—some of whom she would never meet in any other way. With these friends she finds new interests and skills, for her own enjoyment. The friendship the leader has with her girls is the most continuously satisfying part of her job.

She takes part in a real experience in working out democratic principles with her troop and acquires a deeper understanding of what it involves.

She receives increased recognition from the community as "an authority" about its daughters. Parents seek her opinions and value her comments. Girls seek her advice and respect her judgment. If she is a parent herself, this association with young people adds to her prestige in her own family. The church, school, and other civic agencies respect her influence and ask her cooperation.

She learns youth's point of view and a vocabulary that may be priceless when trying to understand other groups of young people. At the same time she shares with the rising generation the ideals, the information, and the attitudes that have permanent value.

And, lastly, it is only fair to say that all the above satisfactions do not come without some moments of painful introspection, hard work, occasional discouragements, and considerable patience. No job worth doing is free from those moments. Group leadership is not easy.

But, to those who accept this form of service and responsibility comes a reward—a reward so unexpected and so satisfying that no one who has once experienced it will ever be content with anything else. For, as each individual puts her talent, be it little or big, at the service of the group, she is aware that she becomes a bigger person. Not only has she a part in that whole that includes all those others who are doing likewise, but, by companionship with them, her own talent is enhanced. Oftentimes a true creative process is set up by which a group becomes able to take steps toward the solution of its own problems. This is indeed the fine fruit of democracy. Far away from this creative process as we often are, it is yet, in essence, the ideal that has drawn people from all over the world to our shores, and has been the guiding star of many of our best Americans.

Chapter Two

First Steps in Starting a Troop

EVEN THOUGH you are impatient to get started as a Girl Scout leader, there are certain practical preliminaries that should have your attention.

In this chapter you will find the necessary information to help you get started with a group of girls. Whether you are beginning with a new group or taking over an established Girl Scout troop here are specific suggestions to help you.

The material includes:

Preliminary steps before meetings should begin.
Leadership qualifications.
Assembling the girls and getting started on the troop program.
Girl Scout membership requirements and registration procedure.
Activities and aids for the early days.

GETTING OFF to a good start with plenty of enthusiasm is important in any enterprise. In forming a Girl Scout troop it pays double dividends in fun and satisfaction. Therefore, it is important that the leader, and the other adults concerned, understand the steps to be taken that result in a full-fledged troop of eager Girl Scouts. There may be moments when you feel everything happens at once, but you will see that there is a logical progression in planning for a new troop. These first steps are:

1. Get in touch with the local Girl Scout council, if there is one; if not, write to Girl Scout National Headquarters.
2. Read the national policies and a few essential facts about the program.
3. Secure community backing.
4. Find adult leadership.
5. Consider any necessary financial support.
6. Locate an adequate meeting place.
7. Get the girls together.
8. Plan the first four to eight meetings.
9. Arrange for prompt registration.
10. Have an investiture ceremony.

You may have been in on these steps from the very beginning. Perhaps you were the person instrumental in promoting the idea for a troop. In that case you would see that all the steps were properly taken. On the other hand you might have come in at step four as the adult leader secured by some sponsoring group. Or you may be taking over an already established troop and would probably start with step seven. In any case, you will want to be familiar with your troop foundations.

After the first few weeks with your troop, when you and your girls are acquainted with each other and with Girl Scouting, you will find it increasingly easier to plan your programs together. This chapter, with its specific suggestions, is only to help you reach that point where you feel sufficiently at home with Girl Scout leadership to pick and choose from this book and from the *Girl Scout Handbook* the methods and the program activities your own particular troop needs.

HELP FROM YOUR GIRL SCOUT COUNCIL
OR NATIONAL HEADQUARTERS

If you are in a community where there is a Girl Scout council, be sure to get in touch with it before making plans to start a troop. It will help you in every possibly way and explain to you any local policies. Some communities, for example, have special organization procedures or expect every leader to take some form of training. Most cities over 25,000 population have a Girl Scout office with a staff member in charge. This is listed in the telephone book, and you can get preliminary information easily.

If you are in a community where there is no council, write to National Headquarters, and it will send you information and help. A troop organized where there is no council is called a "lone troop." There may be other lone troops in your community, however, whose leaders would be glad to assist you.

NATIONAL POLICIES AND THE
GIRL SCOUT PROGRAM

Get a *Girl Scout Handbook,* which contains all the program activities, and read at least the first three chapters. You will use the book constantly thereafter as a companion piece to this book. Every person interested in using the Girl Scout program should read the national policies before organizing a troop. They are made for the greater protection of all girls, and represent the few basic rules that the National Council expects all local units to use. You will find them in the pamphlet, *Policies of the National Girl Scout Organization.*

COMMUNITY BACKING

Since a Girl Scout leader serves the community as leader of girls, it is only right that she should have community support and understanding. Her troop will have more stability and a finer program if the community is interested in it.

[20]

The troop leaders meet with the girls' parents to tell them about Girl Scouting and to enlist their cooperation.

A Troop Committee

One of the best ways to obtain this backing is to have a troop committee consisting of three to five persons interested in a particular group of girls. Often the troop committee is organized first and finds the leader. It depends on where the impetus for a troop originated. But no matter who comes first, troop committee and leaders should work together from the beginning. The committee shares in the responsibility for a suitable meeting place, for financial assistance, for adequate leadership, for interpretation of Girl Scouting to parents and the neighborhood, and in countless other ways. Members of the committee may include parents of the girls, persons representing the school or church where the troop meets, or any man or woman interested in assisting a troop to have a successful program. For further details about the organization and responsibilities of a troop committee see pages 326-332.

[21]

Lone troops must have a troop committee before they can register. A lone troop committee takes the responsibility for selecting and endorsing the Girl Scout leaders, and also assumes certain other responsibilities. Write to National Headquarters for complete information about the function of a lone troop committee.

A Sponsoring Group

Often some civic organization interested in young people will promote, organize, and sponsor one or more Girl Scout troops under the direction of the Girl Scout organization. The sponsoring organization should select one or more its members to serve on the troop committee. Be sure to read page 332 if some organization wishes to sponsor your troop.

The Girl Scout Council

Where there is a Girl Scout council, this group brings the backing and support of the whole community to Girl Scouting, in addition to the neighborhood backing provided by a troop committee. In small towns, the council in carrying out its community responsibilities often knows and cares for the needs of each individual troop. When this is the case, separate troop committees may not be needed because of duplication of effort.

ADEQUATE ADULT LEADERSHIP

Every Girl Scout troop has at least one adult leader over twenty-one years of age and one or more assistant leaders at least eighteen years of age. It is a good idea to obtain and use the talents of an assistant leader from the very beginning.

You do not have to be a trained expert or an unusually talented person to be a Girl Scout leader. The kind of person you are is infinitely more important than the skills and techniques you may be able to impart. The girls want to be sure of the sincerity of your interest and understanding, and you want to be sure of their confidence and respect and liking for you. Then you can plan the program together, and there are many sources of help available to you in carrying it out.

It would be foolish to catalog all the virtues as necessary qualifications of a leader, and if you possessed them all and were the "perfect example" your girls might find very little fun in being with you. They do expect to find in you the very qualities you need most to work with them: sincerity, imagination, resourcefulness, patience, maturity of judgment, and a sense of humor. Possessing these and a willingness to listen to their ideas and suggestions, adding your own and developing theirs, you may be wise enough not to expect too much of yourself or of them.

FINANCIAL RESPONSIBILITY

Both you and your troop committee should have a fair picture of a troop's financial responsibility before starting to organize. There are annual national membership dues of one dollar from each girl, leader, and troop committee member. This money helps develop and maintain Girl Scouting throughout the country. The total membership dues should be collected from each prospective member during the organization period of a new troop. After the initial registration, the girl's national membership dues and troop expenses should come from a troop treasury. Clubs and organizations of any kind need money to carry on a good program; therefore possible troop budgets should be carefully considered. See pages 178-180. Program materials, books, the Girl Scout uniform and insignia, are all matters to be considered. If a troop committee understands how much Girl Scouting is going to cost, and knows the economic status of the troop, it can see at what points it should assist.

Leaders of lone troops may receive training and guidance directly from National Headquarters and from the national staff members in each region. For the privilege of using the Girl Scout program, lone troop committees pay each year a credential fee when the troop registers. The fee is raised by the troop committee, not the girls, and represents the community's contribution toward providing Girl Scouting for its young people.

[23]

When a troop is organized under a council, all adults in the organization usually assist in whatever form of money raising is used to support local Girl Scouting. The council is responsible for paying the annual charter fee to the national organization.

AN ADEQUATE MEETING PLACE

Most of our troops meet in schools and churches, some meet in settlement houses, some in homes, and the most fortunate have a club room of their own. While we should be grateful to and cooperative with any person or organization whose property we use, just "any place" won't do. It is not fair to the girls nor to their program to have weekly meetings in a cold, dark basement or in a school room with desks fastened to the floor. Many a troop has risen above such an environment, but at the cost of energy that might have been used

Girl Scout troops meet in churches or synagogues, schools or other public buildings, private homes, and Girl Scout Houses.

for the benefit of both girls and community. Therefore, make every effort to locate the right meeting place before calling the girls together. Attractive surroundings, space, safety, and accessibility have more to do with the success of your troop than you might ever guess.

LOCATION OF THE MEETING PLACE

It should be easily and safely accessible to the girls and acceptable to the parents as a suitable meeting place for their daughters. It should not be in a place where lively games would disturb anyone, nor where the legitimate noise of other groups could ruin a troop meeting. Sanitary arrangements, light, ventilation, and all other health and safety precautions should be adequate. A yard, park, or outdoor play place nearby is very desirable. A book called *Safety-Wise*, which is sent free to every new Girl Scout leader, gives further help along these lines.

THE MEETING PLACE

It should be large enough for team games and allow for separations into small activity groups or patrol meetings. One large room with a small room and a kitchen occasionally available is an ideal arrangement. These extras might be furnished by the nearby home of a troop committee member or parent. There should be a cupboard, chest, or closet where troop equipment could be kept from week to week. Best of all is a room that can be the troop's own, which they can fix up to suit themselves and where they can safely leave their Girl Scout possessions and treasures. Often several troops meeting on different days can share the same room. It is impossible to overestimate the pride, pleasure, and good results that come from having a room of one's own.

Furniture should be practical, sturdy, and movable. A little paint, gay curtains, and some carpentry may be all the girls need to create for themselves the perfect Girl Scout home.

Paul Parker Photo

GETTING GIRLS TOGETHER

With the confidence inspired by interested adults and a suitable meeting place, you are ready to arrange for the first meeting. Sometimes an announcement of the time and place of meeting is made through the school or church where the troop is to meet, sometimes the leader or troop committee has a list of girls waiting to become Scouts and those girls are notified directly. If you are to be the person to interest a group of girls in joining your troop, talk to a small gathering or to one class instead of a large assembly. You do not want to be confronted with a crowd you cannot handle, unless you are prepared to furnish leadership for several troops. If you can, arrange to have girls of about the same age. Start with ten and eleven year olds or with twelve and thirteen year olds. If you must take in girls with a wide age range at the beginning, be doubly sure to start with one or more assistants. Lone troops of necessity often have a wider age range.

However your prospective Girl Scouts are gathered together, there are a few things to keep in mind. First, find out as much about these girls as you can before the first meeting, so they will not seem like total strangers. If you cannot talk to the girls themselves and thus get acquainted, talk to the people who know them. Questions such as these are good ones to get answered:

How old are the girls?
Have they been Brownie Scouts?
Where do they go to school? In what grade?
Where do they go to church?
Who or what got them interested in wanting to be Girl Scouts?
How limited is their spending money?
Do their parents need interpretation about Girl Scouting?

A Troop Meeting Place

Girls take great pride in a meeting place of their own that they can fix up to suit themselves. Everyone contributes books, magazines, materials for general use. Here they can read, write, work on crafts, have parties, cook over an open fire, and hold regular troop meetings.

Do the girls all know each other, or are they more or less strangers?

What do they like to do?

There are many more things you will learn later about each girl, but you cannot learn everything at once, and this makes a good beginning.

Second, make this first meeting lively and significant. Third, start with the size of group you and your assistant can manage easily. New members can be added when you are all better acquainted with each other. Somewhere between twelve and sixteen girls seems as large a number as most new leaders should try to handle at first. Start with a smaller group if you prefer, but remember you should have at least eight girls to register as a troop, and there are always a few "joiners" and "tasters" in every gathering who drop out before membership requirements are completed.

Leaders who know in advance what girls are to be in their troop like to have a meeting with the parents before calling the girls together. This provides an opportunity to enlist cooperation in advance.

IF YOUR GIRLS HAVE BEEN BROWNIE SCOUTS

If you are taking over a group of girls who have been Brownie Scouts, you can move along very quickly. If they came from the same troop, your girls already know each other and know about Girl Scouting. They will have already completed their Tenderfoot requirements. They are eager and ready to start on Second Class or perhaps badge activities. They are used to planning together and may be ready to form patrols or elect officers immediately.

You will want to find out as soon as possible how their Brownie troop was organized, what program activities they did, how many girls there were in the group. This will help you know just where to start with these girls in planning a happy and progressive program. Brownie Scouts think they are graduating into a wonderful grown-up adventure when they join a Girl Scout troop. They will be very disappointed if they find they are just repeating things they did as Brownies, or are plunged into experiences for which they are not ready.

[28]

Perhaps the girls are seasoned day campers or have been to an established camp. They may know far more than you about how to do things in Girl Scouting, and they will enjoy showing you. That is fine, as it will increase their feeling of growing up and becoming more responsible. Read the *Leader's Guide to the Brownie Scout Program,* especially the chapters on "The Importance of Her Troop to the Brownie Scout," "How to Measure Progress in the Brownie Scout Troop," and "Preparation for the Intermediate Girl Scout Program." This will help you understand these young people.

Former Brownies who, for some reason, did not meet the Tenderfoot requirements and have not had a fly-up ceremony before they left the Brownie troop should have the opportunity to be invested as soon as possible. Girls in one program level should be able to progress easily and naturally to the next, and thus avoid any lapse of membership in the Girl Scout movement. Girl Scouting has unity as well as progression and all age levels select activities from the same eleven fields of interest. Brownies do not have ranks and badges, but they are familiar with the beginning activities. The Brownie pendant has the same meaning as the membership star that is given to a Girl Scout for a year's active membership in a troop.

Series B under "The First Four to Eight Troop Meetings" at the end of this chapter will be helpful for those of you who have former Brownies in your troop.

TAKING OVER AN ALREADY ESTABLISHED TROOP

Many of you will begin your experience as a Girl Scout leader with a troop that is already organized. The former leader may have been with the girls for only a short time or for years. Perhaps the troop has had a succession of different leaders. In any case there are some special considerations in addition to those in the preceding pages. Your girls already know each other and are more or less familiar with the Girl Scout program. They may also have established some traditions and ways of work that they enjoy, and assuredly they will be in different stages of progress.

With this group it is doubly important to learn about the Girl Scout program by reading the *Girl Scout Handbook* carefully, and if

[29]

possible by taking a training course or visiting another troop that is a going concern with a good program. Talking to an experienced Girl Scout leader can be very helpful and encouraging.

Get Acquainted Before You Go

Find out as much as you possibly can about your girls and which ones are considered leaders, what the troop did last year, and its general standing in the community. Read the troop records and if possible talk to the former leader. If the troop has an active troop committee it can help you in many ways to get off to a good start.

One of the most important things to find out is what form of organization the troop has had. Ask the troop officers, patrol leaders, or a group of older girls to meet with you before you meet with the whole troop, get acquainted with them informally, ask for their advice and opinion about troop programs. With their help plan for the first meeting, and prepare a list of program suggestions that could be presented to the entire troop for discussion.

The First Meetings

If you can meet with the girl leaders ahead of time and can go to your first meeting able to call these girls by name and produce concrete program suggestions, things are pretty sure to go well. If this is impossible, ask a member of the troop committee, the school principal, or the minister of the church where the troop meets, to explain that you are the new leader, to express confidence in the good times you will all have together and to say that you count on the girls' welcome and help. Sometimes it is necessary for someone to explain what has happened to the former leader or perhaps bring a message from her.

The suggestions for the *First Four to Eight Meetings* in the following pages will be helpful to you, especially Series B, but there are a few points that you will need to keep in mind.

1. Establish yourself with your girls as quickly as possible. They may be comparing you with the former leader to whom they were devoted and thus have a tendency to be critical, especially if you do things differently. Loyalty to tradition and to trusted friends is very

strong in girls of this age. You do not wish to destroy these loyalties, but to respect them. At the same time you want to make your own contribution as a potential friend and as a person with active ideas. Possibly this former leader may not have been popular or wise in her guidance. You may then find the girls trying "to put something over on you," hard to control, apathetic to ideas, or very vague about Girl Scout standards and ideals. In this case your friendly interest, your positive program ideas, your patience, and your unwillingness to listen to personal criticisms will soon be felt, if clearly demonstrated.

2. Include the familiar and the unfamiliar in your first meetings. For example, if the troop has an opening or closing ceremony it has always used, let the girls show you how well they can do it. They may do it badly, and you will have other and better ideas for the meetings, but make these changes later. Let the girls sing some of their favorite songs, and even if they send a shudder up and down your musical spine, appreciate their attempt, and then ask them if they would like to learn one of your favorite songs, or one that other Girl Scouts sing a great deal. Choose a hiking or action song or maybe an easy-to-learn round. If you suggest games, let them choose and run off one of their own.

3. Whatever form of organization or business meetings the troop has used should be the starting point with you. Even if you are convinced that the patrol system is just what this group needs and their previous method has not been adequate, remember that any satisfactory form of organization grows to fit program plans and the ability of your girls.

By starting in this way you can learn a great deal about your girls, their interests, ability to work together, and at the same time give them a comfortable feeling that you are interested in what they have been doing and can be counted on for new ideas.

GIRLS IN VARIOUS STAGES IN THE PROGRAM

It is quite likely that many of your girls will be at different places in the program and all anxious to progress. The older ones may be approaching First Class rank; others may have a varied assortment of badges; the newer ones may be eager to catch up.

This presents one of the most difficult of all situations for a new leader taking over an established troop. Don't let it worry or confuse you. Make it quite clear to the girls at the beginning that you are anxious to help them progress and that during the year their suggestions and individual desires will be considered. However, during the first month or two it is important to establish troop unity and to plan troop activities of equal interest to all. Say something like this, "Since you are all interested in badges, don't you think it would be fun to choose one badge this fall that we could work on together as a troop—just to start off anyway? I notice that you all like to sing, yet no one has the Minstrel badge, and I believe I can help you earn it." Or, "Since a very important part of Scouting is service and you are all experienced Girl Scouts, how would you like to work on My Community badge? Here are a few things we could all do together." Or, "Since you older girls are well on your way to becoming First Class Scouts, how would you like to work on either the One World or World Gifts badge? Either of these badges could be used to help complete your First Class requirements, and at the same time be a good start for some of the other, younger, girls. All of us need to know more about International Friendship these days." If you have an assistant leader or a member of your troop committee who is willing to help, you may find it wise to say, "What about you girls who are anxious to complete a major in Homemaking working with Mrs. S. who is a real authority on the subject? The rest of us might like to do Games or Troop Dramatics and take over the recreational side of the troop meetings. Then we'll all be having a good time."

After starting with the girls in some such fashion it becomes increasingly easy to plan a program that incorporates the interests of different groups by using program consultants or other troop committee members.

IF THE FORMER LEADER HAS LEFT NO RECORDS

You might inherit a troop where the former leader kept no records about finances, program, or individual girl's progress. She may have thought she could keep it all in her head, but meanwhile she has left town and taken her head with her. This presents certain difficulties too, since your girls may say, "But I've already paid my membership dues"—or—"I've done all my Second Class activities"—or—"We had finished the Foot Traveler badge except for the ten miles we were to do this summer," and so on. Get in touch with the former leader if you possibly can. If not, some member of the troop committee may be able to help you discover the actual facts, or parents may remember whether dues were paid or badge requirements met. Do not seem to doubt either the girls' word or the good faith of the former leader. Your troop committee should tide you over any financial emergency until the troop budget is straightened out—girls should not be penalized for the leader's carelessness. Often a series of quiz games or quick review using the activities the girls say they have "finished" will indicate how far they have actually gone without making them feel they are having to do everything over again. A troop party, hike, investiture, or piece of community service provides an ideal testing ground for many activities about which there is question. Above all remember how devastating it is to the pride of a young girl to have her word doubted by an older person she respects. It would be far better to accept the word of your girls and then later, if you find any one of them untrustworthy, to talk the whole matter over with her, based on statements you know are not true.

Start another set of records and fill in all the gaps as quickly as you can from information obtained from your Girl Scout council, your troop committee, parents, or program consultants who have worked with your girls. Well kept records are very important to a troop and should be considered troop property in which girls and adults have a share; they should not belong to any one leader.

If There Is No Troop Committee

If you are taking over a troop that has no troop committee, get one immediately. Right at the beginning is the ideal time to explain to the parents or to the group that is sponsoring your troop that you must have their help. It is only a fair bargain that, if they need your leadership abilities, you need their backing before accepting the responsibility. Your early days will be far easier under these circumstances, and the community will value you more highly if you make it see that your troop is a community job, not a single-handed effort.

[33]

THE FIRST FOUR TO EIGHT MEETINGS

Troop meetings in Girl Scouting never follow any definite pattern; they are based on what each individual group of girls wants and are guided by the objectives the leader is trying to achieve. However, new leaders just starting out have similar objectives. They wish to get acquainted with their girls and to have them thoroughly enjoy the troop meetings. They want to make sure the girls learn about Girl Scouting and are prepared to become members of the organization as soon as possible. They need to discover what special interests and abilities their girls have, and how capable they are of self-government. Therefore, the following series of suggestions for first meetings with a troop are gathered from leaders who have found them successful. No one leader could use these plans just as they are without

The leader and assistant leader divide responsibilities: (a) by each taking an interest group or patrol.

[34]

The leader and assistant leader divide responsibilities: (b) by the leader taking charge of a troop activity while the assistant talks to individual girls who want help.

modification, because varied circumstances call for various adaptations. Changes will be based on the circumstances under which you meet, the time at your disposal, what you know about your girls, and on what they themselves want to do. These suggestions combine in a series of meetings the fundamental elements in program planning as described in Chapter Six, "What Are Troop Meetings Like?" Perhaps they will help you through the early days of learning about Girl Scouting, of selecting program activities, and the beginnings of troop self-government. Your girls may take anywhere from four to ten meetings before they are all ready to register as a troop, but do not let this period drag out. An impressive investiture ceremony should be eagerly anticipated and not delayed until the fine ardor of their enthusiasm has cooled.

[35]

The leader and assistant leader divide responsibilities: (c) by the assistant leader taking charge of a play rehearsal or some lively activity while the troop is assembling or while the leader talks to visitors or new Girl Scouts.

SERIES A

These ideas have been used where the majority of girls are new to Girl Scouting, more or less strangers to each other, and between ten and twelve years of age. A tentative time allowance for different activities is given because timing is so difficult to decide at first, and often the very thing you wished to do most of all gets crowded out. Change the order or timing of these suggestions in any way that suits your special group. For example, if your girls have been working in school up until the time of your meeting, you will probably find it wise to start with some lively activities to let off steam. If, on the other hand, they walk to meetings or have had other strenuous activity, they may wish to start off with some sit-down activities such as discussions, patrol meetings, crafts, or singing. Your timing will be changed as you discover interest or the lack of it. Many a leader has gone to meetings prepared with many ideas for games and songs to find her girls burning to talk and discuss plans and unwilling to be diverted by "recreation." Equally true are the cases where girls at first will neither listen to a leader or to each other for more than a few minutes.

First Meeting

POSSIBLE ACTIVITIES	REASONS FOR OR COMMENTS ABOUT THE ACTIVITIES
Game—(about 15 minutes) Choose any lively game with simple rules that can be easily explained. Example: Relays, Dodge Ball, Going to Jerusalem. Refer to *Girl Scout Handbook* for suggestions on how to choose and teach games.	This helps everyone to get acquainted and breaks the ice. Also gives you some idea of your girls' sense of fair play, general alertness, and so forth. If girls come straggling in to meetings at first, games to which late arrivals can be easily added are a wise choice.
Talk About Girl Scouting—(not over 10 minutes) Tell about some of the things Girl Scouts do, such as hiking,	Girls want to know immediately what they are going to do as Girl Scouts, for they are expecting that they will have fun and ad-

[37]

dramatics, crafts, community service. Explain that Girl Scouts the world over subscribe to the same code and repeat the Girl Scout Promise and Laws.

Make it clear that knowing these Laws and wanting to live up to the Promise is the most important part of Girl Scouting.

Typical Scout Activities—(about 30 minutes)

Choose one or more according to the time it takes.

(a) Singing

Either an action or hiking song, a simple folk song or round, or a patriotic song suitable for using with the Pledge of Allegiance to the Flag of the United States. Refer to *Girl Scout Handbook* for points on how to choose and teach a song and to one of the songbooks in the *Publications Catalog*.

(b) Outdoor Activity

A brief treasure hunt or nature observation trail around the block or to the nearest open space, using some of the Girl Scout trail signs. See Tenderfoot requirements in *Girl Scout Handbook*.

(c) Simple Dramatics

Such as those suggested in Troop Dramatics badge activities numbered 1-5 in the *Girl Scout Handbook*.

(d) First Aid

How to use a triangular bandage and how to tie a square knot. See other suggestions in the *Girl Scout Handbook*.

[38]

venture, something different from or in addition to their ordinary experiences. At the same time they need to know that they have a code to live up to and an opportunity to be of service to others. They are young idealists, often in complete disguise!

In choosing from this list either ask the girls which activity they would like to try first or select one to start with that you feel you can do well enough so your girls would enjoy it.

A selection of activities will give the girls actual experience with things Girl Scouts do and satisfy their desire for action. It gives you a chance to see what they really enjoy and along what lines their interests and needs might lie.

Watch and see how your girls work together and which ones seem to be natural leaders or have unusual ability in some line. The girl who loves to sing may not be good at games or on the trail, but she may make a fine song leader.

This is a very good time to let your assistant leader or a member of the troop committee help with the program. Perhaps she could teach a song or a few trail signs, while you take a few girls outside to lay a very short trail. Or you could each help a different group prepare a charade or pantomime showing a Girl Scout activity.

(e) Crafts

Using material at hand or scraps. See section on Arts and Crafts in *Girl Scout Handbook*. Make something useful for the home.

Troop Government—(about 20 minutes)

Explain how to join the troop and the membership requirements. Give out the parent consent forms that are obtained free from the national or local headquarters. Ask girls to bring to the next meeting the forms filled out and signed, together with the national membership dues of one dollar. Explain that a girl may get her *Handbook* immediately, but that she cannot be invested as a Girl Scout or purchase her uniform and insignia until—(a) she has completed the membership requirements, and (b) the troop is officially registered.

Ask the girls if they have any suggestions for the next meeting or any questions. Discuss any preliminary steps in troop organization that might be taken next week, such as troop dues or election or appointment of temporary troop officers.

This is the time to explain how a troop is organized and managed; make it clear that it is a joint enterprise shared by leaders and girls.

Help the girls feel the troop is *theirs* by asking for opinions, encouraging suggestions, and working together on program planning. This may come slowly at first, but work toward it.

Explain that being a member of a national organization with her name officially recorded at National Headquarters entitles each girl to the privileges and pleasures of Girl Scouting, just as being a faithful member of her own troop entitles her to a full share in the plans and fun of that particular group.

This is the time and place for leaders to explain and demonstrate the principles, the privileges, and responsibilities of democratic government.

Closing—(5-10 minutes)

Girls standing in circle formation so that all may see, hear, and take part.

Reminder of what they are to bring next week.

Repeat the Girl Scout Promise slowly (girls do not officially take

A dignified ending to a meeting gives a sense of belonging to something important and a sense of unity. It emphasizes the thoughts that should be remembered.

Girls like and need some cere-

[39]

the Promise until they are invested). Suggest that girls learn Promise and Laws by next week and be ready to give examples from their own everyday living of at least one Law.

Sing a patriotic song. If there is a Flag of the United States available, give the Pledge of Allegiance.

monial and often want to plan special ways of opening or closing a troop meeting.

Borrow a Flag from the school, church, or American Legion. Do not buy this at first, since the troop needs its money for books and other equipment.

Second Meeting

Game—(about 15 minutes)
Same type of game as for first meeting or one suggested by the girls. A dramatic or singing game is also good for letting off steam.
Troop Government—(about 25 minutes)
Collect parent consent forms and membership dues. Discuss weekly troop dues. Appoint or elect temporary treasurer.

Discuss regular and prompt attendance at meeting. Decide at what hour meetings shall officially begin and end.

Appoint or elect a temporary troop secretary or scribe.

Encourage questions and ideas.

It may be wise to collect any money or papers before an activity starts, since such things get lost so easily.

The parent consent forms are the beginning of your troop records. They give you the information you need for registering the troop, and help you in knowing more about your girls. They also help parents know more about Girl Scouting.

Let the girls begin to take some share in managing troop affairs. Temporary elections are often wise in a new troop until your girls get to know each other and the jobs better. Leaders need to give plenty of help and supervision to troop officers at first. While the treasurer collects the dues and keeps the troop accounts, the money is turned over to the leader or assistant leader to keep or bank.

Scout Activities—(about 35 minutes)
Choose one from the list given
[40]

Continue to notice what activities the girls like especially. Make

in First Meeting or one of the Tenderfoot homemaking requirements.

Closing—(about 15 minutes)
Tell how Girl Scouting got started and something about Juliette Low. Explain Girl Scout Motto and Slogan. Repeat Girl Scout Laws and ask for examples of observance.

sure all participate. Watch out for the slow or shy girls to make sure they are included.

Repeat any chosen activity until it is done well enough to give girls a sense of accomplishment and pleasure in reaching a good standard of performance.

Continue to add to girls' understanding of the courage and spirit that developed Girl Scouting and their share as Girl Scouts in the future of their country. Urge them to read Chapter One in the *Girl Scout Handbook* carefully so that it may be discussed during these first meetings.

Third Meeting

Demonstration and Practice with the Flag of the United States—
(about 20 minutes)
Show girls how to act as Color guard and discuss respect due the Flag. Practice the horseshoe formation as found in the *Girl Scout Handbook.*
Conduct the Flag Ceremony—
(about 10 minutes)
Pledge of Allegiance.
"Star-Spangled Banner."
Repeat Girl Scout Laws.

Let one or two girls tell about a Law well carried out, preferably by someone else.

Girl Scouts often have occasion to use the Flag ceremony, and you may want to use it in connection with the investiture of your troop. It should be practiced sufficiently so that it moves with dignity and without sense of strain. Correct posture and the ability to walk well and to stand quietly might be brought out here as a requisite for good health and good looks.

While always glad to hear of or to recognize any girls' effort to live up to the Laws, encourage them to notice or report on the good deeds of others rather than their own. Smugness is a most unpleasant characteristic.

[41]

Lively Recreation—(about 15 minutes)

Games, action song, or folk dance.

Girls usually need vigorous physical activity after a period demanding quiet attention and control such as the above.

Troop Government—(about 20 minutes)

Collect any parent consent forms and membership dues that were forgotten last week.

Have treasurer collect weekly troop dues.

Have secretary take attendance and enter each girl's full name and attendance in troop record book.

Discuss form of government troop will use to start with. Possibly a direct form, if a small group (town meeting); if over twelve girls, a representative form (patrol method). See Chapter Five.

Do not try to hurry troop organization. Let it proceed slowly and as need is apparent for various officers and small working units such as patrols; girls often want to elect officers or divide into groups without having the least idea what it means.

Demonstrate or give concrete illustration whenever possible.

Girl Scout Quiz Game—(about 20 minutes)

Divide into two teams or use the temporary patrol groups for a competitive review testing game. The spelling bee, radio quiz, or relay race form might be used for questions that you have prepared in advance. Questions on respect due the Flag, the Girl Scout Laws, the history of Girl Scouting, or those suggested by other Tenderfoot requirements could be used.

Appoint team captains or patrol leaders to be in charge of each team. This gives the girls practice in working together for the good of their team or patrol; it gives you an idea of how much the girls have remembered and where further review is needed.

Closing Song—(about 5 minutes)

This brings the troop together as a unit again.

[42]

FOURTH MEETING

Lively Game—(about 15 minutes)

For sheer recreation.

Troop Government—(about 20 minutes)

Patrol meetings or general business meeting to attend to following matters:

Dues

Attendance

Check on Tenderfoot requirements.

Discuss time, place, and program for first hike or outdoor meeting. See *Girl Scout Handbook* and section on "Begin Early in the Out-of-Doors" in this chapter.

Encourage all girls to complete Tenderfoot rank so that the entire troop may be registered and girls invested as soon as possible. Find out what individuals need extra help.

Let girls have a real experience in program planning by discussing all aspects of hike.

Scout Activities—(about 30 minutes)

Any of the Tenderfoot or Second Class activities in the Out-of-Doors field would be appropriate here.

Undoubtedly your girls have indicated certain preferences, and it would be wise to explore further the Second Class or proficiency badge activities to which they have responded.

Closing—(about 20 minutes)

Circle formation.

Discuss what it means to be a Girl Scout. Point out actual examples of how Laws have been applied (or forgotten) in troop activities of past three weeks.

Learn one or two songs appropriate for the hike, perhaps a marching song, and one to sing around a campfire.

Troop officers should be ready by this time for special meetings with you and your assistant to plan for the next meeting and their responsibility in helping to carry them out. These meetings are usually held after or between troop meetings. See Chapter Five.

[43]

FIFTH MEETING

Lively Song or Folk Dance—
(about 15 minutes)

Tenderfoot Activities—(about 30 minutes)

(a) Final check-up on membership requirements. You, as leader, talk to individual girls to make sure they understand the Girl Scout Promise and Laws.

It is important that you talk to every girl in the troop individually before she becomes a Girl Scout. This is to make sure she has as clear an understanding as is possible for her age and stage of development about what the Girl Scout Promise means. It also helps you to know the girl as an individual and encourages her to feel you are an understanding older friend to whom she can talk freely. Many of these chats were undoubtedly held before, after, or in between meetings, but there always seem to be some girls who can only be reached at the meeting.

(b) The rest of the group can practice games and songs that might be used on the hike, rehearse a ceremony, or review any Girl Scout activity under the direction of your assistant leader or troop committee member or troop officer.

It is probably wise to have another adult supervise this part of the program, even if the girl leaders are taking some responsibility for leadership. Your assistant leader, or whatever adult is going to go with you on your hike, would be the best person.

Troop Government—(about 25 minutes)

General assembly or patrol meetings:

Dues and attendance.

Assignment of specific jobs and responsibilities for hike.

Collecting ideas for the investiture ceremony.

Follow through on troop program planning for hike.

Closing Ceremony—(15 minutes)

This might be the Flag ceremony or the rehearsal of some part of the investiture.

[44]

The leader or chairman of the troop committee fills in registration forms. See the ABC's of registration in this chapter.

Sixth to Eighth Meetings

These meetings should include:

1. A hike or outdoor expedition of some kind.

2. Preparation for the investiture ceremony. This investiture should be held as soon as possible after you have received your troop certificate and the individual membership cards.

3. Plans for future programs, community service, or badge activities. See chapters on "Girls' Interests and Needs" and "Leader-Girl Program Planning."

SERIES B

The following suggestions might be used where the majority of girls know something about Girl Scouting. Perhaps they have been Brownies, are former Girl Scouts, or have members of their family and friends in Girl Scouting. This series is also appropriate for twelve to thirteen year olds or a group of friends who have already expressed definite reasons for wanting to be Girl Scouts. These meetings should be studied in connection with the first set, as they are adaptations of those plans and references but with a different emphasis. If you are a leader taking over an already established troop, work out the adaptations with the help of your older girls or the Court of Honor. In a group of this kind girls are likely to be more varied in their interests and in their knowledge of Girl Scouting. They may need to be divided into interest or age groups immediately. An assistant leader or troop committee member could take one section of program activities or help one patrol with special plans.

[45]

FIRST MEETING

| POSSIBLE ACTIVITIES | REASONS FOR OR COMMENTS ABOUT THE ACTIVITIES |

Lively Game—(15 minutes)

A Girl Scout or Patriotic Song—(10 minutes)

For fun and as a mixer.

Repetition of the Girl Scout Promise and Laws.

Girls who are familiar with Girl Scouting usually want Girl Scout activities and ceremonies from the very start as they feel they already "belong."

Troop Government—(30 minutes)

Discuss form of organization, dues, officers to be elected.

Give out parent consent forms to be returned. If you have received up-to-date records of the girls who have been Brownies or Girl Scouts, these forms need not be given to them.

Remind girls to bring one dollar annual membership dues. This would not apply to girls or to a troop already registered within past year.

Ask girls what Girl Scout activities they like.

This kind of group is anxious to get started at once. Since they are acquainted with each other and with Girl Scouting, they are usually ready for some organization and a temporary election of officers almost immediately.

Remember that Brownies are already members of the Girl Scout organization and may be the most helpful and responsible members of a new Girl Scout troop. They will expect to have a voice in managing their affairs.

Scout Activity—(20 minutes)

One suggested by the girls or one selected by you.

Tenderfoot requirements for those girls who have not met them.

Almost any activity chosen from the Second Class requirements would be appropriate for the early meetings of this group.

Talk on Girl Scouting—(10 minutes)

Have informal discussion on what it means to be a Girl Scout, what the girls like best about it, or what from their own experience the Girl Scout Promise means.

Encourage your girls to do most of the talking. Such a discussion will help you know more about your girls, how they feel, and what their interests and ethical standards are.

[46]

SECOND MEETING

Opening Ceremony—(10 minutes)

One suggested by the girls that they had used previously or had seen other Girl Scouts do. Or you could review the Flag ceremony with them.

This creates a feeling of group unity and loyalty to a tradition that had meaning in their past experience.

Game or Action Song—(15 minutes)

A hiking song, singing game, or lively team game would be good. If the troop is divided into patrols, use the patrols as a team.

For release from tension and for fun.

Troop Government—(25 minutes)

Collect annual membership dues and parent consent forms. Have election of troop officers, such as temporary treasurer, secretary, patrol leaders.

Discuss plans for a hike or other special activity chosen by girls.

Elections should be guided by the discussion of the previous week about the jobs that needed doing and the qualifications of the girls to do them.

Girl Scout Quiz Game—(30 minutes)

Select questions your girls should know from their previous experience as Girl Scouts or Brownies, or take questions about your community that any observant girl should know.

This will help you find out how much they actually know about Girl Scouting or about the community in which they live.

Closing Song—(5 minutes)

Any song appropriate for saying good-night or for singing around a campfire. See any of the songbooks listed in the *Publications Catalog*.

Some of these songs will probably be familiar to your girls, and if you do not know them, let one of the girls lead.

Court of Honor or Executive Committee

After the meeting is over, have the troop officers and patrol leaders stay for a brief discussion of plans for next week. If more convenient, arrange to have this meeting between troop meetings at your house or some nearby place. Explain to them in detail their responsibilities such as how to lead a game, how to conduct a patrol meeting, how to keep troop accounts, what questions to ask in preparation for a hike. See the chapter "Developing Self-Government in the Troop."

THIRD MEETING

Games—(20 minutes)

Familiar games chosen at the Court of Honor and led by the girls.

Start giving girls responsibility for leading some of their own activities as soon as possible. Watch to see how girls respond to each other's leadership and give help where needed.

Troop Government—(30 minutes)

Either in a general assembly or in patrol meetings:

Attendance and dues.

Discussion of plans for hike.

Gather suggestions for Second Class or proficiency badge activity the group would like.

In guiding the choice of a badge, suggest a few that the whole troop would enjoy working on together and one that you can handle. This will help establish troop unity and your friendly relations with the girls. Different patrols might choose different requirements, if they wish.

Example of badges especially good for an entire troop activity: Games, My Troop, My Community, Foot Traveler, Hostess, Troop Dramatics, Back-yard Camper, World Trefoil.

Scout Activity—(30 minutes)

One of the Second Class activities or an activity selected from one of the badges in which the girls have expressed interest.

Or

Tenderfoot requirements.

During the early days of the troop this is the time to try a sampling of activities until the girls have enough information to decide what they want to settle down to first.

[48]

Closing—(10 minutes)
Discussion of Laws and Promise.

Even though the girls may be able to repeat the Promise and Laws, they need to discuss them frequently in relation to their everyday living and their behavior in the troop.

Brief Court of Honor Meeting

A brief Court of Honor may be held to discuss how things are going and to get a report on what activities or badges the girls have chosen. Make any decisions necessary for the hike.

FOURTH MEETING

Hiking or Action Songs—(15 minutes)

With any group of girls who have been in school all day it is usually wise to start a meeting with some form of physical activity.

Troop Government—(25 minutes)
Either in general assembly or patrol meetings.
Attendance and dues.
Assignment of definite responsibilities for the hike.
Choice of Second Class or badge activities that whole group could start on.
Ideas for troop investiture.
Final check on information for troop registration form.

If troop government is carried on in patrol meetings, you and your assistant will need to visit these meetings at first to help keep things moving. It will also help you in training your patrol leaders if you can see what their difficulties are. Withdraw from the picture gradually, and be sure never to dominate the discussion or take the meeting over from the girl leader.

Scout Activity—(30 minutes)
(a) Completion of Tenderfoot requirements for new girls (in charge of leader).

Talk to every girl individually before she is invested. If there is not time in troop meeting, arrange to come early or make special appointment.

(b) First Aid review or nature trail in preparation for hike (in

The older or more experienced members of the troop might be

[49]

charge of assistant leader or troop committee member).

Closing—(15 minutes)

This might be a discussion of one of the Girl Scout Laws with which the girls had difficulty, a good-night circle for a few favorite songs, or a story.

given special responsibilities for the hike, such as having the first aid kit, laying the trail, being in charge of fires, and so on.

Court of Honor

A final check is made on hike plans, ideas for the investiture ceremony, and any necessary plans for getting to work on the Second Class or proficiency badge requirements that have been chosen.

After this meeting the leader or troop committee chairman should be able to register the entire troop.

FIFTH TO EIGHTH MEETINGS

These meetings should include:

1. A hike or an outdoor expedition. The hike could be a longer and more advanced one than suggested in Series A, especially if the girls are experienced hikers. The same preparations should be made, but it might be an all-day affair including a one-pot meal, some cross country games, or a nature trail.

An outdoor expedition might be connected with the badge on which the girls had chosen to work. Nearly every badge suggests some sort of trip.

2. Preparation for the investiture. If the troop is already established and only a few new girls are to be invested, a get-acquainted tea party for parents might be planned instead. The new girls could be invested at that time or at a strictly troop ceremony, whichever they preferred. If the troop is small and wishes to add new members, a game party could be given for girls of the right age to interest them in Girl Scouting.

3. Some piece of community service might be planned or executed during this period. This could also be done in connection with a badge activity.

[50]

BEGIN EARLY IN THE OUT-OF-DOORS

An outdoor program for every troop is an essential part of Girl Scouting. Every girl expects it and wants it. It is fun for all, easier than you may think, and the best builder of troop morale, responsibility, and cooperation you could find. This does not mean just hikes and opportunities to go camping. It means outdoor games, treasure hunts, nature trails, exploration trips during the regular troop meeting. It means leaders and girls doing things together out-of-doors the year around—ice skating parties, swimming parties, gardening, bird walks, exploring the community. It may all culminate in that greatest of all outdoor experiences—camping. But in the meanwhile, for the sake of your girls and for your own sake too, go out adventuring. Activities in the Foot Traveler, Outdoor Cook, or any of the nature badges will give you a good start. Almost all badges have some outdoor activities in them. If you feel uncertain about your abilities along these lines, or if your time and strength are limited, an outdoor-minded troop committee member, friend, assistant leader, or Senior Girl Scout can give you invaluable assistance. Girl Scout fathers are also a grand help in outdoor work.

The First Hike

A hike is usually one of the first things any group of girls will ask for. It is also one of the best ways for girls and leaders to get acquainted and to share in planning a good time together. It is an excellent plan to have something especially interesting to do between the time the troop registration is sent in and the investiture ceremony. Do not let the season of the year put you off. There are leisurely supper hikes for hot weather, or lively cross country hikes for chilly days, or snow trails for the winter time. Since it is important that this first hike together should be successful for all concerned, here are a few hints to help make it so.

1. Plan carefully in advance. General points to consider for hikes are in the *Girl Scout Handbook*.

2. Select a place that is familiar to you or that you are able to visit before the hike takes place.

[51]

3. Make absolutely sure at the meeting immediately preceding the hike that every girl knows (1) just where to meet, (2) what her responsibilities are, (3) what to wear and take (including parents' permission to go). Girls have a wonderful faculty for not listening to the duller and safer responsibilities so dear to protecting adults.

4. Have the hike short, not more than a mile or two in walking distance, and not more than four hours spent away from the troop meeting place. Enthusiastic girls of this age nearly always overestimate their strength and vitality. It is far better for them to come home wanting more than to come home worn out and cross.

5. Include one new skill or adventure and accomplish it. This might be fire building, cooking one simple thing, learning to identify trees that yield hard and soft woods. Do not attempt more than one or two new skills on the first hike. Pride in satisfactory accomplishment is better than a smattering of information.

6. Plan for fun. In addition to learning a new skill, plenty of fun can be provided through outdoor games, singing, story telling around a campfire, working up a good appetite.

THE ABC'S OF REGISTRATION

For New Leaders and Assistant Leaders

Registration means to each girl and adult: (1) the privileges of individual recorded membership in a national and international organization; (2) the right to use the Girl Scout program and wear the Girl Scout uniform and insignia; (3) an assurance that program suggestions, health and safety precautions, and leadership training all measure up to a high standard; (4) an opportunity for individual help either from National Headquarters or from a local council chartered by National Headquarters to serve its registered membership.

By the time you are ready to register your troop you will probably have already attended to A, B, C, and D, which follow. However, the whole story is outlined here, so that you may conveniently check all registration procedure. *All the forms mentioned may be obtained from your Girl Scout council, or, if you are a leader of a lone troop, from National Headquarters.*

[52]

The A B C's of Registration

A. *Establish your status as a leader.*

   1. If you are under a Girl Scout council, find out from it what you should do. Often an interview or training course is required before you apply for your commission.

   2. If you are the leader of a lone troop, write to National Headquarters, and it will send you the instructions you need.

B. *Give out and collect the parent consent form from each girl.*

   This gives you the information you need about each girl to register her when she has completed her membership requirements. These forms make the beginning of your troop record book.

C. *Collect the one dollar annual membership dues from each girl, leader, and troop committee member.*

[53]

D. *Make sure that each girl has completed her Tenderfoot requirements satisfactorily.*

E. *Fill in the form entitled "A Troop and Troop Committee Registration Form."*

Read information and directions on this form carefully. Keep a copy for your troop record book. Send this form or forms completely filled out to your local council, or, if you are a leader of a lone troop, to National Headquarters. Make sure the right amount of money accompanies this form.

F. *Individual membership certificates and a troop certificate will be returned to you from National Headquarters.*

G. *Fill in the membership certificates and present one to each girl and adult.*

These certificates are used when purchasing Girl Scout uniforms and insignia at stores that carry Girl Scout equipment. They are often used as admission cards when special privileges are extended to Girl Scouts. Since these cards are evidence of membership, warn your girls to guard them carefully.

H. *Have a troop investiture ceremony after these registration details are completed.*

Your girls are now members of a full-fledged troop.

I. *As new members join the troop during the year,* obtain the form entitled "Additions to a Troop and Troop Committee" and register these members in the same way. Pay partial dues of fifty cents if there are six months or fewer from the date of registration to the troop expiration month, or full dues if there are more than six months.

[54]

THE XYZ'S OF REREGISTRATION
For Leaders or Troops that Are at Present Registered

X. *If you are already registered as a Girl Scout leader* but are starting a new troop, inform your council. You proceed as described from B to H.

Y. *If your troop was registered last year under another leader,* you proceed as described from A to H, except that B, D, and H apply only to new girls who are not Girl Scouts.

Z. *If you and your troop are reregistering together,* here is your procedure.

1. Make sure that the annual membership dues are in hand well in advance of the troop reregistration date, which is one year from the original registration date.

2. Plan a troop birthday ceremony to celebrate another active year in Girl Scouting. Be ready to present membership stars or service numerals to those girls who have earned them through prompt reregistration each year.

3. Necessary registration forms will be sent you a month before the troop is due to reregister.

4. Read carefully directions for filling out the form or forms. They may have changed since last year. Anyway, refresh your memory. Transfer the necessary information from your troop record book to the registration form.

5. Send the form completely filled out with correct amount of money before the due date.

6. When your new membership cards have been returned, enjoy your troop birthday with the pleasant feeling that your girls have learned something about good budgeting, financial responsibility, and belonging to a national and international movement of young people.

[55]

INVESTITURE CEREMONIES

The investiture is the time when the new Girl Scout officially takes her Girl Scout Promise and is established as an active member of her own troop, of the national organization, and of the association of Girl Guides and Girl Scouts around the world. It should be an important occasion, full of dignity and meaning. There is no one way a girl should be invested, but there are certain things that are usually included in any ceremony that is planned. Since it is a leader's responsibility to see that this ceremony has meaning for each girl in her troop, there are a variety of things you will need to consider in addition to those mentioned in the *Girl Scout Handbook*. First make sure that each girl understands the importance of the occasion, that through her talks with you she understands something of Girl Scouting and what taking a Promise means. She should not be made to feel tense and over-emotional about this. Rather, help her to see she is subscribing to a group code of ethics, which she has thought about and believes in. You and other Girl Scouts who believe in this same code will help her in living up to it.

Whatever ceremony is planned, make sure the form used is one in which everyone can see, hear, and participate. Girls of this age cannot be expected to stand quietly more than ten minutes at the most, so if the ceremony is longer that that, it should provide either an opportunity to sit down or an activity that lets everyone move about. It is equally important that every girl know just what to expect, and if any part of the program needs rehearsal, such as a special formation, a Color guard, or a dramatic presentation, it should be well done in advance. Nothing spoils the feeling of a ceremony more quickly than uncertainty over what to do, fumbling over cues, general confusion.

When it comes time for the girls to be invested, ask the troop officers and patrol leaders to come up first to take the Promise and receive their pins. As you speak to each girl and listen to her as she repeats her Promise, make it seem a friendly and serious conversation rather than a solemn and terrifying speech. We want our girls to think as well as to feel when they make a promise.

Opinions differ as to whether outsiders should be invited to an investiture. Some feel it is a family matter and strictly a troop affair.

[56]

Becoming a Full-fledged Troop Member

INVESTITURE

The whole troop takes part in this ceremony.

STEPS A GIRL TAKES TO BECOME A FULL-FLEDGED MEMBER OF A GIRL SCOUT TROOP

1. She locates a troop in her neighborhood, school, or church. She visits the troop with a friend, or asks the leader if she may go to a troop meeting.
2. She obtains her parents' consent to join the troop.
3. She meets the requirements for the Tenderfoot rank.

   Refer to the first chapter in the *Girl Scout Handbook.*

4. She satisfies her Girl Scout leader that she has fulfilled the above requirements. The leader registers the girl and attends to the Girl Scout pin. Usually the girl pays for this pin in advance, perhaps, when paying her annual national membership dues.
5. She makes her Girl Scout Promise and receives her Girl Scout pin at an investiture ceremony.

Others feel it is an impressive interpretation of Girl Scouting and wish to have friends and relatives present. This may be decided by the troop itself. In the case of a new troop and new leaders, when the leaders and committee members are receiving their first membership certificates, it often becomes a community affair to launch and welcome this new Girl Scout troop. Under these circumstances some local official interested in backing Girl Scouting, the Girl Scout commissioner, or a council member should be on hand to welcome the adult members of the troop, to say a word about the privileges and responsibilities of Girl Scout leadership, and to explain what the troop is going to mean to the community. The official welcome to adult members would come first, and the leaders in turn would conduct the investiture for the girls. Many leaders wish to be invested just as their girls are. Sometimes the leader is invested in a training course or by another leader or council member. A leader may be invested with her own troop and in this case she would receive her pin first as part of the welcoming ceremony to the new troop.

PUBLICATIONS AND PROGRAM MATERIALS FOR THE NEW TROOP* ·

BASIC PUBLICATIONS EVERY LEADER SHOULD HAVE

Girl Scout Handbook
Leadership of Girl Scout Troops
Girl Scout Troop Records and Reports
    This is a book containing all troop record forms. These loose-leaf forms may also be ordered separately and incorporated in the leader's own notebook or a record book made by the troop.

---

*All books in this list may be ordered from the National Equipment Service. See Girl Scout *Publications Catalog.*

FROM GAMES TO BADGE ACTIVITIES

The Starting Point	The Game Is Played	A Possible Result		
		ACTIVITY IN "GIRL SCOUT HANDBOOK"	BADGE	FIELD
Games for Girl Scouts				
"Centerpieces"		No. 16	Home Gardener	Agriculture
"Sealed Orders"		No. 8	Drawing and Painting	Arts and Crafts
"Pedestrian Safety"		No. 8	My Community	Community Life
"Nosebag Lunch"		No. 15	Community Safety	Health and Safety
"Identify the Song"		No. 6	Nutrition	Homemaking
"Foreign Shopping"		No. 9	One World	International Friendship
"What Is It?"		No. 6	Troop Dramatics	Literature and Dramatics
"Tree Facts"		No. 10	Music Appreciation	Music and Dancing
"Halfway Round and Home Again"		No. 1	Tree	Nature
Any Game		No. 11	Foot Traveler	Out-of-Doors
			Games	Sports and Games

SENT FREE TO ALL REGISTERED LEADERS:

Safety-Wise
Minimum standards for health and safety in relation to Girl
Scout program activities.
The Girl Scout Leader
Monthly publication sent to all leaders, assistant leaders, and
troop committee chairmen.
The Girl Scout Uniform and Insignia
Descriptive booklet, telling how, why, and when to wear the
uniform and insignia.

SUGGESTED FIRST BOOKS FOR THE TROOP OR LEADERS' LIBRARY

FOR BOTH LEADERS AND GIRLS:

Sing Together—A Girl Scout Songbook or *The Ditty Bag*
Games for Girl Scouts
Day Hikes
Arts and Crafts with Inexpensive Materials
Dramatics for Girl Scouts
Juliette Low and the Girl Scouts

FOR LEADERS ONLY:

Understanding the Adolescent Girl by Grace Loucks Elliott
Leaders' Nature Guide
Troop Financing in Dollars and Sense

Add other books as the troop grows older and special needs become evident. Books suggested in the classified list in the Girl Scout
Equipment Catalog, in the Girl Scout *Publications Catalog*, or by
your librarian will serve as a guide for further reference material. You
may need more program books, such as *Skip to My Lou*, full of singing games; or *Let's Go—Troop Camping!*; or a specialized book on one
of the crafts or nature fields. You may want more help in understanding how to work with girls and need one of the books on group work
or on girl psychology.

[60]

Program Materials

While the materials needed depend on what the troop has chosen to do, the following items prove generally useful to have on hand and help a wide variety of program plans and spur-of-the-moment ideas:

materials for inexpen- sive arts and crafts	scissors	patrol record books
paper	sewing materials	pack basket or rucksack
pencils	bean bags	(individual knapsacks
crayons	ball	can be made easily)
	first aid kit	outdoor cooking equip- ment

Material for making the troop meeting room more attractive is often needed. This might include such things as a chest in which to keep troop equipment, curtain material, paint, pictures, wall charts, bulletin boards, shelves. The girls can make many of these items from materials contributed by parents or troop committee members. Attics and storerooms often yield the makings of just what a resourceful group of girls can make into troop equipment.

FLAGS

Troops like to have their own American Flag and troop flag, but program materials are usually needed first. It is nearly always possible to borrow an American Flag at the start or to ask some patriotic organization to present one to a Girl Scout troop. Troops may also make their troop flag. Some find this an interesting project in connection with the Sewing badge.

Suggestions for Individual Girls

Girls often need a little advice about Girl Scout equipment that they might need. Parents, with birthdays and Christmas in mind, are often grateful for a few hints. The following suggestions may prove helpful:

1. *Girl Scout Handbook*—unless several copies are available in the troop library.

2. Girl Scout pin—not included in the membership dues and essential for investiture.

[61]

3. Girl Scout uniform.

If the uniform cannot be purchased completely at first, start with the dress, belt, and tie; add beret, then socks and shoes.

Accessories to hang on the belt, such as compass, are often not needed as urgently or as soon as some of the other items, although they often prove irresistible to the proud new Girl Scout.

4. *The American Girl* magazine.

This magazine for all girls has many ideas for troop meetings and badge work as well as a wealth of good stories and articles.

5. Other equipment.

Advice under this heading depends partly on your troop program, but even more on knowing the individual girl. It might be that a paint box, sketch book, camera, diary, outdoor cooking equipment, or book on a special subject would open up new doors and develop valuable hobbies. Personal accessories listed in the catalog are a matter of taste and budget, but you will need to advise girls who are looking forward to going to camp. Refer to the lists suggested in *Let's Go—Troop Camping!* or the folder of the camp to which the girl plans to go.

Chapter Three

Ranks, Badges, and Progression

Now THAT YOU ARE LAUNCHED with your troop, you may be fairly puzzled by the wide scope of the Girl Scout program. This chapter and the next one are written expressly to help you use the program suggestions in the *Girl Scout Handbook*. Since all of the actual badge activities are in the girl's book you will need to have it in your other hand. In this chapter you will find an explanation of the ranks and badges plan, ways of work, and objectives to keep in mind when planning with your girls.

The material includes:

A guide for progression through Tenderfoot, Second Class, and First Class rank.

A guide for earning proficiency badges and the Curved Bar.

Special suggestions for the seventh and eighth grade girls and how to prepare them for Senior Scouting.

Hints to leaders about evaluating progress.

Possible objectives for a troop's first year.

THE PLAN for rank and proficiency badges in the Intermediate program has many advantages for both girls and leaders. Badges are a means of grouping activities under headings related to the girls' interests in a way that can be easily understood. Girls of this age want something specific to work on, a sense of progression, and a guide list they themselves can use. They also respond to standards and to some form of definite encouragement. Badges serve girls as a source of ideas, as a stimulus to achieve because of recognition given, and as a symbol of preparedness for service.

Leaders find badges an invaluable source for troop program material. Since a leader's chief job is to help girls to develop and to become the best possible citizens of our country, she is anxious to have the right tools for the job. The badges are tools that have been carefully selected and tried out over a period of many years. A busy leader can spend more time thinking about her individual girls and their needs if she has tested program material ready at hand. These program activities have been chosen by experts who know what girls want and what is appropriate for their age and ability. No leader can be an authority on all subjects, nor has she time to do research work on whatever subject her girls are most anxious to tackle. The badges are her working outline and her protection. Like all good tools they must be used wisely and chosen to fit the material. Fit your badges to your girls; don't try to fit the girls to the badges. What happens to a girl and her attitudes while earning a badge is far more important than the mere acquisition of knowledge.

You may ask what is the difference between rank badges and proficiency badges. The proficiency badges are designed to increase a girl's information, skill, and appreciation along some specific line. Each badge shows her progress in a single subject or field of interest, using related activities. The rank badges deal with a variety of activities and are designed to show progress in a girl's all-round understanding of Girl Scouting. Rank advancement is to encourage a diversity of interests and thus provide an all-round program experience. As a result, every First Class Girl Scout should be able to demonstrate her understanding of the Girl Scout ethical code, a knowledge of the total range of the program, and real proficiency in several branches.

[65]

GENERAL PROGRAM PLAN

Don't miss this!

Psst!!

ELEVEN PROGRAM FIELDS

	AGRICULTURE	ARTS and CRAFTS	COMMUNITY LIFE	HEALTH and SAFETY	HOMEMAKING	INTERNATIONAL FRIENDSHIP	LITERATURE and DRAMATICS	MUSIC and DANCING	NATURE	OUT-OF-DOORS	SPORTS and GAMES

Under each of the eleven program fields there are two Second Class activities—

and several proficiency badges—

Second Class

A girl must complete one of the Second Class activities in each of the eleven fields.

First Class

A girl must complete Second Class and earn at least twelve proficiency badges, as follows:

1. Four to six badges in one field. (This may be her major.)
2. The remainder from any other fields.

OTHER FIELDS

MAJOR FIELD — FOUR TO SIX BADGES

SECOND CLASS

THE TENDERFOOT RANK

The Tenderfoot rank is a requirement for membership in an Intermediate Girl Scout troop. Its purpose is to acquaint a girl with the ethical code, with some understanding of Girl Scouting and what membership in a national and international organization means, and to give her some experience in sharing in the life of a troop. Suggestions for activities covering the Tenderfoot rank are given on pages 37-45, since they are an essential part of every leader's first month with a new troop. The *Girl Scout Handbook* explains the requirements in detail.

Four weeks is the shortest period of time in which a girl can complete these requirements. Six weeks should be long enough for any girl if she has an opportunity for informal discussion and friendly conversation with her leaders and with other girls. A new girl entering an old troop may take part in other troop activities while she is fulfilling the Tenderfoot requirements. However, until after she is registered as a Tenderfoot Scout, she does not officially use the Girl Scout salute, give the Promise, or wear the uniform. After a girl has earned her Tenderfoot rank she may work on a proficiency badge or on the Second Class rank, or both at once.

SECOND CLASS RANK

The purpose of Second Class rank is to open up to girls a wide range of new experience. Therefore, one activity from each of the eleven program fields must be selected in order to earn this rank badge. The Second Class activities offered are basic ones and may be used as a lead into one or more proficiency badges, if the girls are sufficiently interested. Leaders often ask how long it should take to complete Second Class requirements. This is difficult to predict, but if a new troop of ten and eleven year olds decides to work on Second Class rank steadily, it might take from three to six months to finish. Well prepared Brownies who have become Girl Scouts might take less time. Older girls may progress more rapidly. Often a group stops in the middle somewhere because of interest in one subject and earns a proficiency badge in that field. The girls may go back to the Second

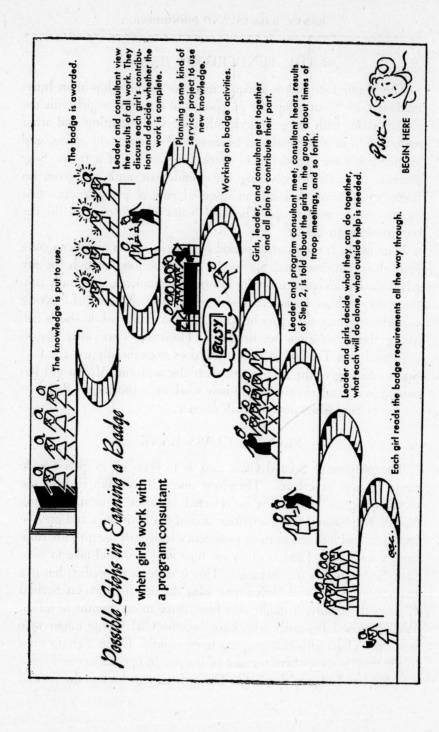

Class requirements after completing a badge or two, or they may work out a program for working on both simultaneously. This combination of interests extends the time for completing any one set of requirements. Second Class activities are especially appropriate for young girls whose attention span is short, or for girls who have not as yet any very definite interests. The requirements should be done as group activities in troop meetings whenever possible and represent a troop or patrol decision. For this reason the Second Class activities often furnish excellent and varied program material for new troops.

PROFICIENCY BADGES

Program material in one specific subject is developed in the form of proficiency badges. The badges suggest activities that girls like and can do well with a reasonable degree of effort. They are distributed among eleven different fields of interest in the Girl Scout program and allow for a wide range of choice. No one girl could possibly earn them all, but any girl, no matter what her background, should find many badges that she could enjoy earning. By having a program broad enough to offer privileges and responsibilities for all girls, such terms as handicapped, over- or underprivileged, foreign, will be lost in an emphasis on personal development and social adjustment.

The majority of the badges furnish good troop program material, as most of the activities are appropriate for groups of girls to do together. Some badges, such as Reader, Writer, Personal Health, put their chief emphasis on individual achievement. However, all badges include some group and some individual activities. This is in keeping with the objectives of Girl Scouting, which aim to develop a girl individually and as a cooperative member of a group. Every citizen in a democracy needs to develop her own abilities and at the same time learn to share and work with others.

A leader's responsibility in using the badge program is to see that a reasonable balance between group and individual activities is kept. If a girl is working alone or under the supervision of an adult on a badge such as Musician or Beekeeper, she should also be having the experience of working with other members of her troop on a badge that calls for many group activities. It is unwise to say that all badges must

[69]

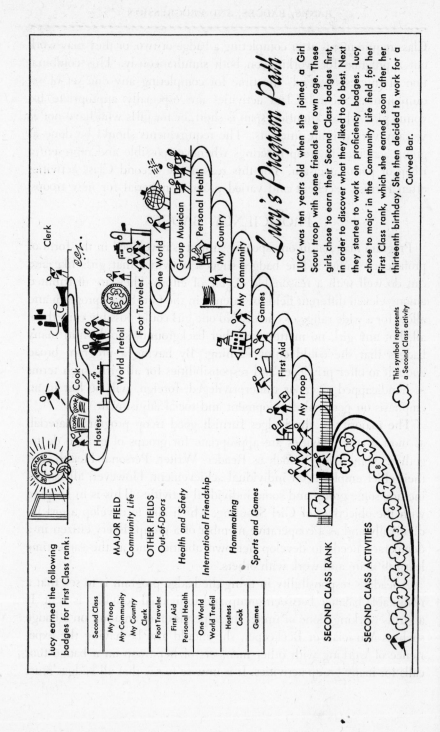

Lucy's Program Path

LUCY was ten years old when she joined a Girl Scout troop with some friends her own age. These girls chose to earn their Second Class badges first, in order to discover what they liked to do best. Next they started to work on proficiency badges. Lucy chose to major in the Community Life field for her First Class rank, which she earned soon after her thirteenth birthday. She then decided to work for a Curved Bar.

Clerk

Cook

Hostess

World Trefoil

Foot Traveler

One World

Group Musician

Personal Health

My Country

My Community

Games

First Aid

My Troop

⬤ This symbol represents a Second Class activity

Lucy earned the following badges for First Class rank:

Second Class
My Troop
My Community
My Country
Clerk
Foot Traveler
First Aid
Personal Health
One World
World Trefoil
Hostess
Cook
Games

MAJOR FIELD
Community Life

OTHER FIELDS
Out-of-Doors

Health and Safety

International Friendship

Homemaking

Sports and Games

SECOND CLASS RANK

SECOND CLASS ACTIVITIES

1 2 3 4 5 6 7 8 9 10

be earned at troop meetings, since this often does not allow variation enough for individual needs. Some girls have special talents or interests not shared by others, some have a good deal of leisure time that should be constructively used, while other troop members may be overburdened with outside activities. It is equally unwise to let girls do the majority of their badge work at home or unrelated to the regular troop program.

The question of credit for work done in school or elsewhere in relation to earning a badge often comes up. Cooking lessons in school, riding lessons at home, may prepare a girl for earning a badge or arouse her interest in it, but they should serve only as a starting point. As part of earning her badge she should practice in a different situation what she has learned elsewhere or choose more advanced activities or demonstrate her abilities by contributing to the troop program.

In selecting the activities in the badges, a three-month period was kept in mind as a reasonable length of time for earning a badge if girls worked on it steadily. Since badges are often combined or interwoven with many other troop activities, it may take up to six months or a year to complete the requirements. Arbitrary rules are dangerous and out of keeping with our general philosophy, but many leaders are puzzled about the interest span and the standard of performance to be expected from the average girl. In general, the younger the girl the more quickly she will need encouragement and definite recognition of progress. She has a short interest span; therefore the badges that can be completed in about three months are usually best for her. Girls over twelve have more success in combining two badges or in developing a longer-term project that might take five or six months to complete.

The badges marked Junior High have been developed particularly for this older girl who is usually in the seventh or eighth grade in school.

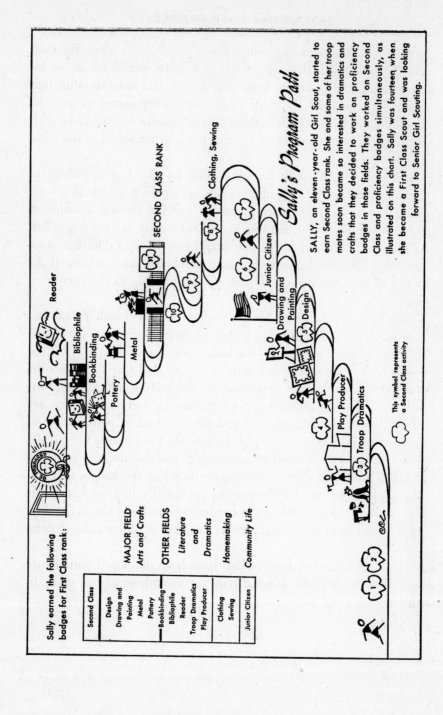

Sally earned the following badges for First Class rank:

Second Class	
MAJOR FIELD	Design
Arts and Crafts	Drawing and Painting
	Metal
	Pottery
OTHER FIELDS	Bookbinding
Literature and Dramatics	Bibliophile
	Reader
	Troop Dramatics
	Play Producer
Homemaking	Clothing
	Sewing
Community Life	Junior Citizen

Sally's Program Path

SALLY, an eleven-year-old Girl Scout, started to earn Second Class rank. She and some of her troop mates soon became so interested in dramatics and crafts that they decided to work on proficiency badges in those fields. They worked on Second Class and proficiency badges simultaneously, as illustrated on this chart. Sally was fourteen when she became a First Class Scout and was looking forward to Senior Girl Scouting.

This symbol represents a Second Class activity

Reader

Bibliophile

Bookbinding

Pottery

Metal

SECOND CLASS RANK

Clothing, Sewing

Junior Citizen

Drawing and Painting

Design

Play Producer

Troop Dramatics

A Guide for Developing a Badge (or Group of Badges) in Your Troop

1. Go over the badge as outlined in the *Girl Scout Handbook* so you will be ready to help the girls choose the activities that would be fun and useful to them. Girls are often tempted by activities that are too advanced, too expensive, or impractical for them. Avoid unnecessary disappointments.

2. Read what this book has to say about that particular program field in order to get the objectives clear in your mind. You will also find some useful hints about handling the activities and resources to which you can turn.

3. Start with a good, lively activity. This may be one chosen by the girls from the badge suggestions, or one selected by you because you think the troop will enjoy it. Try other related activities to see if the interest holds sufficiently to warrant the next steps. If the troop has already chosen many activities that fall under one badge, suggest the possibility of completing that badge.

4. Read and discuss with your girls the selection in the *Girl Scout Handbook* that tells about the field in which the badge belongs. This will help the girls to develop their own ideas and to start work.

5. Discuss which activities could be done in troop meeting and which ones at home or outside of troop meeting.

6. Decide on whether you and your assistant can handle the material alone. If you feel you need outside assistance, read pages 336-342 in this book. If you need books to help you, consult your library and the Girl Scout *Publications Catalog*.

7. Consider the following points in deciding when a girl has completed the badge:

a. Achievement of the objectives set up for the badge.

b. A reasonable amount of time and effort put into earning the badge.

c. Community service or pleasure to others that has been given while earning the badge.

d. Satisfactory completion of the required number of activities.

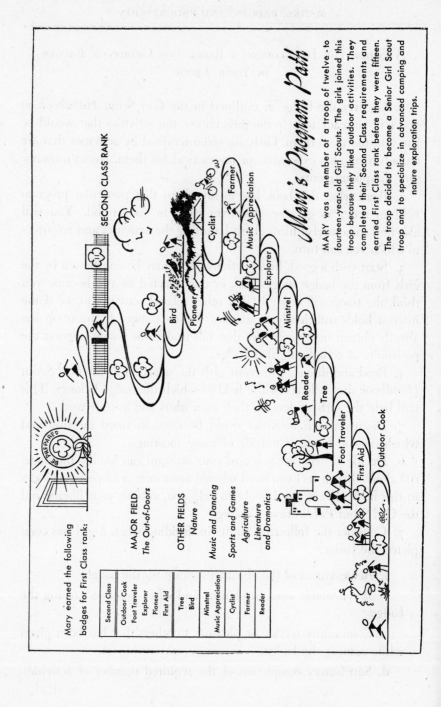

Mary earned the following
badges for First Class rank:

Second Class	
Outdoor Cook	
Foot Traveler	
Explorer	
Pioneer	
First Aid	
MAJOR FIELD	
The Out-of-Doors	
Tree	
Bird	
OTHER FIELDS	
Nature	
Minstrel	
Music Appreciation	
Music and Dancing	
Cyclist	
Farmer	
Reader	
Sports and Games	
Agriculture	
Literature	
and Dramatics	

SECOND CLASS RANK

Farmer

Cyclist

Music Appreciation

Bird

Pioneer

Explorer

Minstrel

Reader

Tree

Foot Traveler

First Aid

Outdoor Cook

BE PREPARED

Mary's Program Path

MARY was a member of a troop of twelve-to
fourteen-year-old Girl Scouts. The girls joined this
troop because they liked outdoor activities. They
completed their Second Class requirements and
earned First Class rank before they were fifteen.
The troop decided to become a Senior Girl Scout
troop and to specialize in advanced camping and
nature exploration trips.

FIRST CLASS RANK

The purpose of this rank is to encourage an all-round experience in Girl Scouting through learning many new skills and at the same time to develop a girl's chief interests and abilities. Two requirements were chosen with this purpose in mind.

1. Complete the Second Class rank.
2. Earn twelve badges, of which four to six are chosen from one program field and the remainder from other fields.

Here is where a leader's guidance is most important. Help your girls to choose a field in which they are really interested and in which they have definite ability. Too often they drift into their "major" because it is the easiest one in which to earn badges, or because they suddenly discover they have a couple of badges in that field and "they might as well" make that their major. After you have known a girl for at least a year, you should have a fairly clear idea of what she likes, what she needs, and what she can do well. On that basis talk to her about choosing a field in which to concentrate a year ahead of the time she would be ready for First Class rank. Make time to talk to her. During that year help her to work on badges that develop her best abilities. Give her an opportunity to share what she is learning through giving service to others in her community. Let her experience some of the intangible rewards for her work, such as social approval, a sense of personal adequacy, the feeling of being needed, and the sheer fun of doing something she enjoys.

The reason for limiting the number of badges in a major interest is again the desire that a girl's experience should not be too restricted. In exploring several other fields, she may choose related subjects or ones that are entirely different. Remember, the ultimate objective is an "intelligently participating citizen in a democratic social order." Attitudes, skills, and information that help a girl achieve that status are the ones to select.

First Class rank should indicate a few fields in which a girl has located and developed her abilities rather than show a mere smattering of information. Normally, most First Class Scouts would have earned the majority of their badges just in the process of sharing in general

[75]

troop program plans and in exploring their own interests. For instance, a girl who majored in Homemaking (five badges) might quite naturally have earned My Troop badge, Troop Dramatics, Minstrel, Backyard Camper, Outdoor Cook, and the Games badges as part of the regular troop activities. She then has ten badges to which she might add two representing a special individual interest, such as Home Gardener and Landscaper. Study the charts in this chapter. A leader's help in interpreting this plan is needed, for most young people are literal minded and inclined to get by with a minimum of effort. A leader who knows the Girl Scout standards and objectives can explain them to her girls in terms of their age, abilities, and local situation. No book written for girls all over the country can do it adequately.

A few other points on helping a girl to get the most from earning her First Class rank concern outside assistance and time allotment:

Make sure that a girl meets several program consultants in the major field she is offering for First Class work. She may do most of her badges under the direction of a consultant. But often much of her work is done at troop meetings under your supervision, or with the assistance of your troop committee. Somewhere along the line she should have a chance to talk with or work under an outside person who has a special interest in that field. Whenever possible use a consultant in other fields where a girl has shown a marked ability. This should widen her horizons and show her how she might continue with these activities beyond Girl Scouting, perhaps developing them as a permanent hobby or considering them seriously in relation to a future vocation. Many a girl has decided that she wishes to go into the field of health education, nursing, designing, or the natural sciences because of an early and interesting introduction to the subject. Both her high school years and her experience as a Senior Girl Scout can be more satisfactory if under wise guidance she has already located and developed some of her real abilities—or discovered her limitations—in an informal atmosphere where school grades do not have to be considered.

A First Class Scout is usually about thirteen or fourteen years of age or in junior high school. Only rarely would a girl under this age be sufficiently mature to have met the requirements properly. The aver-

[76]

age girl entering a troop around her tenth birthday might be First Class in three years if she worked hard. More often it takes longer, for badges should never be the whole of Girl Scouting. Community service, camping, parties, gay good times, and serious discussions are a vital part of our program. Some girls will not be interested in completing this rank, since other phases of the program may suit their needs better. This plan is for girls who need it and want it. Some troops prefer to select from the badges the program ideas they wish to develop in their own way. That is quite all right, if they develop their own goals and standards in keeping with those of the total Girl Scout movement. However, if a girl does wish to complete the First Class rank, she should meet the requirements fully and in such a way as to fulfill the objectives set up for them.

THE CURVED BAR

The Curved Bar is designed for the First Class Scout who wants something definite to work on until she graduates into a Senior troop. The whole plan is especially appropriate for girls of junior high school age who have increasingly grown-up interests. Work on the Curved Bar helps a girl prepare for the kind of Senior program she wants and gives her the skills she needs for advanced standing in a Senior group.

The requirements are:

1. Complete the First Class rank.

2. Earn at least four badges from one of the fourteen groupings under the Curved Bar heading in the *Girl Scout Handbook*. These badges must be earned *after* First Class rank has been completed. The groupings are: Agriculturist, Ambassador, Business Woman, Child Nurse, Docent, Entertainer, Flier, Forester, Homemaker, Nurse, Nutritionist, Play Leader, Sailor, Voyageur.

Each group includes six to eight badges. The one that is starred in each grouping in the *Handbook* must be earned if the girl has not previously earned it.

You will see that a high standard is asked of the girl and that she is expected to spend about a year earning the Curved Bar. She will want to demonstrate both her advanced skill and her ability to give service. A program consultant to advise on activities and standards and to give girls individual help will prove essential.

If you have a wide age range in your troop, you may have only one or two girls working for a Curved Bar. In that case, your responsibility is to help a girl choose her badges and find a program consultant to guide her work. Keep a friendly eye on her progress and make sure she has ample opportunity to fit her new skills and interests into the troop program. Girls working on a Curved Bar should be the most helpful and responsible members of the troop when planning program.

If you have a troop of older girls, you may have a large group working for a Curved Bar. This group is handled like any other interest group, with you and one or more program consultants helping the girls develop their plans and making their activities an important part of the troop program. Often you will find that girls working for First Class and for the Curved Bar are interested in the same badge. This simplifies planning and creates greater unity in the troop.

HELPING THE GIRLS CHOOSE

If you have helped a girl choose her major interest for the First Class rank, you probably know a good bit about her. When this same girl needs advice on selecting a grouping for her Curved Bar, you will want to ask her, and yourself, a number of questions.

Does she still have the same major interests she had a year ago? If she does, should she choose a related grouping? For instance, your ardent camper who chose the Out-of-Doors for her First Class might want to develop these interests further by choosing Ambassador, Voyageur, or Forester. These groupings would also prepare her as a Senior Girl Scout for international and trip camping, or the Ranger Aide program.

On the other hand, she may be in that unsettled state that makes her feel all former interests are childish. Can you help her decide what she wants to do this year and what kind of Senior program she might like to prepare for next year? Suggest another approach, such as Flier, Nutritionist, or Docent. These groupings can use her former skills in a new way, and be obvious preparations for the grown-up Wing Scout and Senior aide programs.

Should she be definitely encouraged to develop new interests because she is becoming one-sided? We all know girls who have become so absorbed in one creative activity, in sports, in nature, or in clothes, that we worry a bit about their all-round development. It is our responsibility to see that these girls are ready for a greater variety of interests before they enter high school. The outdoor girl might be encouraged to choose Homemaker by starting with one of the badges in that grouping that she would naturally enjoy, such as Handywoman, Garden Flower, or Community Safety. The girl whose chief interest is reading or writing or music could find social outlet for these interests in Play Leader or Child Nurse. The girl whose mind lingers unduly on clothes and what is known as "superficial things" would have an eye-opener by finding that the Good Grooming badge leads her into Nurse or Business Woman, and that becoming an Entertainer challenges her best efforts.

PREPARATION FOR SENIOR GIRL SCOUTING

Just as the Brownie Scout looks forward to joining an Intermediate troop, so should the older girl in your troop be thinking about becoming a Senior Girl Scout. A girl is usually ready to join a Senior troop when she has finished the eighth or ninth grade. You as her leader should encourage her graduation into this more mature club where she will be planning with girls of her own age the kind of recreation, service, and self-development that is important to all high school girls. She can, and should, take greater responsibility for managing her own affairs; she is on the threshold of becoming a self-directing adult, with the possibilities of homemaking, a job, and full-fledged citizenship just around the corner. Her younger years in your troop should mean she can move on to the more advanced program with a contribution to make and an ability to keep on growing. The activities and plan for First Class rank and the Curved Bar are excellent preparation for Senior Scouting. Read over these sections carefully with your own older girls in mind.

[79]

Don'ts for Earning Badges

not alone!

not by report!

not the examiner!

Progression from an Intermediate Troop to a Senior Troop

If there are only a few older girls in your troop, help them locate a Senior troop. Talk to the Senior leader about your girls and, if possible, arrange a plan for their graduation. It may be that your girls will be invited to visit some Senior meetings before they join. A joint party might be planned to include an official good-by and welcome. Or a Senior Scout might act as older sister to your girls and be responsible for taking them to her troop. She would introduce them to her friends, make them feel at home, and help them get started in the program.

If you have a large group of older girls who want to stay together, either you or your assistant might like to "graduate" with them and form your own Senior troop. Often a member of the troop committee will help one of you with the younger members until they, too, are ready to become Seniors.

If your entire troop is composed of junior high school girls, it is often possible for the whole group to set a date for becoming a Senior troop. You will need to consult your council about this, since it has the final decision about when girls should progress from one age-level program to another.

Many places feel that this progression should be arranged before the girls graduate from grade school. They will then be established as Senior Girl Scouts when they enter high school and not get lost over the summer months because of so many changes in their school life.

Junior High School Girls

We all know that when a girl goes into her teens or into junior high school she seems to develop as a new personality rather suddenly. She seems to outgrow her former interests and to try on the externals of young womanhood. Girls of this age in our troops either tend to drop out because all former activities seem childish, or they become a disrupting influence in the troop. This is all a quite natural part of growing up and we need to be prepared for it in our program planning. It will help if we remember that these girls have not changed fundamentally but merely wish to appear older.

[81]

Their sudden interest in boys is one sign of growing up, and you should be ready with ideas for possible activities. Many leaders find that including boys in the program is difficult, because boys of this age seldom admit any interest in girls. It is better not to try the dressed-up type of social activity that high school boys and girls enjoy, even if your girls ask for it. Suggest something more informal, such as a joint hike and treasure hunt, a barn dance with plenty of food and lively games, a hay ride with singing and ample refreshments. Boys of this age do like to eat, to make a lot of noise, and to show off their abilities. So do your girls. Both boys and girls can have a lot of fun together, provided they all feel comfortable and at ease with what they are doing. Husbands and fathers from the troop committee can be invaluable at this stage in your planning.

The starred badges in the *Girl Scout Handbook* are just for girls of this age and should be handled in as mature a way as possible. You will find in these badges many ideas for appropriate boy-girl activities, for important community service, and for fun on a more grown-up level. You have already seen that both First Class rank and Curved Bar are designed for girls between the ages of twelve to fourteen. If the girls' eyes could be turned toward Senior Scouting and the interesting, exciting things Senior Scouts do, many difficulties with our young teen-agers would be solved. They are so apt to think that Girl Scouting is what they did as little girls, because that is all they know or see. Most girls envy the clothes, the customs, and the privileges of their older sisters. It is perfectly natural for your older girls to want the dress, insignia, special privileges, and responsibilities of Senior Girl Scouts if they are acquainted with them. You help them get ready for this older program.

Mothers and fathers are familiar with the problem of the girl who wants to grow up too soon. They are also concerned with the girl who clings too long to childish ways and the security of staying with younger girls. Girl Scout leaders face these situations, too. They must find ways to help the first girl enjoy her present experiences while looking ahead, and to help the second girl feel confident enough in her abilities to "be her age" and to step along with her contemporaries.

A LEADER'S PROGRESS

QUESTIONS FOR CONSIDERATION

From time to time in the life of a Girl Scout leader there are moments of discouragement, moments when she questions her efforts in developing her girls. She wonders if the troop is accomplishing what it should. Evaluation of the effect of the program on girls, on herself, and on the community is a hard and thought-provoking job. The following questions may serve as a kind of guide to you in sorting out progress in leadership. You might ask yourself these questions every three months or so and develop a kind of measuring stick and a method for picking out strong and weak points.

Do not be surprised if, as your understanding broadens, you become more critical of your progress. Do not be discouraged to realize that it is hardly possible for all the questions to be answered satisfactorily at any one time. Help in answering these questions is to be found within the covers of this book.

TROOP MEMBERSHIP

Are there evidences of congeniality? What are they?

Are the girls all about the same age? Does this affect the troop program?

Are there differences in background? Does it matter?

Is there good group spirit or do the girls think mostly of themselves?

Are there any groups of girls who do not get along together? Which ones?

Is the troop small enough so that you and the girls really know one another?

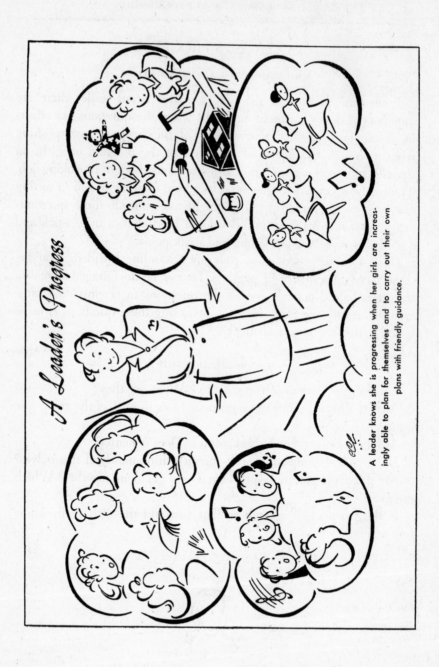

A Leader's Progress

A leader knows she is progressing when her girls are increasingly able to plan for themselves and to carry out their own plans with friendly guidance.

PROGRAM PLANNING AND TROOP MEETINGS

Do the meetings GO easily? What makes this happen?

Do the girls seem to like your ideas? How can you tell?

Do they have as many ideas as you do? Do you like their suggestions?

How do you find other clues to their interests?

Do you try to find out which activities the girls liked and which ones they did not like and why?

Does the year's program include a fairly wide variety of activities?

Are the girls encouraged to take part in a variety of activities or to continue along in one direction, depending on which they need to do the most?

Are some of the activities new experiences, some new ways of making familiar occupations more enjoyable, and some additional experiences along lines already explored?

Do the individual meetings usually include both quiet and exciting kinds of fun?

Do the girls understand the handling of troop finances in a businesslike way?

Are the girls encouraged to take responsibility?

Is each girl encouraged to do her best? If so, how?

Are the girls learning to work better with others or to work better alone, depending on which they need to do the most?

Are the girls encouraged to finish the things they start out to do?

Do the girls feel satisfied and successful when they are carrying out most of the program activities? Have they a feeling of progress?

Are the girls given opportunities to understand, practice, and develop honesty, loyalty, kindness, courtesy, responsibility?

TROOP MEETING PLACE

Is it large enough so that several activities may be carried on at the same time, and is the equipment suitable?

Is it clean, well lighted, well ventilated, and well heated?

Has the troop done anything to make it more attractive?

Is it easily accessible to the girls' homes?

Is there room to store the troop's own equipment?

Is there outdoor play space?

RELATION OF TROOP TO HOME AND COMMUNITY

Have any parents reported ways in which their daughters' participation in some phase of family life has increased because of the troop program?

Have the girls mentioned any instances or occasions when they have shared their troop interests with their families?

Have the parents of your girls helped with any of the troop activities or attended any troop affairs?

If the troop meets in a school, church, or community center, has it been a helpful and cooperative tenant?

Have the girls in the troop found ways of giving thoughtful assistance to organizations in the community or carried out a service project of their own making?

Have the program activities been carried out in such a way that the girls' knowledge about their community has been increased?

Has the troop program made intelligent use of the facilities the community offers?

Has the troop expressed its appreciation in some way to the older friends who have helped in various ways to carry out the program?

Has the troop done anything with other troops?

YOU AND YOUR RELATION TO THE TROOP

Do you enjoy the troop in the long run? (Discount the discouraging moments.)

What new interests or friends have you acquired because of Girl Scout activities?

Have you used good judgment in facing your own limitations as to time, energy, and ability, or have you become overtired or overanxious about your troop?

Have you been successful in choosing persons to help you and in working with your troop committee?

Do you think of the members of your troop as "just a lot of girls" or as separate personalities?

Do you know your girls well enough to understand them in relation to their family backgrounds?

Do the girls feel that you are to be trusted with confidences?

[86]

Do you accept the girls' reaction to program activities even when their idea of fun isn't the same as yours?

Do you respect the girls' ideas and do they know it?

Have you helped the troop to build up any traditions—ceremonies, celebrations, ways of being useful?

Are you friendly to everyone, or is it hard for you not to show partiality?

Does each girl feel free to talk to you?

Do all the girls enjoy working and playing together in troop activities?

The Troop's First Year

Many leaders feel that it is helpful to have a list of definite objectives to be reached by the end of the first year. The intangibles in terms of your girls' development, group morale, and social attitudes are very hard to measure. They are the most important of all, yet they are the by-product of well developed group activities and individual satisfactions. Following are some tangible objectives that could reasonably be reached during the first year and should indicate a healthy, flourishing troop.

PROGRAM

Interesting weekly meetings that girls attend regularly.

Hike or special expedition at least every other month.

Girls' progress in program indicated through earning at least two badges, one of which might be Second Class, depending on age and interests.

Impressive ceremonies developed by the girls that have meaning for your troop. These might include an investiture, an opening or closing for special occasions, a Court of Awards.

Evidence that the Girl Scout Promise and Laws have been understood and practiced.

Prompt reregistration of entire membership.

[87]

ORGANIZATION

At least one trained assistant who could take the leader's place.
A functioning troop committee.
An established troop budget plan.
A troop treasurer who understands the budget.
A troop secretary or scribe who understands her job.
Responsible patrol leaders or planning committee.
Regular meetings of the Court of Honor or planning group.

MEETING PLACE AND EQUIPMENT

An attractive meeting room.
Leaders and Girl Scouts in uniform.
Equipment and books needed to carry out program.

COMMUNITY RELATIONS

At least one community service project located and carried through
to a satisfactory conclusion.

At least one party or demonstration of some Girl Scout activity to
which parents or friends are invited.

Some contact with another troop or group of Girl Scouts to give
girls a feeling of belonging to a national and international organization.

Troop publicity in local or neighborhood paper.

Cooperation with local council activities.

New Ideas for Experienced Leaders

If you have been a leader for several years you have enjoyed the
companionship of your girls and the things you have done together.
You know the satisfaction of a community job well done. But possibly, human nature being what it is, you may feel you are getting
a bit stale on the job. Perhaps you do not have the same enthusiasm
for training a new group of little girls that you had in the beginning.
It may seem to you that your older girls are not as interested as they
used to be. There are even some leaders who feel that their long and
varied experience with Girl Scouts has given them the right to settle

[88]

back and let the troop move along in a comfortably ordered pattern.

Experienced leaders are such a tremendously valuable asset for Girl Scouting that they should occasionally treat themselves and others to a new kind of mental stimulation. If any of the above descriptions fit you, look over the following ideas and try out one or more:

1. Take a training course from which you will gain new convictions about Girl Scouting, new program skills, an opportunity to hold discussions with other leaders, expert advice.

2. Visit some other troop, play groups, or school classes that include girls the ages of yours. Talk to their leaders or teachers.

3. Read any three chapters in this book that you have not read or studied recently. The chapter on "Character Education" or "Group Control," for example, may have new meaning for you now.

4. Select at least one program field with which you are not familiar. Consider what parts of it might be enjoyed by your girls. Stimulate their interest and yours by doing some entirely different activities.

5. Discuss with your assistant leader or troop committee various methods for planning program or presenting material. For instance, give your assistant leader and older girls some new responsibilities; devise a way to give younger girls more voice in troop affairs; try out new teaching methods through discussion groups, dramatics, expeditions, social events, investigation of community resources.

6. Locate and use a program consultant.

7. Take a little vacation from your troop and let your assistant or troop committee carry on. During this vacation you could perhaps help some new leader get started.

Chapter Four

The Eleven Program Fields

HERE YOU WILL FIND ideas to guide you in determining what activities or which badges are the best for your particular group of girls. This chapter, together with the preceding one and the *Girl Scout Handbook,* will give you so many suggestions about what to do and how to do it that ten years with a Girl Scout troop will not seem long enough.

The chapter contains a brief section on each of the eleven program fields, which are Agriculture, Arts and Crafts, Community Life, Health and Safety, Homemaking, International Friendship, Literature and Dramatics, Music and Dancing, Nature, the Out-of-Doors, and Sports and Games. Each section covers three main points:

> *General purpose and point of view.*
> *Suggestions about badges.*
> *Chart showing how to weave group and individual achievement into the troop program.*

A s you can see by the chart on page 66, the rank and proficiency badge activities are distributed through eleven program fields in the Girl Scout program. These fields cover the actual or potential interests of girls and are grouped under eleven headings for the sake of convenience in locating ideas and source material. There is no boundary line between fields; many activities overlap or are so interwoven that their designation under one heading or another is purely arbitrary. In working out a troop program related activities are naturally combined. There is no need to treat the developing interests of a group as reference material that must be classified to be easily found. For example, it is clearly not possible to separate health from sports and games, nature from the out-of-doors, or community life from homemaking and the arts. The Brownie and Senior Girl Scout program use these same fields of interest, though the program pattern and the activities selected are suited to the ages and interests of the group they serve.

You will want to be familiar with the aims and standards for each field, since they will guide you in deciding *when, why,* and *how* to encourage interests in some activities and not in others. The brief description of individual badges will help you decide whether the activities are suitable to the age and interests of your girls. In each field certain badges are recommended for beginners or for younger girls, while others are designed primarily for girls of junior high school age; some badges require standards of physical fitness or preliminary experience; some require definite talent; others need only a sincere interest and willingness to work.

Be sure to read in the preceding chapter the suggestions for ways of developing all badges.

AGRICULTURE

Agriculture has to do with the things we raise for human consumption. It is of paramount interest to all the world.

GENERAL PURPOSE AND POINT OF VIEW

The general objectives of the Agriculture field are to help each Girl Scout to:

Appreciate raising and producing food as one of the most important occupations. Lack of proper foods has caused wars; it breeds ill health and ill will; it keeps people from doing their share of the world's work.

We all have to eat and, in this country, the day has passed when each family raises the greater part of the food they consume. Now, the few feed the many.

Understand food values and costs. Most people have little comprehension of the amount of time, money, and skill needed to get hens to produce good eggs and produce plentifully; or, how much time, skill, fertilizer, spray, and equipment are needed to produce good string beans. Too few people know what a piece of fruit or a vegetable really looks like when it is in prime condition.

Put more variety into family meals, when she is responsible for them. Eating habits are strong and fairly set with most people. An interest in agriculture and the many types of vegetables, meat, and fruit produced in this country should add variety and interest to meals. It is also possible to learn to eat the food that is, at the moment, cheapest and in best condition.

Feel a greater responsibility for humane practices in the raising, use, and slaughtering of livestock. An animal is a living creature that feels pain and fright as we do. We depend upon farm animals for an existence, and we owe these creatures our vigilance in doing all we can to see that humane methods are practiced.

Understand pure food laws. These laws are a great protection to the health of our country and should be understood, improved, and upheld by all citizens.

Have a greater understanding of the need for conservation. We mean conservation in its broadest sense—conservation of food, soil, wildlife, forests, and waterways.

[92]

Food is life. It comes from living things and keeps us on this earth as living things. Wasting food is wasting life and no good can come of it.

To produce such things as livestock, grains, vegetables, fruits, and honey, we have to have soil. We have to practice conservation in using the soil in order to keep the soil producing. This means careful use of the land and fertilizing to replenish the chemicals used by growing plants.

Trees are valuable to us for many reasons, some of which are: keeping soil in place; storing up water; and providing shade for livestock, shelter for various forms of wildlife, and lumber for human needs.

Wildlife includes all forms of wild animal and plant life. Most forms are valuable in the field of Agriculture. We should have very little fruit if it were not for insects, especially bees. We should have too many mice and moles, rabbits and woodchucks, if it were not for the owls, hawks, foxes, and snakes. We should have too many insects were it not for birds, snakes, moles, and skunks.

Those who work for badges in the field of Agriculture will gain a knowledge of the interdependence of plants and animals.

The field of Agriculture is very closely allied with the fields of Nature, Homemaking, and Health and Safety.

The Troop Garden

The smallest plot of land can yield amazing results. Gardening offers a first-hand and worth-while introduction to the great field of Agriculture. Interest in any of the following badges can be developed through a garden that is part of the troop meeting place, or a neighbor's back yard or bit of farm land.

AGRICULTURE FIELD

SECOND CLASS ACTIVITIES NO. 1, 2

Home Gardener Badge

Fruit Raiser Badge

Landscaper Badge

Beekeeper Badge

Farmer Badge

HINTS FOR BADGE ACTIVITIES

The activities in the field of Agriculture—as in any other field of interest—can be group activities or individual activities. For instance, *one* girl, all by herself, may learn how to "introduce a new queen bee into a hive of bees," or she may learn it in a group. Because it *is* more fun to learn along with other people, it would be hoped that groups of girls would work on these activities.

Girls who live on farms or near farms will have a greater opportunity to do things in the field of Agriculture all the year around. Girls who live in the city or in suburban areas and spend part of the year in the country will find that they can do some of the activities in the winter and part of them in the summer. For instance, a girl does not have to live on a farm to "be able to describe the food values of milk and milk products," and "know three recipes using milk products in quantity." But she does have to get somewhere near a cow to "know how to milk a cow by hand or to strip after machine milking."

There is one over-all badge, called "Farmer," which is designed as an introduction to Agriculture. It gives a bird's-eye view of the whole field. Most of the requirements for this badge can be met during a ten-week summer vacation on a farm.

None of the badges in the Agriculture field can be earned by a girl who spends fifty-two weeks a year in a large city. But there are many activities under these badges that such a girl would find interesting and possible to do.

Many a city dweller, old and young, hopes for the day when he or she can live in the country and have chickens, or cows, or sheep, or fruit trees, or a large garden. So it stands to reason that many city girls will be interested to do some of the activities in Agriculture, badge or no badge! Someday those girls *may* live in the country and will have a body of knowledge that will make country living, for them, a success.

An interest in agriculture cannot help but make a person more resourceful. When you live on a farm you cannot run around the corner to the delicatessen, or to the hardware store, or to the cleaner. You have to plan ahead, go without, or make something else do. This

[95]

training in resourcefulness should get into all activities in the field of Agriculture.

There are many sources of help for the Agriculture field, the greatest one being our own United States Department of Agriculture. The headquarters of this department are in Washington, D. C. But it has branches in every state called the "Extension Service." The state extension service can be found at the state college. This extension service is also carried into counties and headed by the "county agent," who helps farmers with technical knowledge to make better farms. His office will be found at the county seat. The "home agent" —at the same address—is a woman who helps farm women learn the best ways to do *their* part of farm work. The state or county extension head will have free publications that will be most useful for the badges in the field of Agriculture. Also, you may write to the Superintendent of Documents, Washington, D. C., and ask for price lists of publications. We suggest the following subjects: foods and cooking; fish and wildlife; animal industry; insects; irrigation, drainage, and water power; forestry; plants; agricultural chemistry and soils and fertilizers; farm management. You will find, in these price lists, mostly booklets and pamphlets at a very low price.

The Extension Service of the Department of Agriculture helped in planning the Girl Scout field of Agriculture. It is the hope of the Extension Service, and our hope, that the Girl Scouts and the 4-H Clubs will find many ways in which they can work together for the betterment of a community. Agriculture is only one of the fields of human endeavor in which these two organizations can work for the common good. We hope to learn as much about each other's programs as possible and share each other's facilities when necessary or desirable. By facilities we mean such things as meeting places, camps, equipment, and personnel.*

---

* See *Memorandum of Relationships Between Girl Scouts and The Extension Service of the United States Department of Agriculture.* One copy, free, from the Program Department, Girl Scouts of the U.S.A.

ARTS AND CRAFTS

Every girl has creative ability.
Give her an opportunity to find it and to use it.

GENERAL PURPOSE AND POINT OF VIEW

The activities offered in this field aim to stimulate an interest in creative activities through individual and group participation, and through understanding and appreciation of the work of others. These creative activities weave naturally and easily into other parts of the Girl Scout program, coloring and affecting the whole pattern as a bright thread is carried on the shuttle back and forth on a loom. For instance, if a Girl Scout is interested in homemaking, she might turn first to the nature program where a quickened observation would see the color harmonies in plants, birds, insects, animals, and minerals—color harmonies that could be adapted to color schemes for room furnishing, table decorations, dress. Design motifs could be built up from the multitude of patterns found in the wide field of nature study and used to decorate textiles, pottery, and other homemaking crafts.

Ability to sketch and design would help in drama and in nature study. Skill with her hands would make the Girl Scout a more efficient camper, Mariner, or even musician, for she could mend or make her own musical instruments, make carrying cases for them, or make portfolios for her music.

In the dawn days of the world, primitive man looked at the earth and all the things that grew on and in the earth. He thought and reasoned about the use he might make of the trees and grasses, rocks, earth, and minerals. Then, with his hands, he fashioned from these earth-gifts many things, rough and crude at first, more finished as his hands became more deft with practice. Shelter, arms, boats, furniture, cooking utensils—little by little he made the great adventure of living less difficult by the things he made. This was the origin of the crafts.

Later, when the beauty of sunset colors, the lilt of birdsong, and the dance of wind-blown trees filled man with joyous dreams, he decorated the things he had made with rhythmic and colorful designs and pictures. This was the origin of art.

[97]

The Troop Meeting Place

Every troop would like to improve its meeting place. Each girl has abilities that can be developed to help this common cause. One or more of the badges below will suggest activities that can help create an attractive troop home. At the same time a girl may be started on a life long interest.

ARTS AND CRAFTS FIELD

SECOND CLASS ACTIVITIES No. 1, 2

Needlecraft Badge

Wood Badge

Bookbinding Badge

Design Badge

Interior Decoration Badge

It is almost impossible, however, to make a definite distinction between the arts and the crafts—we cannot say where one ends and the other begins. In the dictionary we find these definitions:

Craft— Dexterity and skill in a manual employment.

Art—Expression of beauty in form, color, sound, or movement.

The development of dexterity and skill with our hands may eventually give us the ability to express beauty of form. To illustrate: we may work in wood carving until we are able to handle our tools so skillfully that we may produce some exquisite examples of wood sculpture; we may do simple pattern weaving and learn through practice to express creative beauty in a tapestry that would be recognized and given the appreciation due a work of art.

HINTS FOR BADGE ACTIVITIES

In the suggested list of activities, therefore, no attempt has been made to separate the arts from the crafts. Under each of the badges listed, the fivefold objective would be to develop: creative ability, skills, appreciation, lasting interests, and relationship with other program fields.

In all work done in this field, our creed is:

All work shall be original. We will do no copying or tracing of pictures or designs. All work shall be made of real materials used honestly. We will not try to make paper look like reed, or cloth resemble leather. All work shall be honestly and entirely our own. We will not use assembled or cut-out projects that are partly worked out.

At first glance, the amount of material incorporated in the Arts and Crafts field is somewhat bewildering. However, if the Girl Scout leader will consider the suggested badge activities in relation to her own community and her own troop, she will find that they fall easily into an ordered pattern.

They are bewildering because they have been selected with a view to covering a wide range of localities and situations—large cities, small villages, lone troops, farm communities, North, East, South, and West. They fall into ordered patterns when, from the lists, the leader helps the girl to select those activities that can be adequately carried out with the facilities available.

In developing this ordered pattern it will be helpful to consider the various steps to be taken. First and most important is the elimination of fear—an age-old fear that has separated us from the natural joy of creative activity. We fear the unknown. Therefore, the best antidote to fear is knowledge gained from doing an activity. Encourage the girls to try simple pencil sketching, painting, modeling, even photographing the things they see about them. Point out that their first efforts, like their first efforts in learning to swim, dance, or play the piano, are preliminary practice steps and they must not expect professional work with the first try. Encourage them to try again by commenting on the good points in their work and giving a few suggestions about making their ideas clearer. *Pencil Sketching* by Evelyne Geen* will help. The same method may be used in selecting color and developing design for weaving, needlecraft, and other crafts. *Arts and Crafts with Inexpensive Materials** is a small book that will suggest many good beginnings. We must set our standards high, accept them inevitably as our own, and set out toward them courageously and with enthusiasm. Our own courage and enthusiasm as leaders will set the pace for the girls and a spontaneous response will result.

Our second step might well be to consider not what to do but what the community offers; the facilities available may determine the choice of what to do. If there is a well known pottery in your city, you may find it very easy to stimulate an interest in this craft through visits to the pottery, through instruction and guidance from one or more workers in the pottery, through help with firing, and finally through having a place to procure materials. If there is a furniture factory, it may be possible to study the many types of wood and the methods of curing, cutting, and finishing as well as to procure scraps of beautiful wood for carving.

When museum classes offer opportunity for study in painting, modeling, or the study of pictures, the problem is solved, or, should we say, there is no problem. One of the most valuable things Girl Scouts can gain from the Arts and Crafts field is the habit of using museums intelligently. If there is no museum in your community it

* See Girl Scout *Publications Catalog.*

is often possible to obtain by mail from nearby cities helps such as printed lectures, illustrated with lantern slides, that can be delivered by Girl Scouts; moving pictures; books and pamphlets.

Libraries are of the greatest help in this field. If you do not have a public library, the state library may be asked to lend books. See Chapter Eleven, "Working with Your Community."

Professional artists and craftsmen are glad to lend a helping hand, if our activities are of the type that measure up to their standards. In asking help from artists, we must be wise. We cannot expect them to do our work for us, such as conducting weekly classes for our troops, ordering materials, deciding upon programs, and so forth. We should first make an effort to get under way with the subject chosen and then ask them to come in for criticisms and suggestions.

COMMUNITY LIFE

To be a good citizen, a girl should know
and appreciate her community.
Help her to serve it democratically.

General Purpose and Point of View

The general purpose of this field is to help each girl develop a better understanding of and loyalty to the ideals of her country. The activities aim to encourage an interest in the current affairs of her community, a desire to serve her community and nation, and a pride in the epic that is America. They aim to develop a zest for truth in forming opinions on social issues and a faith in the power of American men and women to improve themselves and their surroundings in a modern and changing society.

The feeling that every single American has a responsibility in preserving and safeguarding the heritage that is American democracy is apparent on every hand. This readiness and earnestness undoubtedly affects Girl Scouts and is a spur to them when learning about their community and their responsibilities toward it.

The first chapter in this book attempts to show the importance of citizenship training for every girl; read it over again if you are about

Troop Community Service

Every troop wishes to do community service as a part of its program. Community life and community service branch into every field in the Girl Scout program. This page shows how a girl, or a group of girls, could do many of the Second Class requirements and complete certain other badge activities through a community service program.

AGRICULTURE
Second Class No. 2
Give flowers or plant to hospital or shut-ins.

ARTS AND CRAFTS
Second Class No. 1
Make articles for a community agency or a church bazaar.

COMMUNITY LIFE
Second Class No. 1
My Community Badge
activity 15

HEALTH AND SAFETY
Community Safety Badge
activities 1, 3
Public Health Badge
activities 2, 12, 14

HOMEMAKING
Second Class No. 1
Let the group entertained be younger children in need of a special treat.
Sewing Badge
activity 24

INTERNATIONAL FRIENDSHIP
One World Badge
activities 2, 11
World Gifts Badge
activities 14, 15

COMMUNITY LIFE FIELD

MUSIC AND DANCING
Second Class No. 1
Could be used in entertaining young children.
Group Musician Badge
activities 9, 13

LITERATURE AND DRAMATICS
Second Class No. 2
Offer services to library.
Troop Dramatics Badge
activities 12, 13

THE OUT-OF-DOORS
Foot Traveler Badge
Earn by getting acquainted with the community and while giving service.

NATURE
Any of the conservation activities.
Conservation Badge

SPORTS AND GAMES
Cyclist Badge
activity 7
Games Badge
activity 14

to start on this field. One of the basic tenets of the Girl Scout program is service to others, and the activities in this field are definite suggestions of ways to bring these objectives to actuality. Nearly every chapter in this book has amplifications of these objectives and examples of how troops have developed these activities. In a sense the entire Girl Scout program comes under this heading, since our overall purpose is preparation for community life.

HINTS FOR BADGE ACTIVITIES

All the badges listed in this field should result in some real value to the girl's community, such as actual improvement of living in her own community; desire on the girl's part to share actively in her community's responsibilities appropriate to her own age and ability; awareness of some of the underlying causes of the problems of social welfare, whether conservation of national resources or care of persons needing special assistance. Every community is filled with challenges for service if girls but look for them. Girls need a constructive outlet for their energies. Without the sense of "belonging" in the more serious phases of living, without the responsibility of making a contribution to a larger group, girls cannot develop the character traits so necessary in an American democratic society.

For most Girl Scouts the starting place is most naturally an increased awareness of their troop or their patrol group. If it is the latter, the leader must be very sure that the patrol helps rather than hinders the solidarity of the whole troop. There must be no such thing as a socially most desirable clique that keeps out certain others. Instead, the patrol, even though it may have certain interests of its own, should be still very much alive to its membership in the troop and eager to do its part toward building up troop morale. On the other hand, the idea that strikes fire may be the thrill of feeling oneself a member of something much bigger than one's own little group.

For this reason almost any activity in the My Troop badge makes a good beginning. Here a Girl Scout learns more about group living in her own troop and about her troop's place in a national and international organization. She must be a contributing member and do her part with others in making her troop better because she is a mem-

[103]

ber of it and can take responsibility in its self-government. The Speaker badge is especially helpful for older girls in developing leadership ability and training in citizenship. My Community badge suggests ways to explore a girl's town, village, or city and to learn more about its educational and recreational facilities, its people, occupations, and the interdependence of communities. Interest in community service can either lead into this badge or be interwoven with it. The activities in My Country badge are to acquaint a girl with a geographical section of the United States different from her own, such as the Northwest, New England, the deep South. The story of the building of America is full of colorful romance and poetry, and all young Americans delight in it. Perhaps the most important and the most profitable badge from the standpoint of citizenship training is the Junior Citizen badge. It includes activities about taxes, voting, forming an opinion, care of public property, citizenship status, and our patriotic symbols such as the Flag, the national anthem, the Statue of Liberty. In general this badge should be preceded by or earned in conjunction with one of the others. The Aviation, Radio, and Traveler badges deal with the activities that bind together the people of the nation and world. Every girl today is vitally interested in radio, in telephone, and in air, land, and sea travel, and in all the factors that make all peoples increasingly interdependent.

Other important badges belonging jointly to this field and Health and Safety field are the Public Health and Community Safety badges. They suggest many activities for community service and for understanding and appreciating one's own community.

Refer to the guide for selecting effective community service on pages 348-349. This guide is particularly important to use in connection with the badges in this field.

HEALTH AND SAFETY

Health and happiness for oneself and others.
The Girl Scouts' motto is "Be Prepared."

GENERAL PURPOSE AND POINT OF VIEW

The general purpose of this field is to help each girl develop wholesome ideals of health, regarding health as a means to an end, not an end in itself. She should appreciate health as well adjusted living through which, despite possible handicaps, she may attain usefulness and happiness. The activities offered aim to establish desirable habits and skills and to increase her knowledge of health and safety through study of scientific principles, through appreciation of the family physician, and through the functions of public and private agencies. Each girl should be helped to accept responsibility for the health and safety of herself and others, to understand the common causes of accident, and to make a concrete contribution to the general safety of the community.

Health and safety in the Girl Scout program are not topics to be talked about but are ways of "doing" that bring enrichment of life. Health is more than mere physical well-being. It includes mental, emotional, and social aspects of development. The leader of a Girl Scout troop has a valuable opportunity to observe her individual girls and to meet their health needs through activities that are related to their own interests that are centered around their daily life in home, school, and troop.

An effective safety program has a vitally important part to play in the promotion of human well-being. In guiding such a program do not make a girl overcautious or overconcerned about dangers but help her to recognize problems that involve safety and to maintain a sane attitude toward them. Encourage her to avoid creating accident hazards beyond her ability to remove. She should realize the value of meeting these unavoidable hazards intelligently and courageously. These results may be achieved by learning just what to do in actual situations, as part of her everyday experience.

Many of the activities in this field have been purposely selected as introductory to those of a more complicated or specialized nature,

[105]

Troop Hikes and Expeditions

Every troop goes on hikes into the country and on expeditions around town.
While the girls are having a good time exploring their countryside and community
they may cover much of the Health and Safety field. Activities chosen from one
or more of the badges below make these expeditions more than just fun. They
contribute to a girl's physical fitness, self-reliance, thoughtfulness of others, and to
an appreciation of how her community protects its citizens.

HEALTH AND SAFETY FIELD

SECOND CLASS ACTIVITY NO. 1

Personal Health Badge

First Aid Badge

Outdoor Safety Badge

Community Safety Badge

Public Health Badge

which require mature judgment, poise, ability, and skill. A Girl Scout may pursue this specialization in the Senior Girl Scout program or in the field of a selected vocation.

The Personal Health badge is basic not only to other badges in this field but to many in other fields, such as the Out-of-Doors, and Sports and Games. In helping a girl to choose concrete activities that will promote her well rounded growth there are four things to be kept in mind:

1. Importance of a leader's own example of healthful living.

2. Appraisal of the girl's health and vigor through the leader's observation; reports from a physician, dentist, the girl's parents, and possibly school cooperation. A Health Examination Record form has been developed by the National Health and Safety Committee and may be ordered from the National Equipment Service.

3. Use of the girl's interest as a guide in selecting activities. For example: does she want to be good at sports, dance well, or be attractive looking?

4. The need for directing a girl to reliable and authentic sources for information.

Obviously, the test of the program is not found in the girl's acquisition of knowledge, but in its effect upon her actual health and happiness.

The Home Health and Safety and the Farm Safety badges suggest many stimulating possibilities for the girl who is interested in homemaking and her own environment. It is well to remember that the number of fatal accidents occurring in and around the home nearly equals the highway accident toll. Orderliness, cleanliness, courtesy, and alertness to hazardous conditions all appear in these activities and should be the points of approach and emphasis.

The Home Nurse and Child Care badges are best suited to the more mature Girl Scout, although the activities that require techniques and responsibilities too advanced for the twelve- to fourteen-year-old girl have been definitely excluded. However, a junior high school girl earning the Home Nurse badge should be able to give ordinary bedside care, to cooperate intelligently with a physician in following his orders for the patient, and to help adjust the home situation to meet the needs of the sick person. A girl earning the Child Care badge should understand the essentials of the protection, care, and feeding of normal infants and children. She should also know enough about the behavior and interests of babies and little children to be able to look after them and amuse them successfully for short periods of time.

The Public Health and Community Safety badges are closely related to activities in the Community Life field and to the desire to be of service. Any troop looking for practical ways to be of service to its community will find a wealth of interesting suggestions in these badges.

The Outdoor Safety badge is an excellent one for the lively outdoor-minded troop. It can be earned in combination with many other badges, particularly those in the Out-of-Doors, Nature, and Sports and Games fields.

The First Aid badge takes into account two important reasons for giving first aid instruction to every lay person:

First: The increasing accident toll of today. This increase is evidence of greater need for emphasis upon accident prevention and the proper care of injury.

Second: The practical importance of knowing what to do first in the ordinary emergencies of everyday life.

Obviously it is praiseworthy to care for the injured. But since there are many injuries that need not have occurred in the first place, it is wise to give thought to the prevention of accidents. All possible causes should be eliminated. The best advice on accidents is, therefore, "Don't have one." The idea of having an accident-free record should be presented to the girl as a matter of pride and satisfaction. She should also be guided to analyze all accident situations to discover possible causes and means of preventing similar occurrences.

Proper first aid, promptly given, is a safety measure designed to prevent needless complications. Training in first aid should, therefore, equip the girl with knowledge of the first simple, sensible, and effective things to do in an emergency until the doctor arrives, and should train her to be expert in performance of such first aid.

Indirectly, these activities should also help to prepare the girl to act with poise and to render intelligent service in time of possible emergency or disaster.

Instruction in first aid is given by an especially qualified person usually in cooperation with the American Red Cross. Any girl completing the Junior Red Cross First Aid Course will have covered the activities in this badge. But girls too young to be admitted to that course may earn this badge under a qualified instructor, since it is especially designed for younger girls.

The First Aid to Animals badge is designed for the girl who has a pet in her home or who lives on a farm. It combines well with the Cat and Dog badge or with those badges in the field of Agriculture that deal with domestic animals. It must be earned under the guidance of a veterinary.

HOMEMAKING

A woman's greatest job is that of homemaker.
Help each girl to understand the attitudes and the skills
that will make her home a pleasant place.

GENERAL PURPOSE AND POINT OF VIEW

The general purpose of this field is to help each girl feel an increased enjoyment of her home through understanding what is involved in caring for the needs of a family, and to increase her security in family relationships through broadening her interests in her home and her ability as a homemaker. The activities aim to develop greater skill in caring for the health and comfort of a family; in the art of hospitality and the acquisition of social poise; in the selection and care of household furnishings and equipment; and in the purchasing, making, and care of suitable and attractive clothing.

People live in houses but all people do not live in homes. Throughout life a woman must make a home for herself and perhaps others. Oftentimes that home is only one room; again it may be a small apartment, a modest cottage, or a large house. Whatever the size, all attitudes and activities should aim toward creating a real spirit of homelikeness.

The Girl Scout has a wonderful opportunity to contribute toward the establishment and functioning of a real home. It is her instinctive gift to create a certain atmosphere that means home, whether it is a hotel room, a tent at camp, or an emergency shelter, and we must help her do this. Homemaking activities have many appeals. The girl may be interested in daily home activities because of the personal satisfaction they bring, she may see herself as a responsible citizen by having homemaking tasks of her own, she may want the security in her social life that a knowledge of homemaking can bring. No matter what her motive, there is another aspect to be considered: the girl is in a profession, the most important profession of life—that of homemaking. It is with the present as well as the future in mind that leaders of Girl Scouts may work with their girls in this program field. All young girls, however, are not automatically interested in their homes or in the variety of concerns that center there. Almost all persons discover when they are quite young that experiences that seem dull as a part of everyday living gain greatly in interest when they take place in other surroundings or are shared with friends.

Hints for Badge Activities

Most school systems include homemaking in their curricula, but the completeness of their program varies from school to school and community to community. The use of the homemaking activities in the Girl Scout program should vary similarly, since it would be foolish to attempt to duplicate a very complete homemaking program carried out under trained leadership in the schools. The two programs, however, can dovetail nicely, for it will be valuable to use in troop meetings many activities that girls first learned in school. By repeating activities under different conditions, or by choosing more advanced ones, there should be no reason for a girl to request "credit" for school work, or to feel she is asked for needless duplication of effort. Whatever a girl learns in school she learns for the very purpose of using somewhere else.

In all phases of the program the need to keep the activities real and readily accomplished by many girls is of tremendous importance. A very decided effort has been made to relate the activities to social

A Parent-Daughter Supper

Mothers and fathers should have an opportunity to see their daughters' troop in action. Nothing is more satisfying to both parents and daughter than a demonstration of a girl's ability to be a charming hostess and an efficient cook. A well planned dinner party, often with special entertainment, may be the high point in earning one or more of the badges below.

HOMEMAKING FIELD

SECOND CLASS ACTIVITY NO. 1

Hostess Badge

Cook Badge

Foods Badge

Troop Dramatics Badge

Group Musician Badge

trends, such as the rapid growth in the number of people living in apartments, and the diminishing of services performed in the modern home. With the objectives of this program field carefully in mind, the following badges have been developed around home needs and responsibilities. In addition, four badges in other fields belong jointly to this one. These are Home Health and Safety, Home Nurse, Child Care, and Interior Decoration badges.

The Cook and Foods badges are in a sense twins, and troops often elect to work on them together. Girls between the ages of ten and twelve are young to consider the finer points of cooking as an art, but some use of this approach could be quite entertaining and stimulating, especially to those girls to whom cooking at home or in school may seem like an old story. The romantic aspects of the family diet, not very evident at first, can surprise the Girl Scout who embarks on the Foods badge. She discovers that fruits and vegetables, meat and eggs, can become as interesting as characters in a play. For the girls over twelve, the Nutrition badge offers a more serious and thorough approach to the subject of good eating.

Satisfactory home membership frequently rests on appreciation of the home itself and of the contribution of the parents and brothers and sisters to the running of the home. Both the Housekeeper and Handywoman badges suggest activities that are practical and point toward useful home service. In the Handywoman badge especially, there are activities in which father and daughter find a common bond. For a troop wishing to fix up its meeting place, or for a girl with a mechanical or manual gift, this is a fine badge.

We cannot overestimate the importance that appearing well dressed has in the eyes of the young adolescent, nor the connection between suitable clothes and satisfactory social adjustment. For that reason, there are three badges related to the subject, two especially designed for the junior high school age. Girls of this age all recognize the fact that clothing budgets are limited and that good taste must be combined with the ability to make or purchase becoming clothes that will wear well and fill the most needs. There are few girls of this age who do not want or need help with some phase of this subject. The Sewing badge is for the girl who has, or who would like to develop, a gift with the needle. There is a section for beginners, and one for advanced sewers who would like to make their own clothes. The Clothing badge is devoted to the subject of planning and selecting a suitable and attractive wardrobe with an eye on the budget. The Good Grooming badge is full of practical suggestions and activities; it points out the relation between posture, poise, good health, and good looks and how a girl may look her best in every detail.

The activities in the Hostess badge offer many opportunities to develop that ease in social relationships on which so many phases of social adjustment depend. Everyone wants to give a good party but the young hostess of Girl Scout age needs to develop an understanding of hospitality based on graciousness and the knowledge of social customs. Important as the details of party giving—good manners, menus, decorations—are to the hostess, these are but secondary to her real concern, which is the enjoyment and comfort of her guests. This is an important badge for any troop interested in homemaking, since it may be related to or interwoven with any of the other badges. It provides activities in which the whole troop can share, thus checking any tendency toward choosing too many individual or outside activities unrelated to the troop program.

INTERNATIONAL FRIENDSHIP

Every girl must feel her responsibility for world citizenship. Girl Scouts and Girl Guides in every land build toward international understanding and friendliness, the basis of world peace.

GENERAL PURPOSE AND POINT OF VIEW

The general purpose of this field is to develop an understanding of other countries and peoples, based on a knowledge of their culture and their customs and a respect for what each country and its people have contributed to the world family of nations in which we take our own place. The activities offer each girl an opportunity to learn more about the contributions that other countries and the United States

[113]

of America have made to each other, and to discover more about girls and Girl Scouting in other countries.

A basic point of view in this field is that the attitudes for international good will are developed close at home by friendliness and understanding of people in our own community who come from different racial, national, or cultural backgrounds.

The suggestions aim to develop a knowledge of factors that make for friendly or unfriendly relations between nations; of cooperative undertakings for peace; and of the work of the United Nations and its efforts toward settling disputes between nations amicably.

Never in the history of the world has there been a greater need for young people to work toward the above objectives. Training for world citizenship· is the greatest task that confronts us all, and the people of the United States are now realizing this responsibility. Our country, as hostess to the United Nations and with tremendous resources at its disposal, is committed to aiding and developing a worldwide "good neighbor" policy. Girls whose relatives and friends have served overseas have acquired interest in and information about all corners of the globe. Not one of your girls is too young to understand the importance of world peace and the attitudes necessary to maintain it.

Girl Scouting in the United States, as a member of the World Association of Girl Guides and Girl Scouts, has an already established organization operating to develop international understanding among young people. Our Juliette Low World Friendship Fund has always had this emphasis. The fund is in memory of our Founder, whose greatest hope was to bring girls of all nations together as comrades so that, when grown to womanhood, they would be an influence for sympathy and understanding among nations.

While realizing that all peoples of the world must understand each other better and that national selfishness must be broken down, you may be in doubt about your individual share in bringing this about. You, as a leader of young people, know that any ideal becomes actual fact only when it is accepted and worked for by the youth of the land. Therefore, you have before you an ever-growing opportunity with far-flung horizons. The interests of girls in the peoples

Any Troop Meeting

The songs, dances, crafts, food, customs, and thoughts of our world neighbors deserve some place in nearly every meeting. The young people of the Western Hemisphere, Scouts and Guides from other countries enjoy knowing more about each other. Suggestions from the badges below can be incorporated in all sorts of troop programs.

INTERNATIONAL FRIENDSHIP FIELD

My Community Badge

World Gifts Badge

World Trefoil Badge

One World Badge

World Neighbor Badge

Interpreter Badge

and customs of other countries is a natural one, beginning with folk and fairy tales and with pictures of children dressed in picturesque costumes. Stories about children in other lands have always been popular from Brownie age on up. Unfortunately in the past the difference between ourselves and others tended to be exaggerated and often became "funny" or "queer." It is important that our present emphasis should be on locating our many similarities, with a recognition that we are all members of the same human race. Differences in color, creed, nationality, or cultural background should be understood and accepted as natural variations in a diverse and complex universe.

HINTS FOR BADGE ACTIVITIES

The badges in this field are of special interest to the World Association and to those troops who want to know more about the young citizens of other lands. The One World badge is designed to show the interdependence of different countries and why the ideals of the United Nations are important. The activities promote friendliness and understanding among young people of different backgrounds, as well as of different nationalities.

The World Neighbor badge is based on an interest in one country, and the Interpreter badge on an ability to speak a foreign language with ease. The World Gifts badge is designed to interest Girl Scouts in the heritage of their own communities and the many contributions of other countries to our own. The World Trefoil badge involves knowledge about Girl Guiding and Girl Scouting in the countries belonging to the World Association.

While not forgetting the old world, whose culture has contributed so much to our own, your girls must also know, appreciate, and develop this new world in which they live. The Western Hemisphere badge helps them to do this. Our next-door neighbors in Canada and Mexico, as well as the islands along our coast, furnish a good starting point. Both Canada and Mexico have active Girl Guide organizations. Central and South America are now developing Girl Guide and Girl Scout movements. In recent years there has been developed for every country in the Western Hemisphere a wealth of new, colorful literature that is easy to obtain.

We recognize that probably the best way to know and appreciate any country is to visit or live there for awhile. Few of your girls will have this opportunity, but there is another good way—become acquainted with people who live there. We like a country primarily because we admire or respect its people and their inheritance. Young people especially are far more interested in personalities than in scenery. Try first of all to find someone who has lived in another country to come to your troop meeting. Perhaps a young bride from overseas would welcome this opportunity to get acquainted. If she can talk interestingly about her native land, that is fine, but better than a set speech is to ask her to share a song, a dance, a bit of handcraft, a game, or a favorite recipe with your girls, explaining the life and customs of the country in connection with the activity. Any one of the badges in this field, worked on with program consultants who have lived in and loved the countries chosen, would be a great step in promoting international understanding. If there are any girls from another country in your community, search them out and make a point of being friendly. Perhaps they can become members of the troop. In any case, they can be made to feel welcome in the community and included in its affairs. Many a foreign-born youngster leads a lonely life in our American communities.

While learning more about other peoples and enjoying their music, dances, and crafts, the interest is much deeper if one or more members of the troop could correspond with girls of approximately the same age living in those countries. An International Post Box is maintained at National Headquarters for the purpose of arranging correspondence between Girl Guides and Girl Scouts in different countries where the movement is organized. This common interest makes letter writing easier and more productive on both sides. In general it is suggested that girls be over twelve before writing to the Post Box. There are many other ways of locating "pen pals" in other countries, such as through school teachers, friends, or relatives living there, or through other international organizations. Contributions to international service projects, with a note attached to the gift, often produce a lively and mutually appreciated correspondence.

Letter writing may be disappointing to your girls unless you help them a little. In the first place they need to understand that it often takes quite a while to get the correspondence going, and immediate results cannot always be expected. Use other activities suggested in the badge material to keep the country "alive" until letters are received. Secondly, girls usually need help in the kinds of things to say or not to say. It might be a good plan to have the first letters read at troop meeting and let each girl imagine she was living in another country and decide whether the letter told her things she would like to know about her correspondent. Encourage the girls not to be stiff or formal, but to tell about themselves, their family and school life, what they do as Girl Scouts, what they most enjoy doing. Photographs or sketches of themselves or their homes and small clippings about school or Girl Scout activities would add greatly. If any of your girls are studying another language, get them to try their hand at writing in that language, even if they are not very proficient at it.

Above all, caution your girls not to sound boastful either about themselves or the United States. Don't let them talk about how much they have or use such adjectives as "biggest, fastest, most powerful" in connection with describing their community. You might discuss the odd impression that some countries have of us, gathered from our movies, and suggest they do their best to remove the impression that we are a nation of millionaires, gangsters, cowboys, or any of the other special characters so often featured in motion pictures. Help the girls to remember that they are ambassadors of good will and that the purpose of their letters is to gain the friendly respect of a citizen of another country.

Many troops contribute annually to the Juliette Low World Friendship Fund. The fund has made possible international camps and gatherings, opportunities for Guides and Scouts to live together at Our Chalet in Switzerland, aid to Guides and children in war-torn countries, exchange trainers, help in starting Scouting in new countries, and many other practical demonstrations in world friendship. Every girl can have a share in it. Contributions are often turned in during February, the International Girl Scout Month, and make a natural tie-up with international program activities.

The annual report of the Juliette Low World Friendship Fund gives a vivid picture of how the money is spent. A copy is sent free to every Girl Scout council. Your girls and you will find this report a source of excellent program ideas, as well as a source of great pride in the movement to which you belong.

International Friendship Troops linked with other countries, over-the-border camping, and international encampments all over the world are increasing rapidly each year. While many of these opportunities are only for qualified Senior Girl Scouts, the older girls in your troop will want to be ready to take advantage of them. The best possible preparation is for your girls to learn about their own community and to make friends with people of different races and backgrounds. Discuss with your girls what it really means to be international-minded in tomorrow's world. Encourage them to learn another language. Unless you have a specific country in mind, French or Spanish would probably be the most useful foreign language. Develop international programs based on the badges in the International Friendship field and give Troop Dramatics, Folk Dancing, Explorer, and Reader badges an international emphasis. Develop your troop's camping skills so that the girls would be good campers under primitive conditions.

The World Association of Girl Guides and Girl Scouts publishes a biennial report that gives up-to-date information about the movement in all countries. It also publishes a quarterly magazine called *The Council Fire,* which has stories about Girl Guides and Girl Scouts in various parts of the world. If you are interested in our international ideals in action, you will find these publications of absorbing interest and full of material you can use with your girls. *Hands Around the World—International Friendship for Girl Scouts* is a recent publication that contains facts that every Girl Scout should know about the World Association; sample activities for international programs of various kinds; and short accounts of Girl Scout and Girl Guide programs in member countries. The Laws, Promise, and Motto, with English translations, and illustrations of pins and uniforms of most of the countries are also given. Though primarily designed as a supplementary book for Intermediate Girl Scouts working on badges in the International Friendship field, it is also an excellent source book for Senior girls, Juliette Low chairmen, leaders, and adults wanting to know about the Girl Scout movement. All publications may be ordered through the National Equipment Service.

LITERATURE AND DRAMATICS

We learn and we share all we know by the written or the spoken word. The world of books and the art of drama are a priceless heritage.

LITERATURE

GENERAL PURPOSE AND POINT OF VIEW

The purpose of the activities in the Literature section of this field is to offer each girl an opportunity to advance with a sense of adventure into the world of books and to discover the power of the written word. We hope that reading and writing for both fun and purpose will become a natural habit; that taste and discrimination will be developed; that knowledge will be increased, perceptions deepened, and individual resources enriched.

How the young reader fares, once a response to books has been awakened or increased, depends largely upon her continued interest and the amount of pleasure she gains from book activities. The leader and the book-wise persons she finds to help her awaken curiosity and sustain interest need, in addition to a knowledge of books, an understanding of girlhood. The rewards for the adult leader, as in all true leadership, are surely self-evident. She might well find many of the badge activities an invaluable personal project. In working with a Girl Scout troop the next best thing to knowing the answers is how to go about finding them.

By the term the world of books, we mean all aspects of this field as suggested by the badges: exploratory visits to libraries, newspaper and printing offices, pulp mills; learning to type and print; participating in community life through reading aloud and telling stories to children and helping with Book Week and other such activities; reading and talking about books; writing poetry, stories, reports of troop activities, and so forth.

[120]

The art of reading is so important an endowment that we have been purposely slow in the past to attempt its cultivation in the Girl Scout program for fear of repeating the failure that many other reading programs have experienced. The flexibility of the present program, however, has given us courage to approach this important subject, for it is a living part of every one of the other ten program fields. A search for information about some chosen subject may lead a girl who is indifferent to reading for its own sake into an interest in books. A girl who already is too bookish may learn the satisfaction of sharing her treasures.

The art of writing is a social and community asset that cannot be ignored. The written words may take the form of a friendly letter, an accurate recording of events, an amusing story. They may be a deeply felt conviction or pure imagination. Ability to express oneself clearly and accurately on paper gives personal satisfaction to the writer and helps to keep the pen a mightier weapon than the sword.

HINTS FOR BADGE ACTIVITIES

The activities in this field, as in all other fields, are planned so that the girl may go on from where she now stands. The mechanics of reading and writing are learned like other skills, but taste and discrimination develop slowly; they cannot be forced. A person may be forced to read, but he cannot be forced to like to read. Young people need to be exposed to good books; to be guided skillfully in using their reading imaginations; to be encouraged in their appreciative rather than critical comments. The natural urge to keep a diary, which many girls have, can often be broadened into keeping the troop log, reporting special events, cultivating a pen pal. Friendly discussion on effective use of words may encourage the young writer to try a troop play, poem, or short story.

It will not be possible to measure to any extent a Girl Scout's growth in matters of taste and discrimination. We can only hope that the badge activities relating to books and writing will help her experience her proportionate share in the joys that may lead to adult purposeful reading for knowledge, enrichment of life, escape from care, emotional outlet, human understanding, and companionship.

[121]

The Troop Play

The troop, or one patrol, wants to give a play or to dramatize a ballad. Everyone can take part. There may be a reader or prompter in the wings, actors on the stage, costumers, stagehands, and singers. Use activities from one or more of the badges below so that the girls can see how to weave badge requirements into interesting troop programs.

LITERATURE AND DRAMATICS FIELD

SECOND CLASS ACTIVITY NO. 1

Troop Dramatics Badge

Play Producer Badge

Reader Badge

Writer Badge

Player Badge

The Bibliophile badge aims to help the "book lover" to understand the history and importance of books, the care and respect due them, and the appreciation of the books themselves—their authors, illustrators, publishers. The young adventurer in the world of books may find her curiosity whetted and her inclination to read deepened by a glimpse into the absorbing realm of printing and bookmaking. The badge may be combined with several activities in Arts and Crafts, notably Bookbinding.

In the Reader badge no definite list to choose from has been given, because no one list could possibly be a successful guide. Books chosen should provide those experiences that the girl can associate with her everyday life. They must satisfy, in addition, her interest in the adventurous and the unknown. Lists made out by the local public library are especially helpful because those books are immediately available. More important than either lists or adult guidance is the enthusiasm that a girl herself can kindle in her group about books that have really caught her imagination and become real to her.

In presenting these badges relating to books, we have tried to remember the wide differences in community facilities. Librarians and reference books are invaluable, but they are not indispensable. It is hoped that the activities for this field offer enough choice to make progress in this art possible to any Girl Scout.

Whether the Girl Scout experiences the glow of creative work or not may very truly depend upon the older person who helps her work out the Journalist and Writer badges.

The Journalist badge, as its name implies, is concerned chiefly with the basic principles of writing a news story and the business of editing and publishing a newspaper. Although not limited to the junior high school age, it is a good badge to help older girls make a well prepared contribution to their school, camp, or local paper. The Writer badge is designed primarily to encourage original writing and facility in the use of words. As with reading, it is difficult to measure growth in taste and discrimination, but not impossible. The chief attitude in any adult toward a girl doing creative work of any kind is to evince appreciation rather than criticism and to encourage an appreciative attitude rather than a critical one on the part of the girl.

Many of the requirements for these badges should be worked out only as group activities, while others may be handled as individual projects. The latter can be shared with the group as the work progresses or after its completion.

DRAMATICS

General Purpose and Point of View

The purpose of the activities in the Dramatics section of this field is to develop a knowledge of the skills needed for a gratifying performance of any kind of play, and a realization that the success of dramatic endeavors is based on group activity, patience, good sportsmanship, ability to accept criticism and to get on with other people. The suggestions offered aim to develop resourcefulness in making the most of materials at hand, and an appreciation of the fact that such things as a pleasant voice, careful articulation, a graceful carriage, good taste, and enthusiasm for life are fundamentals for playing any part on or off the stage.

Hints for Badge Activities

The Dramatics badges are so designed that every girl with a desire to act, secret or otherwise, may have an opportunity to express this interest. Girl Scouts may act in troop meetings, simply and without a great deal of preparation or study, or they may go more deeply into the subject and undertake projects that challenge their resourcefulness and ingenuity.

Girls of this age should not attempt long and elaborate plays. Too much memorizing and carefully directed rehearsal is apt to squeeze the spontaneity and pleasure out of the performance. What happens to the girl while preparing for acting out the play is more important than a finished production. While we are striving for an artistically satisfying performance, we are primarily interested in helping girls to develop their personalities.

Dramatics is a broad road with many by-paths. One opens into a world of design, pattern, and color; another into a world of effect and illusion—often achieved with little more than an old tin can,

[124]

Beginnings and Endings
of
Troop Meetings

For a good time while girls are gathering, for a gay and unified start, for a thoughtful closing, try suggestions from one or more of the badges below. Girls interested in the different badges can select and take charge of the activities.

MUSIC AND DANCING FIELD

SECOND CLASS ACTIVITY NO. 1

Minstrel Badge

Group Musician Badge

Music Appreciation Badge

Folk Dancer Badge

Dancer Badge

light bulbs, and a gelatine slide! Many talents are necessary to the play, and not all of them are on one side of the footlights. Of equal importance are the girls who can act or help backstage, and those who enjoy seeing plays and observing the technique of the theatre. It is as often through one group as the other that standards of play production in the troop and later in the community are raised.

The activities in the Troop Dramatics badge provide many opportunities for girls to act out in troop meetings dramatic situations created from incidents that are familiar to them. This form of simple creative dramatics serves as a wholesome outlet for girls who find it difficult to express their feelings and yet are uncomfortable when they cannot do so. This badge is not only fun for the entire troop but it gives a leader unusual opportunities to learn more about her girls and to develop attitudes, tastes, and abilities.

The Player and Play Producer badges are for older girls whose interest has grown beyond informal troop dramatics and who have a feeling of kinship with the professional theatre. The Player badge offers opportunities to practice the techniques that are associated with a good stage presence and the ability to act. The Play Producer badge takes up the subject of stagecraft—that is, skill in the direction, production, and business management of a play.

The Dramatic Appreciation badge offers suggestions for observing movie, radio, and stage plays with discrimination. It will help girls have a real purpose in mind as they read or make scrapbooks of clippings that concern actors, actresses, the theatre, and motion pictures.

MUSIC AND DANCING

Music and dancing are two of the oldest arts; their appeal is universal. Every girl needs cultural and social experience.

General Purpose and Point of View

The general purpose of this field is to help each girl become more aware of the beauties of sound and rhythm, more familiar with her own heritage of music and the dance, and more understanding of what must go into the making of a fine performance. Group and individual performances are suggested that provide satisfaction to those taking part and to their audiences; break down self-consciousness; and lay the groundwork for a cultural interest that may become part of a girl's everyday life. The activities aim to widen a girl's knowledge of the world through the universality of music and the dance and to give her a better understanding of the ethics of music and the respect due musical material, copyrights, and sources.

MUSIC

Hints for Badge Activities

A girl does not need a beautiful voice or unusual ability with an instrument in order to enjoy the Girl Scout music program. There is a definite place for active listening in our badges, as well as for performing. We all know the very human aptitude for half-listening to others while we are burning with impatience to deliver our own next epoch-making remark! In music it is the same. The happy medium is to be a good performer and an appreciative listener; that makes for a balanced faculty.

Probably the most important and most desired result of participation in the music activities is that girls get to know some great music well enough to feel that it is "theirs" and thus break down the needless barriers that surround music for so many persons.

Music experts who have worked with children say that the approach should be through entertainment that reaches their imagination and stirs them rhythmically—"The Flying Dutchman" or Strauss waltzes for example. The gay and lively music of Mozart and Haydn are popular. So are compositions such as Beethoven's "Fifth Symphony," Wagner's "Tannhäuser," and Schubert's "Unfinished Symphony," if they are presented in single movements.

All the music badges consist of three phases: (1) The girl receives from others. (2) She absorbs and works with what she has received. (3) She passes on to others some of her new experiences. Music is at one and the same time a highly personal thing and a communal thing. Whether one lives in Times Square or on a farm, there are

[127]

certain nation-wide facilities of which the musically inexperienced may avail themselves; the use to which these aids are put remains with the individual.

The moral support and practical help of music teachers, supervisors, church choir leaders, and other professional musicians is an ines- timable boon. Artistic people may often be inveigled into the honorary position of music consultant to a troop and, upon closer knowledge of our cultural aspirations, become active members of the movement.

Troops in isolated communities might pool their efforts and resources to form a joint music library. It is not during a concert but *before* that one wants to study what to look for in the program. College and university libraries having no state affiliation are often most generous in lending materials to neighboring towns and villages; you may be one of their lucky neighbors. A hunt among members of the local council and other friends might result in the unearthing of untold treasures in the way of instruments and phonograph records to which the girls might be allowed occasional access; unsuspected talent too may lurk among their possessors. Intelligent use of the radio is made possible by foreknowledge of the season's programs; and sometimes local stations can be prevailed upon to supply the kind of programs most desired. Association with other organizations having music activities and participation in Music Week might result in a lively game of community "Musical Chairs" from which, incidentally, troops might get stimulating help. The Junior League, for instance, has arts projects in many cities and towns, and its members are often eager to cooperate with youth movements interested in the same fields.

The activities in the Minstrel badge stress the romantic or story phases of music and have a general appeal to all girls through their informal and sprightly nature. Leaders feel this badge to be the most readily popular in the music field and if these activities are enjoyed, girls will probably wish to go on to other music badges.

The Music Appreciation badge aims to show that real listening involves as much activity as any other form of musical enjoyment. Radio music and the great revival of interest in phonograph records now make good music a normal part of everyday life that should be deeply and actively appreciated. The Group Musician badge is concerned with developing musical group activities that allow for individual contributions. Girls who can sing or play will find many suggestions here for combining their talents into good programs. The activities in the Musician badge call for a greater familiarity with the technicalities of music than the other badges do. It is designed primarily for the girl with some musical talent and should be earned under the guidance of a music teacher or consultant.

DANCING

"Dancing," says Havelock Ellis, "is the loftiest, the most moving, and the most beautiful of the arts, because it is no mere translation or abstraction from life; it is life itself. It is the only art of which we ourselves are the stuff."

It is also the most universal of all the arts. Many people are afraid to touch a paintbrush; some even claim that they cannot sing; but few there are who do not think they can learn to dance. We seem to approach this art with an instinctive understanding—which we should bring to all the arts—that the joy of the doing is the primary reason for it. Dancing is an art that must be caught as well as taught, and so, while numerous books of directions have been published, the best way to learn to dance is from a person who dances well.

There has been no attempt to provide badges for dances that are done chiefly for the interest of an audience, such as ballet and the many forms of the "modern dance," because such dancing is usually taught in private classes by professional teachers and seldom lends itself to troop activity. No solo dances such as the Highland Fling, Sailor's Hornpipe, tap dances, are used in earning the two dance badges, since they are more an individual than a cooperative social activity.

Folk dancing is a wide field, with possibilities of life-long interest, and it should be presented to girls as such. In considering the activities in the Folk Dancer badge three points should be kept in mind:

First, *if it is at all possible,* boys should be included in the dance group. This may be difficult, but unless both sexes participate, folk dancing will please only the younger girls. If available, let the girls

[129]

observe groups of grown men and women dancing folk dances. In trying to get boys to take part, it is best to avoid the term "folk dancing"—call it square dancing or barn dancing or a shindy—and put the emphasis on the strength and vigor required. And don't mind a little roughhouse!

Second, the dances should be worthy of the effort of the particular age group. Remember that young people can learn difficult steps more readily than adults.

Third, in localities where there is a living tradition of folk dancing, the girls should be made to feel themselves a part of it. This may be either American country dancing or, in communities with a large population of the more recent immigration, the dances commonly done in other countries.

Since the popularity of folk dancing has spread far and wide in recent years, particularly in large cities, program consultants are not too difficult to find. Possible sources of contact in large cities are International Institutes, nationality clubs, foreign-language newspapers, and churches. Foreign-born parents of troop members may be able to make suggestions.

Especial care should be taken to see that Girl Scouts learn only authentic folk dances. The name of a dance may not indicate its origin at all. A living folk dance, however, may have many variations. Since folk dancing is a vigorous activity, only girls who are able to participate in active sports should take part in it. In some dances, the man occasionally lifts his partner; this figure requiring so much strength should be omitted when only girls are dancing.

The Dancer badge is concerned with social or ballroom dancing, and if boys join the learning group, all will enjoy it more, and many informal parties may grow out of the meetings. In guiding the activities of this badge, local customs should be regarded, for they may vary in different parts of the country, and each section has its own correct ways. The chief emphasis in this badge is on the foxtrot and the waltz, since these are the basic rhythms of modern social dancing, but the popular variations are not thereby excluded. Some of today's dancing may seem frenzied to the generation that knew not swing, but it takes a real dancer to do it.

The best sources of help with the Dancer badge are older sisters of troop members, college students, the Junior League, young married women, and dancing teachers.

NATURE

Nature is something we can enjoy no matter where we go in the world. Show girls how to take care of the woods and be gentle with living things.

General Purpose and Point of View

The general objectives of the Nature field are to help each Girl Scout to:

Appreciate and interpret her natural environment. We should like to have each girl be reasonably familiar with the things in nature that she sees every day. Depending upon where she lives or goes to school the nature may be a patch of woodland, a prairie, a mountain, a suburban street and flower gardens, or a city street with such things as window boxes, fruit stands, and mice.

Develop her powers of observation, investigation, and reason. Anyone who works with nature has the added satisfaction of feeling her powers of observation increase. The subject of nature has a way of prodding one on to investigate into why things do what they do or are what they are. The "whys and hows" of nature are numberless and leave one plenty of opportunities to exercise her reasoning power.

Realize her debt to and responsibilities toward all other living things. No one type of life—earthworm, maple tree, beetle, fish, or human being—can live in this world all by itself. One kind of thing depends upon another for its life and sustenance. Therefore, a study of nature without learning this fact—and appreciating it, too—is like a compass without a needle. And all young people can learn, by reading and practice, responsibility toward other living things through the household pet—cat, dog, fish, bird, turtle—or through feeding wild birds, tree planting and trimming, or soil conservation.

[131]

Back-Yard Nature

Nature is everywhere—for everyone to see and enjoy. Any back yard has enough nature in it to keep a troop busy for months. There will be birds, plants, insects, cats and dogs, rocks and minerals, stars, weather, and a few other things.

NATURE FIELD

SECOND CLASS ACTIVITY NO. 1

Tree Badge

Bird Badge

Wild Plant Badge

Cat and Dog Badge

Star Badge

Weather Badge

Enjoy the out-of-doors as the result of increased knowledge and understanding. The Girl Scout organization is rightfully proud of its camping and outdoor program. One of the things that will strengthen our outdoor program, whether it is camping or short hikes, is feeling acquainted with and at home with the animals and plants and minerals that are to be found "where'er you walk."

A knowledge and enjoyment of *living* things and the *way* they live is the basis of any good nature program and it is hoped that all the activities will lead to a program of this kind. Dr. Bertha Chapman Cady, in writing on the Girl Scout nature program some years ago, said: ". . . the tendency has been all in the same direction—away from rote, from standardization, from the mere acquisition of the names of things, from the acquiring of 'collections' to stow away for moth and dust and decay. More and more our progress has been toward the understanding of the living thing; toward an appreciation of its beauty, without desire for possession; toward preserving a memory or record of the object through picture, line, or word, instead of possessing its dead form; in short, toward conservation in every sense of all beneficent or harmless life, toward a love of things as they live, and a search for an understanding of their function in the great scheme of nature.

"If we can but stir the curiosity, start the search, and free the imagination for the common, everyday nature objects, we have given youth one of the greatest possible gifts. Through eye and ear, through touch, taste, and smell, life is broadened, and this means the acquiring of as great an amount of firsthand experience as possible."

To appreciate nature does not mean that one should try to attain the impossible—to know the name of everything from clouds to lizards. An appreciation comes quite early through acquaintanceship with some things and an awareness of all things.

A great knowledge of nature is not necessary in order to interest a group of young people in it. In fact, it can sometimes be a hindrance instead of a help in that questions are often answered that should, in all fairness to the person concerned, be left to discovery.

Our conception of nature should be a broad one to include all things—bears, birds, ink, glass, sheep, vanilla, and so on. This makes

[133]

it possible to use almost anything to stimulate an interest in this field.

There seems to be no special age at which nature is a primary concern, but when a girl reaches the point of great awareness in her surroundings there seems to be a consuming curiosity about all natural objects. There is no particular age at which any one phase of nature is more absorbing than another. For example, it is impossible to say that a girl will want to know about stars at ten years of age or at fourteen. Every phase of nature can be taught at any age.

Hints for Badge Activities

Nature study lends itself to group activity as well as to individual activity, and, since it is usually more enjoyable to do things with other persons of like interests, the Girl Scout organization hopes that group participation will be emphasized in the nature program wherever and whenever possible.

It is hoped that the nature program will be initiated and carried through in such a way that it will be fun to all who participate in it. This can only be accomplished if we keep it simple, take our time, make our own observations, and do as much of it out-of-doors as possible.

It will be noted that the number of things to be identified is not of primary importance in the list of activities for each badge. If, in any case, the number suggested as fair for most parts of the country seems too difficult or not sufficient, the number may be changed by the joint decision of the girl and the person who is helping her in the subject. *It is hoped that, wherever possible, knowledge gained from watching or caring for some living thing over a period of time will be considered of more importance than identifying a given number of things.* This is a decision that should be left to the girl and her leader. Instead of too much emphasis on numbers, let us watch for a development of understanding and appreciation, an effort to help someone else to become interested, and an accumulation of interesting facts through observation and reading.

There are thirteen badges in the Nature field—each one in a little package by itself and labeled with such words as "bird," "tree," "star," and so on.

While a study of nature can begin almost any place, a leader may have difficulty in deciding just how to start with her troop. The Cat and Dog badge makes a natural beginning for young people who are interested in pets and adds to their appreciation of all living things. The Rambler badge serves as an excellent introduction to many nature fields for girls that like general exploration. The Weather badge is of interest to all who like outdoor life, sports, hikes, and trips over land and sea. The segregating of subjects is for convenience and clarity, but it must be remembered that a person interested in nature will not find it too easy to keep everything in such orderly pigeonholes! A bird perches in a tree and the tree often takes on as much importance as the bird. A snake eats a frog and they both become a matter of interest to a nature student. To help make some kind of tie between these nature subjects an effort has been made to list one activity in each badge that will lead directly and obviously into another in the Nature field. By using our common sense it will be found that practically all the nature badges can be done in the city as well as in the country. Make the changes necessary to make the badge practical and enjoyable in any given community or situation.

The question of help with the Nature field is of paramount importance in the mind of every leader. The most important assets in the community are the nature objects to be found there, such as grass, trees, toads, jewels, vegetables, dogs, and even cockroaches. The next most important assets are the people in the community who are interested in nature or any section of it. Then will come the libraries, museums, zoos, botanical gardens, aviaries, fish markets, jewelry stores, flower stores, and organizations such as Audubon societies, garden clubs, granges, city or state department of forestry, fish and game commission, Department of Agriculture, state agricultural college, state teachers college.

It is most important to find as many channels as possible through which an interest in nature may be diverted to the betterment of the community, such as tree planting, flower preservation, gardening, and bird protection.

As for nature books and magazines, there are many listed in the book mentioned below. It is impossible to list *all* of the books useful in each subject for *all* parts of the country. Each public library will or should have additional books useful to nature students—young and old.

We should like to suggest that every leader who is about to embark on the Nature field should purchase a copy of the *Leader's Nature Guide.** In this book you will find the help you need to make the subject of nature enjoyable and worth while to the leaders, the girls, and the community.

THE OUT-OF-DOORS

Our aim is an outdoor program for every troop.
Have at least one outdoor activity each month.

GENERAL PURPOSE AND POINT OF VIEW

The general purpose of this field is to help each girl realize the fun and possibilities of outdoor experiences and to encourage her self-reliance and resourcefulness through the skills needed for comfort, safety, and pleasure while living out-of-doors. The activities aim to promote good health, a deeper interest in and responsibility about her own countryside, and the satisfaction of cooperative effort through planning and carrying out trips with friends her own age. We hope each girl will learn to appreciate simple, natural things and see herself in relation to the universe.

The out-of-doors has an almost universal appeal to the average girl between ten and fourteen, who normally has a desire to "do"—rather than to talk or listen—to experiment, to go adventuring, and to be a member of a congenial group in search of fun. Every Girl Scout should have many opportunities for hikes, games, woodcraft skills, and adventure out-of-doors. The wide range of activities in this field can be adapted to town or country without great expense or elaborate equipment, and suggests interests that can be developed during the vacation periods, when the girl really has some undirected leisure. School can seldom give much attention to outdoor activity; therefore we have a great opportunity to fill a definite need.

---

* See Girl Scout *Publications Catalog.*

[136]

The Troop Goes Camping

To go camping is the ultimate goal of every girl who likes to be out-of-doors. Troop unity, fun and many badge activities can be woven into preparing for this great adventure. Each girl in the troop can find things she wants to do in one or more of the badges below.

THE OUT-OF-DOORS FIELD

SECOND CLASS ACTIVITY NO. 2

Tree Badge

Campcraft Badge

Personal Health Badge

Pioneer Badge

Outdoor Cook Badge

Camping has its greatest appeal for girls of this age, yet for various reasons many girls have not been able to have this experience. Offer as troop activities as many of the good camping fundamentals and outdoor program skills as possible. In this way, any girl who is a member of an active troop may experience many of the same pleasures as the seasoned camper, be more ready and eager to go camping, and, when she is an older girl or an adult, have keener appreciation of the out-of-doors. We should also keep in mind that our activities, as well as our objectives, should be year-round ones. There has been a tendency to think that a few short weeks in the summer, possibly spring and fall weekends, and occasional hikes were the best we could do. A good year-round outdoor program depends on (1) the inclusion of more outdoor activities in the troop program; (2) activities sponsored by the local council, such as winter carnivals, spring festivals or playdays, holiday activities when regular meetings are temporarily suspended; and (3) camping made available by established, day, or troop camp facilities.

Our chief aim is to develop continuously a girl's love of the out-of-doors and to help her find recreation and refreshment in some form of outdoor activity, whether it is camping, gardening, farming, sports, or games.

HINTS FOR BADGE ACTIVITIES

The Foot Traveler badge aims to make more interesting a delightful form of exercise. Walking costs nothing and can be practiced in all parts of the world and in any community. It is fast becoming a lost art because of the rush and hurry of modern life, but to those people who enjoy walking it satisfies an amazing number of needs and desires, all free of charge. A girl of this age is physically capable of taking long hikes if they are lengthened gradually and if she is suitably equipped. Since the very term Girl Scouting implies an ability to get about easily in the out-of-doors, it seems sensible to put more emphasis on this time-honored and ever-available form of getting about. Frequently in the past Girl Scout hikes have been merely rides to the city limits in a street car or bus and a very brief walk followed by a large meal and possibly a few games. That sort of expe-

[138]

dition can be fun and have real value, but it is not really hiking. Let a hike be the trip where the main idea is to get somewhere on foot. It can be pleasantly combined with outdoor meals if elaborate cooking is omitted, but, if combined with strenuous games and sports, energy is usually overtaxed or dissipated in two directions.

In earning this badge some girls ask if they can count the walk to school, to their music lessons, or to the stores. Provided each walk is one half mile or over, it may be counted under that done in "town or city streets." However, since a girl selects at least three areas for hiking, these town walks should not be more than one third the total amount.

To eat out-of-doors, to try to cook something of one's own choosing, and to feel the sense of mastery and excitement that comes from lighting and controlling an open fire are desires common to every boy and girl. Something very fundamental is satisfied in all of us by achieving skill along these lines. Satisfying one's hunger is always a popular pastime, and when it is intelligently done in a pleasant or new environment through one's own efforts, it becomes sheer delight. Fire and its uses have a constant fascination, perhaps because of a kind of primitive instinct, and when we are old enough to be trusted to create, control, and use it properly, we have achieved man's estate. The Outdoor Cook badge aims to develop these skills so essential to any real camper. Housekeeping standards take on a new significance, and it is a wise leader who emphasizes not only the cookery but also the standards of cleanliness, service, and courtesy that are just as applicable out-of-doors as in the home.

The activities in the Back-yard Camper badge are for the group that wishes to practice camping skills in its immediate neighborhood and would like the adventure of sleeping out. It is designed either for the beginning camper or for the troop that cannot easily get to a primitive camping spot.

The Campcraft badge is for the younger camper and suggests that the overnight or weekend camping experience should be in a cabin or cottage already approved by the local camp committee as meeting the Girl Scout camping standards. Primitive conditions, in which a site is selected and the group cares for its own shelter and sanitation,

[139]

belong to the more seasoned camper or to the girl over twelve. It is our belief that a real distaste for outdoor living is often engendered by plunging a girl too soon into primitive camping. It is a romantic and exciting experience, but those without the right introduction are apt to return home worn out with memories of hard work, no sleep, and a sense of being inadequate or a poor sport. To the average new camper, spending a night in the country with a group of her friends and dealing with an environment that is very different from that at home is excitement enough. The activities in this badge are within the range of the most limited budget, particularly if the troop committee helps with the plans.

The American heritage and the spirit of the early pioneers are of interest to every girl. The character, imagination, and stamina that are developed by facing unknown conditions, dealing with the elements, and caring for oneself adequately without the trappings of modern civilization are as much needed today as they ever were. Real democracy and intelligent group cooperation develop and flourish under primitive conditions because here they are related to that most powerful of all instincts—self-preservation. In the Pioneer badge every member of the group needs the help of every other member up to the limit of her capacity. The activities are designed for the girl who has the Campcraft badge or other adequate camping experience, and who is at least twelve years of age. It takes more physical strength and staying power than a younger girl usually has. Even the girl between twelve and fifteen, because of the growth and changes natural to this age, needs practice in the preliminary camping skills until they seem easy to her. We should be sure she is in good health before she attempts this badge, and should watch to see that she does not attempt anything beyond her physical strength. Primitive camping probably has its greatest natural appeal to a girl of this age. Unless she has acquired a real enthusiasm for camping in early life, she may have better success pioneering in other fields, such as nature study, community life, or the arts.

The activities in the Explorer badge are based on the desire for new experiences, for adventure, and for feeling independent that is at a high peak with the twelve to fourteen year old. She is more mature than her younger sister in her understanding of the world at large, more eager to get away from home, more demanding that her fun should be in new pastures. It is at this age that tremendous admiration is felt for persons who have lived spectacular, noble, or exciting lives. This admiration is an expression of her own desire to win recognition, to do important things. Her sense of values is unconsciously being established. It is important, therefore, to call her attention to the men and women whose lives of exploration, discovery, and service have been full of courage, patience, and persistent effort. The details of the trips in the Explorer badge have intentionally been left flexible, since in this way the girls are allowed more opportunity to do real planning, to relate the expedition to their own interests and locality, and to make it as ambitious as any individual group feels is desirable.

Before starting on any of the outdoor activities be sure to check any plans you make with *Safety-Wise,* the booklet that is sent free to every registered Girl Scout leader. If you are considering either of the camping badges you will need *Let's Go—Troop Camping!**

SPORTS AND GAMES

Good teamwork, fair play, and physical fitness are American ideals. Let us develop a nation of players, not observers.

GENERAL PURPOSE AND POINT OF VIEW

The general purpose of this field is to help a girl enjoy health-building activities that are suited to her present stage of physical, mental, and emotional development, and that contribute to her understanding of good sportsmanship and good teamplay. The activities suggested will help her to acquire body balance and coordination, together with standards for developing skill in a given sport, including good form, proper etiquette, equipment, and safety precautions. They aim to give her the sense of achievement that results from learning to master herself and her equipment under many conditions and situations.

---

* See Girl Scout *Publications Catalog.*

Good sportsmanship and enthusiastic interest in games and sports are among our cherished American ideals, for they promote good social attitudes, physical skill, and stamina—all important attributes of citizens in a democracy. To have everyone participate under proper conditions and observe fair play, friendly competition, and sensible safeguards is a desirable ideal for any group of people. There has been, however, a tendency to get too much of our satisfaction from the side line and grandstand. We want girls to have an opportunity to develop their own abilities and general well-being by active participation in the sports that interest them.

Hints for Badge Activities

The Games badge is concerned with games of two types—those of simple organization, such as circle games and ice breakers; and those of higher organization, requiring special equipment and definite space or courts. The girl between ten and fourteen is in the transition stage between an interest in free play and games of simple organization and highly organized team games and competitive sports.

The younger or less mature girl might be encouraged to choose the bulk of her activities from the simpler group, while the older, well developed girl might naturally wish to major in sports. An effort has been made to suggest activities that do not plunge a girl into too highly competitive and organized games yet offer an opportunity to practice the skill and develop the bodily coordination so important to any good athlete. Competitive impulses are keen at this age and must be used constructively. *Games for Girl Scouts** will give any leader more ideas than she can use. The general approach to the subject is that a girl be encouraged to develop her ability so she can enjoy and help others to play these games, instead of placing emphasis on winning or being better than anyone else. The list of games in the badge only attempts to suggest the more popular or desirable games for this age group. Substitutions in the list may be made locally on the advice of an instructor of physical education who works with girls of this age. Some leaders ask why separate badges have

---

* See Girl Scout *Publications Catalog.*

A Troop Play Day

Cross country games, relay races, treasure hunts, water sports, may be part of a troop play day. Winter vacations and week-ends are just the time for ice skating parties and snow trails. Often two or more troops plan a play day together, and double their fun. Activities from one or more of the badges below can be used in making a good program.

SPORTS AND GAMES FIELD

SECOND CLASS ACTIVITY NO. 1

Games Badge

Swimmer Badge

First Aid Badge

Winter Sports Badge

Folk Dancer Badge

not been developed for each sport, such as archery or tennis. Any appropriate sport may be used in earning this badge, but it seems wiser to give to this age group a good grounding in teamplay and in a variety of games. Many of the highly individualized or competitive sports cannot be incorporated in troop programs because they either require elaborate equipment, serve comparatively few girls, or are more appropriate for the high school age.

The Cyclist badge deals with a sport that has gained new impetus in the past few years, but it has always been popular with teen-age boys and girls. With the increase of motor traffic and superhighways, there is greater need for safety precautions than ever before, and the activities of this badge will help to point out the reasons for precautions. Bicycling may be enjoyed in a group or individually and is related to many of the other program fields. It will appeal to groups in all but the most mountainous sections and can be enjoyed most of the year. Once a girl owns, or has access to, a bicycle there need be little expenditure for this activity. Winter activities may include preparations for trips and equipment making.

As in all the fields that require strenuous physical activity, a leader must safeguard her girls by being sure their experiences progress gradually from short excursions to longer trips, and by checking carefully on the health of those who go on trips.

In developing the Horsewoman badge the suggested activities are in relation to saddle horses. Riding has a great appeal to girls. Horse lovers the world over will keep this sport alive no matter how much the machine age may reduce the utilitarian value of horses. Saddle horses are accessible and the equipment available to our girls throughout the country. There is sufficient variety or choice in the activities to care for the difference in Eastern and Western riding and for differing interests in various sections of the country. Adaptations in the wording may be made locally without changing the quality of performance. Encourage girls not only to become good riders but also to learn to give horses proper care.

Today many Girl Scouts are participating in winter sports. They are learning the techniques under the supervision of well qualified instructors. They are learning how to take care of their equipment and how to meet emergencies. Skills involving balance, coordination, and quick reactions are easily and safely learned in childhood or early adolescence. A pattern of good form can be established at this time, which will make a great difference in the ability to perform at an advanced level. Our aim is to encourage an invigorating recreation that most young people and many adults long to enjoy.

The Winter Sports badge could be an important part of the troop year-round outdoor activities in many sections of our country. New opportunities for participation are opening up all over the United States. The artificial ice rinks and winter sports centers make these activities available to an increasing number of persons each year. Even the more expensive winter sports are far cheaper over the period of a year or two than the accumulated bill for movies, magazines, and ready-made amusements; and now that it is customary to have ski outfits or winter sport suits for everyday wear, the problem of extra clothes has vanished.

Anyone interested in young people is constantly looking for desirable rivals that will compete with the commercialized and passive recreation so popular with boys and girls of this generation.

Aquatics is the Number One sports activity in the world today, and it provides a basis for health and happiness.

The Swimmer badge contains activities basic to all forms of water sport, and a girl must earn her Swimmer badge before she is eligible to work on the Boating or Life Saver badges. Physical fitness must be evidenced by a certificate from a licensed doctor of medicine before undertaking any of the activities connected with the water. Since skill is a keynote to safety, these activities must be developed under trained leadership and wisely supervised. The Life Saver badge is only available to girls over twelve who have satisfactorily completed the Junior Life Saving Course given by the American Red Cross or its equivalent given by the Boy Scouts or YMCA under a qualified Water Safety Instructor.

The desirable qualities of confidence and self-assurance are developed by swimmers and boatmen. They are constantly aware of any hazards that may exist and do not overestimate their abilities or run risks. Their confidence and self-assurance are a direct result of knowledge, skill, and effort.

Aquatic activities vary from those based on individual achievement and fun to group competition. Games may vary from simple group play to more highly organized team games. Water pageants encourage artistic and graceful demonstrations of skill and also provide an opportunity for dramatics, costuming, and creative writing.

Before starting on any of the badges in this field be sure to check any plans you make with *Safety-Wise*, a pamphlet that is sent free to every registered Girl Scout leader.

Chapter Five

Developing Self-Government in the Troop

SELF-GOVERNMENT! responsibility for others! group participation! fair play! teamwork! talking things over together! When we think of training young democratic citizens, we are somewhat overwhelmed by our ambitions and responsibility. But we Americans always feel better when "we do something about it." This chapter will help you translate your democratic ideas and methods to the girls' level, since our Girl Scouts are both the heirs and future trustees of democracy.

The material develops six main ideas and illustrates their practical application in troop meetings when leaders teach their girls to:

1. *Select and use a simple democratic form of troop government.*
2. *Participate in group activities in a cooperative way instead of in a competitive way.*
3. *Discuss group plans and make group decisions before taking group action.*
4. *Take responsibility for others.*
5. *Understand patrols and the Court of Honor as a method of representative government.*
6. *Budget, earn, and spend their troop money.*

A SIMPLE DEMOCRATIC FORM OF
TROOP GOVERNMENT

EVERY GROUP NEEDS enough organization to get things done and to define the rights and responsibilities of its members. In the Girl Scout organization, where training for democratic citizenship has always been one of our first responsibilities, teaching Girl Scouts how to select and use a simple form of democratic troop government becomes an important part of every leader's job. We do this by making use of the patrol or other subdivision plan, or by working with the troop as a whole. This goal is not accidental, but stems from the use of the two forms of democratic government we do have in the United States of America. Young American boys and girls should be able (1) to use both forms of self-government and (2) to understand something of the purpose and spirit behind them. The two forms are:

1. The town-meeting type, where each member of the group discusses and votes directly on an issue or rule or law; a democratic form of troop government that works directly with the troop as a whole.

2. The representative form or type, where each member of the group helps elect a person to do a thing for the group, or a democratic form of troop government that uses the patrol or other subdivision plan.

BRIEF REVIEW OF PRINCIPLES OF TOWN MEETING
AND REPRESENTATIVE TYPE OF GOVERNMENT

To help you review briefly the idea back of town meetings and representative forms of government, the following is included.

In a town meeting we see democracy in its purest form. Instead of sending men and women to conduct affairs for them, as in a representative government, the people are there in person. Young and old, rich and poor, take part in the proceedings, and any citizen present may exert the full force of his character and influence. Every matter that is brought before the meeting is discussed and criticized. Those in favor of the measure state their arguments for it; those

[149]

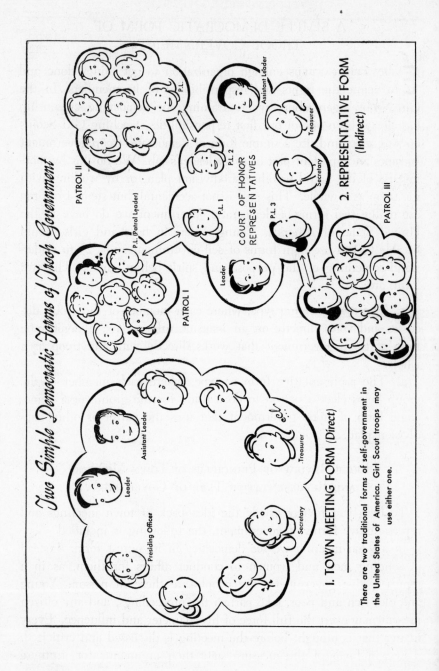

Two Simple Democratic Forms of Troop Government

1. TOWN MEETING FORM (Direct)

Presiding Officer • Leader • Assistant Leader • Secretary • Treasurer

2. REPRESENTATIVE FORM (Indirect)

PATROL II • PATROL I • PATROL III

P.L. (Patrol Leader)

COURT OF HONOR REPRESENTATIVES

Leader • P.L. 1 • P.L. 2 • P.L. 3 • Secretary • Treasurer • Assistant Leader

There are two traditional forms of self-government in the United States of America. Girl Scout troops may use either one.

opposed to it state their objections. When the discussion is at an end, a vote is taken, and, whatever the results may be, all present feel that the will of the people has been expressed.

In a representative democracy the people rule no less than in a pure democracy, but they rule indirectly, i.e., they elect a person to do a thing for them. Our legislators, our President, our governors, our mayors, and, in most instances, our judges are chosen agents of the people. The system of representation works out as follows:

1. A representative is chosen from a certain district—a village, a city, a county, a congressional district, a state—and he usually must be a resident of the district that he represents.

2. In the choice of representatives, the principle of the majority rule prevails.

3. A representative acts not for this or that class, nor for this or that interest, but for the people as people.

4. Representatives in the law-making bodies are apportioned according to population—so many people, so many representatives.

5. A representative is chosen for a fixed definite period of time, usually a short period.

Now that we have reviewed the two basic forms of government and the main ideas back of each, let us turn to young Girl Scouts to see if we can get this across to them in spite of their inexperience and simpler vocabularies.

The Town Meeting Type of Troop Government

Young Girl Scouts, girls new to group life, and small troops with unified interests are often happier when all work together. They prefer the directness of the town-meeting type of self-government. However, this form is most often used when a troop is small (having fewer than from twelve to sixteen girls); and when little structural organization is needed for all girls to help manage the troop affairs quickly and with a "oneness" in their short troop meetings. Yet, there are times when leaders deliberately choose the simpler form for larger troops. They may find that representative troop government requires more experience in taking responsibility for others and more willingness to be represented by others than their girls have yet developed. A few troops may need the direct rather than the indirect guidance of an adult leader in all their activities at first.

The important things to remember about the town-meeting type of democratic troop government are:

1. Every member, girl and adult, connected with the troop is there in person to discuss, criticize, and vote *directly* upon all troop business and plans. The girls need to see why this direct representation is the simplest and purest form of democracy; how this type of self-government prevents one person, or a small group, from dictating to others; why it does not work in their troops when they are selfish, lazy, or absent.

2. A chairman or moderator presides. In a new troop, the leader often presides at the first two or three meetings; then encourages different girls to try—always teaching them how when they do not know; then holds an election for a permanent chairman when the troop is ready to vote. This gradual process gives both girls and leader time to see what the chairman's job is, which girls preside best, when the troop as a whole is ready to elect and respect a chairman of its own age "in the chair." In simple truth, this means that *everybody*—not just the girl in the chair—is on trial and is learning how, and this must be made clear to the girls from the start.

3. A few rules for taking part in discussion are necessary. "Talking things over" in groups, a willingness to learn the facts and listen to others' opinions, trying to decide what is best for all, are necessary rules girls will have to practice in good democratic government.

4. When the troop is ready to vote, each girl and adult does her own voting. The majority rules. At this time, nearly every leader will have a chance to teach girls how the minority, or "the losers," may have their turn another time, and why the minority's ideas and rights must be respected in their troop as in larger community life.

5. Responsibilities are usually delegated to individual girls or a small group temporarily. The number of permanent officers or committees is kept to a minimum, because so few are needed. Most troops have a treasurer or secretary; some have both.

The Representative or Patrol Form of Troop Government

The patrol and Court of Honor system is the representative form of troop government that Baden-Powell evolved for Scouting. It is very adaptable and flexible, and there are many variations upon the main theme as you will see from the description that follows. However, some troops prefer having a president, secretary, treasurer, and committees. With either terminology the form is the same, and the members rule no less than in a town-meeting type of troop government—but they rule indirectly instead of directly.

New leaders usually ask when it is better to use the representative rather than the town-meeting form. Experienced leaders say certain signs indicate the need for representative troop government. Here are a few:

1. If the age range within the troop is greater than two or three years.

2. If the troop divides naturally into several groups of girls who obviously enjoy working together.

3. If the troop has more than ten or twelve girls with fairly diversified interests.

4. If there are enough girl leaders who can assume responsibility for others as well as for themselves.

5. If the troop has demonstrated its understanding of teamplay and a small group is able to work under the responsible leadership of several of its members.

6. If you feel a few girls are managing everything and wish to make more individual participation possible.

7. If all the girls are leaning too heavily upon your leadership instead of learning to elect and respect leadership their own age.

8. If you think it is a good plan to see what different groups can accomplish on their own.

9. If you think the time has come for your girls to have some experience with representative government.

The principles of the representative type of democratic troop government parallel those of our United States Government.

1. A representative to the Court of Honor, or central planning group, is elected by girls in the patrol or sub-group. Experience has

[153]

shown that girls recognize leaders their own age more quickly than adults, especially when time is taken to discuss qualifications of a patrol leader. The girls may make a mistake, but they can learn to correct it just as adults often do.

2. In choice of representatives, the principle of majority rule prevails. It is probably wisest for the leaders to conduct an election by secret ballot so no one will know how others are voting.

3. A patrol leader represents—i.e., speaks, acts, or votes for—not this or that interest, nor her particular friends, nor her personal preferences, but members of her patrol.

4. Representatives to the Court of Honor are apportioned according to troop membership: so many members, so many patrols or subgroups, so many representatives.

5. A representative is chosen for a fixed definite period, often six months or a year.

Basis for Division of Troops into Patrols or Interest Groups

Troops are usually divided into patrols or committees upon the basis of age or school grade, interest, and friendship. The thirteen- and fourteen-year-old girls, especially, feel their age and try to impress the younger girls and leaders with their maturity by insisting upon a patrol by themselves. This is normal development in early adolescence, and the understanding leader will respect and recognize this growing independence. Then, too, the younger girls have more chances to develop if they do not always compete with girls several years older when taking responsibilities or choosing leaders.

When girls become interested in a particular field of interest, and when they want to specialize or become First Class Girl Scouts, they may want their patrols divided according to interests. However, the interest spans of ten to twelve year olds are not as long as those of thirteen to fourteen year olds; therefore, interest groups for them are more temporary and usually last while they are working on one badge, a play, or a crafts project. In such cases, girls sign up for a temporary interest group, but retain their permanent patrol or committee groups, which operate as part of the troop's self-government.

[154]

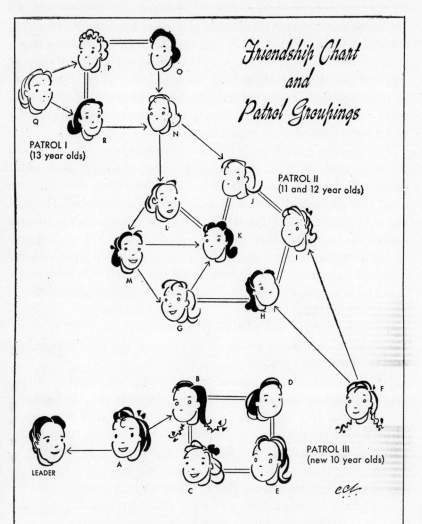

Friendship Chart
and
Patrol Groupings

PATROL I
(13 year olds)

PATROL II
(11 and 12 year olds)

PATROL III
(new 10 year olds)

LEADER

The leader asked each girl to name two girls she liked to be and work with most. Double lines (=====) joining two Girl Scouts above indicate mutually-recognized friendship. An arrow indicates the girl named by a Scout who is not named in turn. See the text for a leader's description of this device and its possible use in placing girls in patrols, locating leaders, and helping isolated girls make new friends.

Organizing the troop's work and play upon the basis of friendship is very important to girls. They like to be with their friends. Research with adults in industry and with children in school has found that the best and fastest work is done with the least effort when friends work in small teams. To gain insight into the girls' friendship, you might study the accompanying Friendship Chart with the leader's interpretation of how she used this technique.

The leader reports: "I asked the girls to name two girls they would prefer to work with and their reasons. Some of their reasons were: 'because she can get things done'; 'she does everything well'; 'because I am sure she would work with me'; 'we wouldn't quarrel'; 'because she is big and strong' (from a wee girl); 'we always agree with each other'; 'she will work when she is supposed to instead of wasting time trying to figure an easy out'; 'she's full of fun'; 'she is my good friend.' This last came from my admiring small Scout, and put me into the chart for this reason: 'Mrs. W......., she is my good friend, she is very good educated about Girl Scouts and she knows her bisiness, I want to be like her when I grow up.' Incidentally, she is my most provoking child, but she bears no ill will even if she gets 'straightened out' practically every meeting!

"As you can see, their reasons reveal a desire for congenial friends and interest in getting the work done for the most part. If you study the chart, you can see that several girls are misplaced in their patrols or need to develop stronger friendships there. This chart also reveals which girls are most likely to influence others. My girls work or play well together, and we have come far in group unity and morale the last three years, but I think this is a fine way for a leader to check up on relationships between girls. I got some surprises, and I feel that I am well acquainted with my girls in the neighborhood as well as in regular troop meetings."

THE COURT OF HONOR

The Court of Honor is made up of patrol leaders and adult leaders —a small executive planning committee of both girls and adults. Assistant patrol leaders are often invited to attend, but do not necessarily belong by virtue of their office. The adult leader acts as chairman, and sometimes a patrol leader may take the chair. The troop treasurer may attend when needed. The secretary of the Court of Honor may be the troop scribe, a patrol leader, or possibly the assistant leader in a new troop.

The Court of Honor meets, preferably, at the end of every troop meeting, or at least every two or three meetings. Court of Honor is usually preferred at this time in order to consider reports from patrol meetings, to catch up with any loose ends, and to prepare the program of next meeting in light of one just held. Once every month or two longer Court of Honor meetings are held to outline the troop activities over a longer period of time, and, later, details are filled in and readjustments made in shorter Court of Honor meetings.

Procedures in a Court of Honor are orderly but simple and informal. As chairman, the leader gives everyone a fair chance to be heard, draws the threads of discussion together, and sees that all important matters are covered in the allotted time. Many Courts of Honor use a simple order of business or "agenda" such as this:

1. Minutes of last meeting read and approved.
2. Reports from each patrol.
3. Leader's remarks, notices, and so forth. (If the adult leaders speak after the patrol leaders have reported, the girls usually feel more responsible for making suggestions.)
4. Discussion of matters brought up by patrol leaders, adult leaders, and any necessary voting.
5. Program for next meeting gone over for final arrangements.
6. Agenda for next patrol meetings drawn up.

THE PATROLS

The Court of Honor is closely linked up to and represents the patrols. The troop is divided into patrols having approximately five to eight girls each. Each patrol elects its own girl leader and assistant leader. Read over the section on the patrol leader in the *Girl Scout Handbook*. Sometimes the patrol feels that the patrol leader should choose her own assistant. The length of time a patrol leader serves varies with the troop, but often six months or one year is the troop's decision on this, with the possibility of re-election for another term.

Patrols usually meet during a part of every troop meeting. They must do *more* than check attendance and collect dues if their representative form of democratic government is to mean anything to them or be an asset to the troop. Briefly, patrols do some of the following:

1. Talk over things they would like to do in their coming troop meetings—such as hiking, camping, community service, so that their patrol leaders may take their suggestions to Court of Honor.

2. Attend to any routine business of the patrol, such as collecting dues, checking attendance, reporting on Court of Honor meetings, delegating patrol responsibilities.

3. Plan patrol projects, practice Girl Scout skills, prepare for their part in larger troop activities.

In a new troop the girls' ideas are often few and halting or wildly at random. But they will improve amazingly as the girls discover that they actually furnish the ideas and plans out of which their programs are made. As leader, you must believe in your girls, trust them, let them learn from their own successes and their own mistakes, and have a heroic capacity for allowing young Girl Scouts to "try out their wings." Democratic government is no cut-and-dried plan in a Girl Scout troop, but arises from a special attitude of mind—a belief that democratic training should be evolved from within rather than imposed from without. The girls must, in fact, make themselves into democratic members of the troop with the leader's guidance.

A GIRL SCOUT PARTICIPATES

The Girl Scout organization feels that one of its first responsibilities is to "help Girl Scouts plan and carry out all their troop activities in a democratic way." The democratic way in a Girl Scout troop, or any other group, seems to mean that all members will have an opportunity to participate, according to their age and ability, in planning, carrying out, and judging the results of their own activities. But to get this idea over to Susie and Mary and the other girls in your troop is not a quick or easy job, and you, their Girl Scout leader, may be the first person who has tried to show Susie and Mary what democratic participation, as defined above, means.

If one of our leadership jobs is to help educate Girl Scouts in a democracy, then we are concerned with educational procedures; that is, the way we work out this idea of participation with Susie and Mary and the other girls in a Thursday afternoon troop meeting. Howard Wilson, one of the nation's foremost educators in training youth for citizenship, says we must get a feeling for citizenship into "youth's spines as well as their minds." W. H. Kilpatrick, another great educator, speaks in much the same way when he says, "Until a child (1) sees what needs to be done, (2) learns how to do it, and (3) is willing to do it, he has not learned sufficiently to meet life's demands."

With this in mind, let us turn to our own field of performance, i.e., how we proceed as we teach girls to take part in troop activities. There are two starting points where leaders need most help, and of which they need to be made more acutely aware.

First Susie, Mary, and all the other new Girl Scouts may need to have the idea of democratic participation explained to them in *simple* words, *and in terms of their everyday experiences,* very soon after they enter the troop. Leaders too often omit this explanation and fail to get the practice over because the girls do not understand what they are trying to do. It is extremely difficult for adults to realize the big gap that exists between the way a ten- or twelve-year-old child and an adult thinks. Yet, every badge within the covers of Susie's *Handbook* requires a girl to participate in activities with others in order to earn her badge. What does "participate" mean to a ten or twelve or fourteen year old? Is earning a badge in a recreational, leisure-time program like earning "A" in arithmetic? If not, why not? Nothing a leader can do is more important than bringing the ideas of democratic participation into Susie's everyday living so that she may see how to be a useful and responsible citizen in school, in troop meeting, or in neighborhood play.

Second, Susie, Mary, and all the other girls will learn democratic participation by *practicing it—week after week, month after month, year after year.* This means that you, their leader, will consciously plan to include this practice in weekly troop meetings. You will not omit it or "let the schools do it all," or take the chance that the girls will get it anyway, or choose the quickest way to get things done re-

[159]

gardless of the procedure. You will be willing to take the slower, but in the end quicker, way of letting Girl Scouts learn how to take part in their troop activities.

A Girl Scout Keeps Her Own Group Activity Record

To get over the idea of democratic "participation"—a big word for a ten year old—you will have to think out your own procedure and begin practicing at least as simply as the following leader did:

She said: "I have found that one of the first things I need to teach new girls is *working together* as a group. Last year it took me quite a while to show the girls the difference between passing a school test and earning a badge. Most of it was my fault, so this year I worked directly and to the point from the very start with the seven new girls who joined the troop. My girls come from homes and schools where being 'at the top of the class,' 'being first,' 'getting A' is the coveted state of their being.

"I tried this kind of talk last winter, and it seemed to give us a good start—

"'Let us look at our badges. You will notice at the beginning of every badge a sentence that reads, "To earn this badge, do ten of the following activities." This means *to take part* or *do your part* in an activity—such as folk dancing, a hike, a play—with others. To earn a badge or your Second Class rank is different from the way you make "A" or "B" in arithmetic all by yourself. We enjoy our parties, hikes, and community service *together* instead of trying to be first, make "A," or get ahead of the others. We do not have report cards, but if there were a report card on earning badges, it would read something like this card I am giving you, and *you* would grade your own Group Activity Card.

"'When you do, or participate in, the first three fall activities—a party, a hike, and service for the Red Cross—I want you to check yourself on this card at home after each troop meeting just to see how you are taking part as a member of *your* troop. This troop is *yours*, and when any one of you forgets, is too lazy, or refuses to do your job, our parties, hikes, or Red Cross service will not be nearly so good. But it is very easy when every girl does her share—and lots of

[160]

fun! At the end of the month I would like to see your cards; and you may write on the back three things you wish your troop could do and that you would like to take part in during the year.'

"This worked for my troop. It seemed to mark the steps in participation for the girls. We referred to the activity card again and again the first few months, but after a while we did not need to check ourselves so carefully. I also found it a very useful device in watching potential leaders, since girls scoring high on this card are apt to be fine leaders. It also helped convince my 'bossy' girl that a leader did not sit back and tell others what to do; although it took two months of record keeping between us to correct this idea."

How I TAKE PART in MY Troop's Activities During October

Girl Scout's Name	Short Hike Trailing Games	Halloween Party	Service with Red Cross
1. Did I want to do the activity?			
2. Did I help make any suggestions? (Can use own ideas, ask other people, look up October magazines for party ideas, read about Hostess badge in *Girl Scout Handbook*, etc.)			
3. Did I help with details of plans?			
4. Did I help decide or vote for the plan?			
5. Did I help carry out plans we made?			
6. Did I help judge results, and offer some ideas for doing things a better or different way if this activity is done another time?			

7. What did I enjoy most?..

The Leader Keeps a Group Activity Record of Girls' Participation

	Mary	Virginia	Susie
1. *Did she want to do the activity?*	Yes.	Yes.	Yes.
2. *Did she make suggestions?*	Yes, she had ideas for working out the dramatization and planned her own costume.	She plays the accordion and made suggestions and found suitable music for her own part.	No.
3. *Did she help in planning?*	Yes.	Had little to say about the rest of it.	Yes.
4. *Did she help decide the plan?*	Yes.	Yes.	Yes.
5. *Did she help carry out the plan?*	Yes, she took much of the responsibility.	She took full responsibility for her own part and helped a younger girl get her costume and plan her act.	She came to rehearsals, but as the time came nearer began to develop stage fright. She was to be in the gypsy chorus ("couldn't find anything") and would not go on the stage, but helped with the singing backstage.
6. *Did she help judge results?*	Yes, but was overcritical of the girls who did not do as much as she did.	Had little to say.	No. The other girls were pretty critical of her attitude, but she said little except she was afraid.
7. *Did she acquire any new interests?*	She sang a solo part for the first time, and became much more interested in dramatics.	Not that I know of.	No.

Many leaders have kept activity records of individual girls from time to time. They say it helps them see at what points a girl is performing well or poorly, and also gives a brief sketch of what the girl actually did.

The preceding brief picture in the life of a troop reveals some of the possibilities for developing girls as they take part in their troop activities with others. After studying the accompanying activity record, re-read the very first paragraph in this chapter; then see if you think Susie's, Mary's, and Virginia's activity records suggest to a leader ways she she might help girls in her own troop become more useful and responsible members.

This record was made by a leader whose troop is in a coal mining town. It shows how three of her girls participated with the rest of the troop in a dramatic ballad, "The Wraggle Taggle Gypsies," as a part of their community Halloween celebration.

LEADING A TROOP DISCUSSION

Just now we are hearing a great deal about "discussion groups." It seems that the town and county meetings of our early forefathers are appearing in a new cloak labeled "discussion groups." This "talking it over" is considered a very healthy sign for our democracy. From America's earliest beginnings "the people" have always talked it over. We have records of famous debates and speeches, and the people going to town and county meetings with earnestness and pride in the part they played as American citizens in making their own town or county, and nation, a better place because they were members of it.

How can we teach our Girl Scouts this first lesson in American citizenship while managing the affairs and solving problems of their own troop? A Girl Scout troop has to solve problems, discuss, and make plans just as any other group does. The American principles of democratic government are the same whether they are in the Senate, the PTA, or the Girl Scout troop. One young Girl Scout explained the Court of Honor and patrol meeting to her mother by saying, "It is just like the United States Government, only more so."

Observation records have been kept of girls at the point, "Does she make suggestions when troop activities are being planned?" Leaders

[163]

observing girls who were more difficult than average in their troops answered this question the same way, "No"; "Once in a while"; "Yes, but too many"; "Yes, but they are silly"; "Yes, but she does so to get attention and giggles or makes faces while she does it." None of the leaders seem to be writing a simple yes. It would seem that we might spend more time talking things over in patrol and troop meetings, and giving every girl a chance to make suggestions. If they do not, encourage them to take part, and show them how if they do not know. Leaders usually reported signs of success with the more difficult girls when they made efforts to include them in discussion of troop plans.

A Few Obvious Benefits of Group Discussion for the Girls

1. It gives every girl a feeling of *belonging* and having taken part in the troop's affairs. If our training is democratic, and that is one of our aims, this feeling of belonging must happen to all the girls in the troop—new girls, shy girls, girls now avoided by the group. Can the troop be taught to find out what new girls, or shy girls, have to give, and learn how to use all girls' abilities and talents in their troop?

2. It helps girls get better and more accurate information, and prepares them for any group action resulting from the group discussion. A girl taking part in discussion needs to listen carefully; consequently she learns more and can report more accurately. Some people call this "active listening."

3. It trains girls to voice needs and pass judgment where group opinion is needed. Girl Scouts who have been trained in troops with a good patrol system are very often active leaders in their school student government. Educators believe that this ability to participate in a discussion does have a carry-over effect into similar experiences.

4. It makes girls more tolerant and broadminded. They soon see that there are usually at least two sides to a question. Opinions of others differ from theirs. They can be led to do a little more "finding out" rather than grasping at their first opinion. This give-and-take of ideas in discussion and planning has to be learned and practiced just as certainly as give-and-take in playing games or in sharing equipment in a crafts project.

[164]

You might encourage your girls to try number seven activity in My Troop badge, which says, "Take an active part in your Court of Honor, patrol, or troop discussions. Help to put on a skit for the troop, showing successful ways of taking part in a discussion, noting such things as courtesy, expressing thoughts clearly, taking no more than one's share of time."

A SIMPLE PROCEDURE IN LEADING TROOP DISCUSSIONS

"Talking it through" with your girls includes (1) describing the problem or situation, (2) bringing out the underlying reasons for the problem, (3) bringing out ways of meeting it, and (4) planning a way to put the group decision into action. This will vary from situation to situation, but the general procedure is the same whether the troop is talking about how we conduct ourselves on a trip to the telephone office next Friday, planning a hike to Cooper's Creek, how to choose leaders in our troop, or what we do when a school operetta rehearsal comes on the same day as our troop meeting.

1. *In describing the situation,* you might ask questions such as: Why are you interested in this? Why are you eager for us to do this? Is the entire group, is one patrol, or are several individuals concerned? What seems to be most important in the desires of girls wanting or opposing it? What does each girl or group involved fear if group opinion or voting does not go her way? What is really at stake?

2. *In getting at the underlying issues,* you can go further and ask: What reasons do different girls or groups give to back up their opinions? Are these reasons sound? What do other people think about this who have had more experience in this particular kind of thing? Will it be the wisest thing for the group or for certain individuals?

At this point in a discussion, the group either does or does not have enough information or experience to continue. It is here that club members, and committee members, often make decisions too quickly or ramble and waste a lot of time. It is extremely important for a *leader to take hold firmly at this point.* A leader and girls must acquire an attitude of "finding out" and "wanting accurate information" about whatever they are discussing and planning. Much is gained in group

morale and timesaving if discussion is stopped here and continued at another meeting, if it is evident that the group only knows what it wants and not enough about how it can be achieved. A leader goes into details here, and helps them define clearly the difficulties they are up against.

Exactly what is it we need?
From what sources can we get help on this?
Whose advice shall we ask?
Who will volunteer to find out about the different things and report to the group at next meeting?

3. *In bringing out ways of meeting the problem*, you might ask: What are the different ways in which we can do this? Which one of these seems to be best for group or individuals involved?

In many adult discussions, talking over common interests does not mean that the group is planning to take group action at the end of the meeting, or even eventually. In such cases, individuals draw their own conclusions as they see fit. However, many troop discussions grow out of program activities. The purpose in talking things over is often to decide what we will do next or how the group can successfully accomplish its desires. Action is more immediate for children than adults, as their interest span is shorter. They live in the present to a greater degree. They want to solve their problems as they come up. "Talking it over" must be "made into action" for ten or twelve or fourteen year olds. Otherwise, it has very little, if any, meaning for them. The purpose here is to teach them to think and agree as a group before they act as a group.

4. *In putting the decision into effect, you might ask:* What changes will we have to make in what we are now doing? How can all those concerned be helped to see its worth? What girls or patrols will take the most responsibility?

CHECKING YOURSELF AS A DISCUSSION LEADER

If you are interested in checking yourself, or someone else, as a discussion leader, you might consider some of the following points:

How many were present? (Any number over fifteen or twenty limits participation, since neither adults nor children talk much in large groups, nor is there time for each member to talk.) . . . .
. . . .

How often did each girl take part? . . . .
. . . .

What girls influenced the discussion most? . . . .
. . . .

How much of the total time did the leader talk? (Often it is too much!) . . . .
. . . .

To what extent did the leader influence the discussion or decision?
. . . .

How many leading questions did the leader ask? . . . .
. . . .

Did she encourage certain individuals to take part? . . . .
. . . .

What did the girls seem to feel that they accomplished? . . . .
. . . .

Was the discussion method a good device at this time? . . . .
. . . .

Would another method have been as good or better? . . . .
. . . .

LEADER'S RECORD: A TROOP DISCUSSION

The brief picture of the patrol and troop discussion that follows is a very photographic one. It is not as good as a sound movie film or actual observation would be, but it can serve as a good substitute. It may seem long at first glance, but to get any idea of the conversation piece between girls within a patrol and troop, or between girls and their leader as they discuss and manage their troop affairs, requires a series of film shots before it tells the story. Human relations in a group are complex, and to assume that they are not is to miss the point.

Certainly, this brief record should prove to you that young girls have some very good ideas and can demonstrate their good judgment if given the opportunity. Notice how this leader helps them clarify their thinking and talks it over with them, yet does not make any decisions or rules for them. Notice where the leader enters into the discussion, and where she closes or postpones a discussion when the group acts a little too severe or is not yet ready to make a decision. The leader reports:

"Three girls had been giving us trouble. One was entirely uninterested, and the other two followed in all she suggested. From the very start, the girl who was acting as leader of this clique had never seemed to get into the spirit of the organization. It may be counted as failure on the part of all the leaders, but appeal to reason and interest had been tried to no avail. Her entire interest seemed to lie outside the Scout group, and her two friends followed. They came when there were special activities and parties, which was just often enough to keep their names on the roll. They frequently brought no dues. (A girl must be absent three consecutive times to be dropped from the roll.) The girls in their patrols were complaining. In fact, the entire troop was dissatisfied with their behavior.

"At one meeting, when these girls were present, a list of questions was handed out to each patrol to be discussed, answered, and returned. The question list with the patrols' answers is given on page 170.

"At another meeting when these three girls were present, the first five questions were put before the troop as a whole for discussion. When the leader asked the girls if they would like to discuss the questions on the check list, they enthusiastically answered yes.

"The leader then told them that all had agreed that it was not fair play to enjoy the privileges of troop membership if the responsibilities were not attended to at the same time.

"She then read the two statements that the majority had agreed upon for question two. One girl remarked, 'If they won't pay their dues in the first place, they certainly won't pay a fine.' The girls agreed with this and dropped the suggestion of a fine.

[169]

LIST OF DISCUSSION QUESTIONS

Things to Discuss in Patrol Meeting	*Patrol Responses*
1. Should a Girl Scout who does not come regularly, pay dues, or take responsibility enjoy the privileges?	Unanimously "No."
2. Give suggestions as to what should be done about girls who do not keep dues paid regularly.	"A fine should be added." "They should be deprived of privileges for the month, or until dues are paid."
3. List excusable reasons for not attending Scout meetings.	"Sickness"—"out of town"—"if your mother needs you"—"conflicting schedules in case of called meetings."
4. List unexcusable reasons.	"Movie"—"staying in at school"— "to do some other activity"—"sleigh riding"—"I forgot."
5. If something interesting to all Girl Scouts occurs, how would you like to go as a body of Girl Scouts instead of skipping meetings as individuals?	"Yes"—"Good idea!"
6. Do you like the suggestion of paying for the crafts you made in order to reimburse the crafts treasury?	"Yes"—unanimously.
7. Do you believe it would be better to do all craft work in the troop room or at home? Give arguments pro and con.	"Could we be given about one-half hour at each meeting to work on crafts?" "We think we should work on them in our troop room, but that we should start work earlier."

"They also agreed to answers to questions 3 and 4 as they were, but this brought forth more discussion.

"The leader asked, 'What should be done with girls who miss without an excusable reason?'

"One girl vehemently declared, 'Kick them out!'

"Another, more mildly, 'Drop them from the roll!'

"The leader: 'But we can't unless there are three consecutive absences. It is a rule, you know!'

"A girl: 'Any girl who comes just enough to stay on the roll, and comes when there is fun and won't do any work, ought to be asked to resign!'

"A girl: 'Anyone who does that way isn't a very good member!'

"A girl: 'She doesn't really belong in Scouts, and, if she doesn't like it, it looks like she'd resign without having to be asked!' "

The leader took over the discussion at this point, asking all the girls to think over these things and see if anyone might be getting lax in these things and could improve.

"When the fifth question was taken up, one girl said, 'It would be fun, but how would we know in time?'

"A leader: 'We might plan it the meeting before.'

"A girl: 'Yes, but suppose it were coasting. You can't know about snow a week ahead!'

"A girl: 'And if we came to the meeting to find out, then went home to get ready, and came back, it would be too late.'

"A leader: 'How about just sending an announcement around at activity period in the various schools to let you know?'

"A girl: 'That would be fine, and, if it were good coasting, we'd be expecting it anyway.'

"So that point was settled.

"A girl then remarked, 'I think going to a good movie together would be fun!'

"A girl: 'If the rest are like me, they won't know if they'll have any money left that long off.'

"A girl: 'Money doesn't last long. You can't always get it when you want it!'

"A leader: 'Perhaps if enough of us wanted to go, and we planned a week ahead, one of the leaders might see Mr. .... (manager of the local theatre) and arrange to get it cheaper. He gives reduced rates, I believe, to a large crowd.'

"A girl: 'I believe I could manage that. Let's try it some time.'

"Girls of this age are so very easily influenced by the opinions of their friends and associates. This very frank, candid discussion made all the girls think about how they were taking their own responsibilities. Most of them returned with added zest and cooperation. The girl mentioned in the beginning and one of her friends dropped out of the troop, leaving room for two smaller girls who were very interested in the organization and had been waiting long to enter. The third girl remained in the troop and her Scout spirit seemed entirely revived."

TRAINING GIRLS TO TAKE RESPONSIBILITY FOR THE TROOP

Leaders' problems in this area, i.e., giving troop responsibilities to individual girls, patrols, committees, or "letting the girls do it," seem to stem from the fact that leaders expect young Girl Scouts to do what experienced club women cannot always do successfully. Mary Elizabeth and Nannette may be jumping up and down with excitement over being "It," patrol leader, committee chairman, hike food buyer, but neither one may have much idea, if any, about how to proceed without a leader's help and guidance.

In teaching girls to take responsibility, leaders seem either to do a fine, thorough job or to omit it entirely. Those who tackle this job usually select Mary Elizabeth or Nannette, or the treasurer, or the shyest girl, or the bossiest girl, or all the patrol leaders, or the ablest girl, either in turn or several at a time, and consciously work to develop them. They try to do at least one thing at each meeting to help these particular girls, and usually work with them over one, two, or three months—sometimes longer, before they take on another girl or small group. This is all they feel they can concentrate upon at one time. As to the way they usually go about it:

[172]

First, the leaders see that the particular girl (or girls) gets a responsible job she should be able to do without too much individual coaching from the leader.

Second, they see that the girls understand and prepare themselves to do their small troop jobs successfully. At first, the leader usually gives more direction and help, and checks on the girls more often than she does later.

Hundreds of leaders work with their girls in this simple way meeting after meeting over a period of time. Nearly always the girls develop noticeably traits associated with responsibility, such as resourcefulness, unselfishness, dependability, poise, self-respect, leadership. These same leaders almost always report that the girls' parents and teachers see "a big difference" or "change for the better," too.

Leaders who do not deliberately plan to teach girls to take responsibility often say they "have not gotten around to it," or "have one girl who has developed a lot this year, probably because her aunt or parents help her a lot more than other girls' parents can." Yet, helping girls do the troop jobs they either volunteer for or are elected by the troop to take is one of a leader's major jobs, and one of the most exciting! But, whatever the true picture is, perhaps it will help leaders who have not "gotten around to it" to have as photographic a word picture as possible of what is done by the leaders who do train girls to take responsibility.

Detailed records are purposely used here. Notice especially how much time, patience, and detailed planning go into teaching girls to take responsibility. Every leader believes in it verbally, but at what speed must we adults gear ourselves to inexperienced ten to fourteen year olds as they learn to manage their own troop affairs. Can we develop girls in our troop to take enough responsibility the first year so that we can say the girls do more for themselves than they did a year ago, or six months ago?

Leader's Record: Training Girls to Plan an Agenda and Conduct Patrol Meetings

"Our inexperienced little patrol leaders, during their first few months, could not get anywhere in patrol meetings. We leaders started typing a list of things for them to refer to while having their patrol meetings. It helps us get things straight. They finish one thing, write notes or anwsers, then go on to the next. And, if they waste a lot of time talking about outside things, of course they do not have their answers completed."

The following was used:

PATROL MEETING (GREEN LEAVES PATROL—ELIZABETH)—APRIL 1:

1. Attendance and dues.
2. Did you think of a good way to thank everyone who helped with our birthday party?............."Thank-you card"............
3. Did you think of a way to entertain the Brownies and when? ...."First Monday in June, treat (us)"..............
4. Are any of you ready to make cook books?......"Yes"......
5. Do you know any ways of earning your first aid kit money? Remember, you have fifteen cents to start with. If each girl in your patrol sells one box of cookies for the first aid fund, will you have enough? Kits are eighty-five cents................"Yes".................
6. Next week is to be given over to a scavenger hunt. What kind do you want?............"Scavenger Hunt"............ Is there something you would rather have instead because we have had such bad weather?............"no No NO"............
7. What do you think of the Camp Scholarship? How many of you would sell another box of cookies and turn in the ten cents to this fund to send someone from Troop 5 to camp for a week next August? ...."5 of 7"............
8. Would you like the troop to get together to see a good movie? ...."Yes"............
9. Does your patrol wish to visit the Standard Building?......... "Yes"............

This leader, like most others, found her inexperienced patrol leaders floundering, and was forced to start in the simplest way—but she did give the girls a fine standard for planning agenda and conducting their patrol meetings, wrote it so that votes by members of patrols had to be taken, asked the patrol to suggest plans for their troop activities, asked for volunteers to take extra troop responsibilities, asked the patrol to make up its collective mind several times, expected them to follow directions and get through on time. At first glance, you may say, "She did it for them," but how much, and what, did she expect them to do? You will find one or two places where the patrol gave poor answers, as in number 6, the scavenger hunt question. Offhand, we might say, "Of course, a group of new Scouts wouldn't have any idea about the kinds of scavenger hunts there are! Why did she ask?" We really don't know why the leader asked. She could have asked this to provoke further discussion, or to force them indirectly to read the game book for ideas on scavenger hunts. She may have expected too much of them. But, whatever her expectation, she found that the Green Leaves Patrol needed some help at this point, and would not be able to plan a scavenger hunt for the troop without some help. Starting with item number 6 in the Green Leaves Patrol may be a slow procedure. It may be a ten year old's speed in taking responsibility at this point, but it is at such points a leader must start in her troop and teach in detail (1) what the job is or can be, and (2) what steps must be taken to prepare for its success.

A LEADER'S RECORD: TRAINING A NEW SET OF PATROL LEADERS IN AN OLD TROOP

"I have very sketchily jotted down the general idea I used in training my patrol leaders, scribe, and treasurer in their duties. My troop has registered for the third time, and I believe that the patrols are working better now than ever before. There are four patrols and twenty-eight girls, ages ten to fourteen years.

"I invited the patrol leaders, scribe, and treasurer to my house for special help. We then decided to meet two afternoons a week for two weeks, and later have one long Court of Honor a month to plan the troop meetings and activities carefully." A report of four Court of Honor meetings follows:

[176]

FIRST MEETING

1. Explained again the idea of patrols and Court of Honor and suggested some of the duties of patrol leaders.

2. Explained the duties of treasurer and how dues, troop income, and expenditures were recorded.

3. Explained the duties of scribe and helped set up minutes for this meeting.

4. Talked about importance of attendance and learned how to use patrol record book and troop record sheet.

5. Asked each patrol leader to tell about her own hobbies and interests. (What did you do this summer? What was the best movie you saw? What magazine do you like best?) Then asked them how well acquainted they were with the girls in their patrols, and to see how much they could find out about them before the next meeting.

6. Explained that patrol meetings could be organized and conducted in the same way these Court of Honor meetings were.

SECOND MEETING

1. Minutes of last Court of Honor read by scribe.

2. Explained duties of leader and assistant leader; told them when to come for individual help.

3. Asked for report from each patrol and discussed real leadership. (Did the girls have ideas, or did they agree to everything? How can patrol leaders give every girl a chance to help plan and carry out patrol and troop activities?)

4. Discussed in general the outdoor badges, since troop had decided it would like to take advantage of warm fall weather. Patrol leaders decided to discuss one badge at the next patrol meetings and suggest two activities they would like to do.

5. Went out-of-doors, gathered tinder and wood, and built a fire for toasting sandwiches.

THIRD MEETING

1. Talked about a place to hike and people who might help us with some outdoor activities in badges.

2. Built a wigwam fire in the back yard and made cocoa.
3. Answered questions about anything we had already done.

FOURTH MEETING

1. Discussed how mothers and friends could help with Juliette Low birthday party at Halloween.
2. Explained about first aid kit for hikes and talked about fire prevention. Discussed visiting forestry headquarters near here.
3. Asked for a report from each patrol and then planned to have a long Court of Honor meeting once a month to plan troop meetings and activities carefully.

OTHER LEADERS' RECORDS IN DEVELOPING RESPONSIBILITY

See chapters "Character Education" and "Group Control, or Discipline." One of the main emphases throughout these two chapters is developing responsibility in (1) individual girls, and (2) the troop as a whole.

THE TROOP'S FINANCES

The cost of carrying on Girl Scout activities is not great, but, no matter how small or large, troop financing has great possibilities for the training of girls in the use of money and group responsibility. To be active in an organization means assuming one's own share of the expenses and obligations; being an earner and giver as well as a receiver. Acquiring and handling troop funds is a vital part of the program—just as important as any one of the listed program fields, and should be treated as such.

The troop treasurer is responsible for keeping an accurate account of the troop funds. She often needs considerable help from an adult on how to do this. The actual cash should be deposited in a bank to the account of Troop ...., Girl Scout Council ...., or otherwise safeguarded in a way that seems best to leaders and troop committee. The treasurer handles the troop funds in consultation with the troop leader. Usually both the treasurer and one adult sign the checks. The entire troop needs to understand the importance of records, receipts, and regular financial reports. It is the business of the whole troop to understand and vote on the troop budget. A small pamphlet called *Troop Financing in Dollars and Sense* may be ordered from the National Equipment Service if you need more help on troop financing than space permits here.

The Need for Money

Girl Scout troops need money for three reasons:

1. *To meet the costs of program activities.*

These might include equipment, such as books, a first aid kit, or a pack basket; money for trips or camping. The amount varies according to the activities chosen.

2. *To help with service projects.*

Every troop takes part in some form of service. It may be direct help to some group in the community or a national service project.

3. *To pay the national membership dues.*

Just as each girl in the troop shares the cost of her troop activities, so each person, adult or girl, belonging to the Girl Scout organization shares in the cost of extending Scouting to many local communities through her annual membership dues.

Individual badges, pins, and uniforms are usually the responsibility of the individual girl to whom they belong. In cases where girls cannot afford to buy uniforms, a plan for making or buying them is worked out with the troop committee.

Sources of Income

The main sources of income are:

1. *Regular troop dues.*

The amount of dues is decided by the girls after a troop budget has been made. When they see how much money is needed, they discuss how much each girl should bring each week and how much the troop as a whole should raise. The amount usually varies from two to ten cents a week.

Some girls need help in earning their dues, as well as their uniforms. Most troops need additional money to balance their budget if they have ambitious program ideas. The leader and troop committee locate desirable ways for individual girls to earn money and sponsor troop money-raising events. The local council, if there is one, should approve the plans.

Some troops prefer monthly or semi-monthly dues. Whatever the amount or the frequency of payment, a system that provides for regular payment of dues seems to have great advantages for most troops.

2. *Money-raising events.*

A few interesting ways troops have earned money are: bake sales, benefit parties, pet shows, doll shows, flower and vegetable markets, bazaars, garden parties, plays, exhibits of antiques, movie benefits. It is important to remember that money-raising projects should:

Be of real value to the girls.

Have some connection with other program activities.

Suit the age and interests of the girls.

Give full value for money received.

Keep within the national policy on money raising by Girl Scouts; (see statement of this policy in the chapter, "Your National Organization").

Be approved by the local council, if there is one.

Be limited in number during the year so the public will not become tired of too many appeals.

3. *Contributions.*

Generally these are made by the troop committee, a sponsoring organization, or other interested civic groups or persons. Contributions are apt to be used for larger troop expenditures, such as camping or expensive equipment, since troop dues cover most of the running expenses.

THE BUDGET

See the *Girl Scout Handbook* for sample budgets.

[180]

Chapter Six

What Are Troop Meetings Like?

IF YOU ARE WONDERING what to keep in mind when planning troop meetings, this chapter will answer some of your questions. Each leader is encouraged to make the fullest use of her abilities, talents, and imagination as she builds and varies her program upon a few main ideas.

The material shows what we aim to do in weekly meetings and why, and how the combination of the following makes a Girl Scout meeting different from other groups:

1. *Include fun.*
2. *Vary the program of action.*
3. *Stress learning by doing.*
4. *Develop self-government.*
5. *Reinforce the Girl Scouts' personal and group code of behavior.*

A LEADER ASKS, "What is a troop meeting like? Show me a typical meeting. How do I know whether I am including the right things in a Girl Scout meeting? What makes a Scout meeting different from an arithmetic class in the fifth grade, a sewing club, or a Sunday school class?"

We quickly assure a leader there is no typical Girl Scout meeting. Then, why does the Girl Scout organization keep its identity and interest thousands of girls in so many different towns over a period ·of years?

A leader does not need to bother about a typical meeting, but she does *build and vary her troop meetings upon a combination of a few larger ideas.* She will hear these same ideas expressed again and again in slightly different ways, but they are of long standing and do not seem to go out of style. We usually speak in terms of what we want girls to (1) become and (2) do. In our zeal we may sound as if we are working with the finished Girl Scout product, but leaders who work with eager, active, growing girls do get enthusiastic and prideful about what their girls can do and are becoming. The table that follows will help a leader see the combination of these larger ideas.

As you build and vary your troop meetings upon these larger ideas, remember that one of the most grown-up and convincing experiences young Girl Scouts can have with their leader is to share, or at least be introduced to, their leader's hobbies or interests. Remember that you, as leader, are a very important person to your girls, so, if you can grow the best chrysanthemums in town, bake a fine chocolate cake, do a creditable figure eight on the ice pond, refinish old furniture, or exhibit a small collection of teapots, the chances are great that your girls will be delighted to be introduced to these same activities. You may find that some of the girls will adopt one or two of these hobbies as their own.

Especially is it wise for a new leader to start with some of the activities that she is best able to share and direct with her girls. In our eagerness to have children learn by doing versus being lectured at, we have used such expressions and part-truths as, "They must decide everything themselves," or, "The girls do it all," which have intimidated parents, teachers, and leaders somewhat and discouraged them from sharing their hobbies or interests with young girls and boys.

[183]

WHAT WE AS LEADERS WANT GIRL SCOUTS TO BE AND BECOME

OUR AIM:

To have Sally, Susie, Arabella, and all the other girls in our troop (1) be, and (2) become, more and more useful (1) to themselves and (2) to others. (This educational goal we share with the girl's family, school, church, community, nation.)

In working toward this large goal, we as Girl Scout leaders use a *combination* of ideas (not one or two) upon which we build and vary our Girl Scout program. There are others, but the ones listed below are very important and are enough to keep a leader busy for a while.

Girl Scouts have a Promise and Laws.	Girl Scouting is fun!	Girl Scouts can do things	Girl Scouts learn by doing.	Girl Scouts use a simple, democratic form of troop government.
From the very beginning we have had an ethical code, stressed duty to God and country, and emphasized citizenship training of an active type. It is important to remember that Girl Scouts and Guides all over the world have the same Laws and Promise. The group code is in the Girl Scout Laws; each Girl Scout's personal code is her Promise.	We have a leisure-time program. It goes on in a girl's free time—and when she comes to troop meeting she expects Girl Scouting to be fun! Leaders need to be acutely aware that play is a significant part of every child's education—and has been in all forms of primitive society as well as our modern and complex one.	We say, "Girl Scouts can do things—they can bandage a sprained ankle, bathe a baby, help cook and serve a meal to a hundred people." The activity program with its many badges is in truth a program of action that experienced leaders and program specialists have found active, growing girls (1) are able to do and (2) enjoy doing.	We use informal methods of education with an emphasis on Learning by Doing. The idea is to give girls first-hand experience and practice in everyday activities of life in addition to talking or hearing about them. We are interested in a girl's performance—performance that is good enough to be useful to herself and to others.	We want girls to have a chance to practice democracy in the small—and to learn to plan and manage their own troop affairs under the guidance of their own leaders. This democratic way of doing things is the girls' heritage, and we must be doubly sure that we gear our democratic ideals to the girls' level.

As you can see, these same ideas are deeply rooted in our American culture, our belief in what young American girls can and should do. Often new leaders say, "I don't know a thing about Scouting." To say that is to say you do not know how to be a useful citizen, to use your leisure time, cannot work and play with groups, have never learned by doing, cannot plan a program. These very important things you do know, and we are eager to have Girl Scouts learn them from you.

GIRL SCOUTS HAVE A PROMISE AND LAWS

The group code is in the Girl Scout Laws, and each Scout's personal code is her Promise, "On my honor, I will try . . ." to live up to the group code. As we help young Girl Scouts build their group and personal code of conduct, we must not worry too much if a ten or twelve or fifteen year old does not comprehend all we do about honesty, or obedience, or thrift. Many times we expect more of children than their age and experience can take; but we start where we find them and build upon what is there. We begin by respecting each Scout not simply as she is but even more with respect to what she may become. We start with her present shortcomings and immaturity, but also with her present promises. We must think of each Scout's actions and moods in terms of development—as a moving-on-ness.

(See chapters "Group Control, or Discipline" and "Character Education" for more detailed help with individual and group codes of behavior in troop meetings.)

GIRL SCOUTING IS FUN!

How Much Work? How Much Play?

To young girls, Scouting is fun. Girls come to troop meetings from school, where chances for muscular activity have been limited, and suddenly find themselves in an informal atmosphere where chances for active play are great. Our Girl Scout organization is proud of its program of leisure-time activities. Our nation is so anxious for children to have a free and happy childhood that we have child labor laws to guarantee this protection. But, whatever we say or believe, or pass laws about, there is always a continuous pull between age and youth over how much work and how much play is "good for them." While adults urge young boys and girls to grow up, be responsible, work hard, a child's world often excludes with impish glee those worth-while things about which adults get so serious. The struggle is to some extent inevitable, but Girl Scout leaders need to understand it to the point of applying it in Thursday afternoon troop meetings and on Saturday morning hikes. The adult is part of the problem. If youth furnishes one element, age furnishes the other. Each has something to contribute. Neither is right in itself.

SIGNIFICANCE OF PLAY FOR CHILDREN

How significant is play for children? How valuable is the emotional release that comes through joyous physical activity? How do children develop through stages of all-play to a combination of play and work, and then to mostly work as they arrive in the adult working world? How does this affect the play and fun we have in our troop meetings?

Play is a child's work, thought, art, relaxation. It is an outlet for a child's emotions—love, hate, anger, fear, jealousy, joy, and a socially acceptable way by which a child is allowed to externalize his feelings and deal with the world. The more a new leader applies these ideas to a group of twenty-four Girl Scouts as they come bounding into troop meeting the less often she will say, "What can I do with them? All they want is play. They won't settle down and do Scout work." A slightly more experienced leader will say, "I can't get them to settle down to work unless we play games the first fifteen or twenty minutes."

Children repeat in their play everything that has made an impression on them in actual life; i.e., they want to be grown-up and to be able to do what grown-up people do. The unpleasing character of the experience does not always prevent its being used as a game. All of us have read stories of children making up games called "air raid shelters," "bombs," and "blackout." Adults are frequently puzzled by such forms of play, may think they are silly or even gruesome. But childhood is a time for experimenting and playing with ways of the grown-up world. It is one of the ways children learn. Play, in its broadest and deepest sense, is the bridge over which children must pass from childhood to adulthood. Play has always been a part of any true system of child education from primitive cultures to our present complex society. We need not feel that we are somehow neglecting our educational duty toward children if we allow them generous time for play.

The Child's Versus Adult's Ideas of Play

To adults, all the Girl Scout program is a recreational one. Yet a leader finds that her troop, or certain girls within the troop, will label an activity work or play with sharp distinctions and attitudes. These attitudes can surprise the most experienced leader. For instance, parties, hikes, and games are fun, but scrubbing a very dirty floor may be fun, too, if girls are fixing up a new troop meeting place or are allowed to go barefooted and swish a lot of water about as they work. Notebooks are usually labeled as unpleasant work—"too much like school." Many ten-year-old Girl Scouts' idea of fun is limited to games as they enter a troop, and sometimes a leader's effort to stretch this idea of fun to include dramatics, crafts, group singing, sketching, or service to the community is not enthusiastically received, and may be rejected. Sometimes girls will label games fun and the new activity the leader introduced as work. It is the leader's idea of fun, not theirs. They will not know it is fun until they try it.

Substitutes for Noise

The discipline problem new leaders ask help with most frequently is noise. Much of this is a need for active play after sitting in school most of the day. Girl Scouts are in the same mood when they arrive at troop meeting after school as they are when let out for recess. All of us are familiar with the noise school children make at recess on playgrounds. This need for physical activity must have expression, and unless a leader can quickly offer substitutes for noise, she has discipline problems. Group singing is acceptable, while shrieking and shouting are not. Singing games, songs with motion, sea shanties, cowboy songs, folk songs, and rounds are vigorous substitutes for noise. In

[187]

The Leader Stretches a New Girl Scout's Idea of Fun!

place of jumping, pushing, wiggling, running about, or banging on the piano, girls can enjoy team games, folk dancing, impromptu dramatics, cross-country games, treasure hunts, a brisk walk or race out-of-doors. Thus, feelings of power, joy, hate, that adults keep children from expressing directly, have a healthy release. These same activities—music, games, and dancing—are educational and worth while, too, are they not?

As one watches leaders outline and plan their meetings, it becomes apparent that many leaders usually include three things: (1) play, (2) work, (3) troop business and program planning. As leaders describe these three and their relation to each other, they seem to interpret play most often as activities girls prefer; work as part of troop meeting program that the leader is ambitious for them to have—"to widen their horizons," "it is worth while," "they need"; troop business or program planning as management of this group work and play. But young Girls Scouts do, in time, teach a new leader to respect the significance of play, and the leader in turn stretches the girls' limited ideas of play as they try out more and more activities in the Girl Scout program.

GIRL SCOUTS CAN DO THINGS

As girls approach the ages of ten, eleven, or twelve years, the age of skill develops. Children become eager to make and do things that are useful and have some relation to the play and work of adults. Younger children paint, act, draw, to satisfy themselves. Ten to twelve year olds begin to care how what they make looks—if it is right, if it works, if it is of any use. They begin to compare what they do with what adults or older boys and girls do. To be able to do things— swim, build an outdoor fire, cook an outdoor meal, ice skate, sew for the Red Cross—is to gain status in the eyes of their playmates and confidence in themselves. If troop meetings are not active enough the leader soon hears the complaint, "Why don't we ever do anything?"

(See chapters "The Eleven Program Fields" and "Ranks, Badges, and Progression" for detailed help with your activity program.)

GIRL SCOUTS LEARN BY DOING

The Oldest Method of Learning

Learning by doing is probably the oldest method of learning we have. It was in practice centuries before anyone ever thought of schools. In simple truth, to learn by doing is to get first-hand experience. Only recently have parents, teachers, Girl Scout leaders, the nation's far-seeing educators and leaders been desperate and anxious for boys and girls to have work experience, learn how to do something —"use their hands," "get busy," and "do something besides just sitting at movies and listening to radio." Young people have been just as anxious to do something that really counts.

As our civilization in America changed from an agricultural to an industrial one, our new civilization stripped many children's work and play at home of its rich content. Sally says to her Girl Scout leader, "Mother won't let me cook. She says I'm in the way." Sally is in the way in a modern kitchenette. She does not have the everyday tasks and after-school chores children had twenty-five years ago. Hence parents, teachers, and Girl Scout leaders must deliberately provide these work experiences so boys and girls may learn about the everyday world in which they must grow up, live, and make their way.

A leader can provide the experience and see that her girls learn by doing as well as the next person if she remembers that to learn by doing is to do a thing as life demands it. This, in turn, controls the space, tools, equipment, adult guidance, number of girls working at one time, and the number of meetings to acquire a skill. For instance, if girls want to do activity number thirteen in the Clothing badge (doing their personal laundry), they must do this not in the regular meeting place, such as the church basement, but by washing and ironing clothes in somebody's home laundry; use the same kind of laundry equipment adults use; be taught by someone who is willing for each girl to practice and learn by doing, not by just watching someone else wash and iron clothes or remove stains; be allowed to practice enough times so they can acquire skill to wash and iron their own clothes or little brother's or sister's. Almost any Girl Scout leader, Girl Scout mother, or troop committee member can teach girls such simple skills

[190]

if they teach them as life demands it. Leaders err most frequently in this area by (1) stopping just short of allowing the girls to do it themselves, and (2) trying to work with sixteen or twenty-four girls instead of six or eight when equipment and space are limited.

The Test of Performance Versus Written Tests

If Girl Scouts learn by doing sufficiently to meet life's demands, they must:

1. See what needs to be done.
2. Know how to do it.
3. Be willing to do what is needed.

You cannot judge all three in a written test. This is the test of performance—performance that is good enough to be useful to a Girl Scout and others.

W. H. Kilpatrick says, "The predominant stress in any activity at any time is just what life under the given conditions of age and experience would demand, no more, no less. To think of an activity in any other way is simply to miss the whole point."

Four Types of Activities in Terms of Purpose

Activities, however, do vary in purpose. Most leaders do not seem to sense this difference between activities until they begin to judge their girls' performance of them. Leaders then ask, "How do I know when girls earn a part or all of their Second Class badge? You say it is not like passing a test in school. Then, what is it?" If you turn to the badges, you will recognize these four types of badge activities:

Appreciation—where the purpose is to enjoy some aesthetic experience, such as listening to a story, going to a good movie or play, watching a sunset, or taking a moonlight hike in the snow. This is the spiritual or inspirational part of the program.

Creative—where the purpose is to have the group or an individual set its own goal, make the plan, carry out the plan, and judge the results of the activity. To be truly creative, all four steps must be experienced. Try not to think of creative activities only in terms of an individual writing an original poem or play, or painting a landscape. Group activities can be creative, too.

Problem Solving—where the purpose is to straighten out or solve a problem, such as activity number eight in My Troop badge, in which girls do something about any rules the troop has that girls resent or find hard to keep, or solve problems as they arise in the troop from time to time, even though they are not suggested in badge activities.

Skill Activity—where the purpose is to obtain some degree of skill or knowledge, such as rowing a boat or bandaging a sprained ankle. We can never learn to row a boat without repetitious practice. We can never render simple first aid without careful and correct practice beforehand.

APPRECIATION TYPE OF ACTIVITY

The appreciation type of activity differs from others in that the activity is for the child rather than of the child. They become listeners and seers rather than doers. It appeals to the aesthetic emotions through a demonstration of beauty, harmony, movement, tone, truth, perfection, religion, patriotism, and the idealistic. It is an excellent modifier of the attitudes and ideals of children.

In the badges My Country and Junior Citizen, there are many activities where the main purpose is a better appreciation, through music and drama, of the epic that is our own America. There are also Music and Dramatics Appreciation badges. Many of the activities in the last half of each Arts and Crafts badge are primarily designed to increase a girl's appreciation of that particular medium. While any activity has some effect on appreciation or attitudes toward whatever is being done, the above named are samples of those written with appreciation in mind as the predominant goal.

Several Hoped-for Results in Appreciation Activities

When appreciation is the goal, there are several hoped-for results. You cannot force them, but an enthusiastic person can use her influence and set the stage. Try hard not to be impatient at first. It just takes time for anyone to appreciate, admire, respect, or comprehend enough to be moved emotionally.

1. The girls should have a wholesome respect for the thing desired, whether it is nature, a fine movie, a view from a mountain top, a fine personality, or a religious or patriotic ceremony.

2. The girls should want to repeat such an experience, learn more about it, or go more deeply into the subject. Proper appreciation stimulates action.

3. The girls should realize what it can mean to an individual, and to their community. For instance, a visit to a national or state park would be fine to help Girl Scouts realize what the park offers in natural beauty to its citizens, how many thousands of people use it each year, what recreational and camping facilities there are, why conservation of a nation's beauty is important to its people and why they are willing to buy the land and protect it.

A Leader's Record of Appreciation Activity

"One way in which we have tried to make our activities count is to explore each one chosen to its fullest capacity. For example, in My Community badge we decided that we would talk with an early settler to find out about the beginning of our town. The girls first took a survey of the town to find out what houses were the oldest. They had such a good time talking with the people who lived in the houses that we spent a meeting exchanging stories. Then they narrowed their choice to see if they could find a house in which the original family still lived. We discovered the N—— house, while not the oldest—being only ninety-seven, was the oldest house in which a member of the original family was still a resident, and she was born the year the house was built, was an invalid, very deaf, but remarkably keen. At the girls' request, I asked her daughters who live at home if we might come and see the house. They were most enthusiastic and set a day and hour when 'Mother' would receive.

"One daughter met us at the door wearing her mother's wedding dress, a beautifully kept silk with large hoops. We were taken into the 'sitting room' where 'granddaughter,' also in period dress, sat knitting a sock for 'Father.' Daughter had considerable trouble with her hoops, which our girls found not at all amusing but very impressive. The hostesses told the girls about the building of the house from lumber cut on the place, mostly whitewood, or what we in Ohio call the tulip tree. Black walnut was considered good enough only for the pantry shelves and the rail fences, which still border the maple-lined road.

"Up in the low attic the girls measured the floor boards with a yardstick and found several that are thirty-two inches wide. We looked down the well and unwound the bucket and explored the lovely big, spicy-smelling pantry. Then, in the dining room we found the big table spread with a red and white cloth. The plates were all turned down, and the spoons were bunched in a spoonholder in the center.

"'Why are the plates turned down?' asked one of the girls.

"'Why, child,' she was told, 'this road out in front was often two feet deep with dust. We did it to keep our plates clean. And then we had no screens, of course, for they hadn't been thought of.'

"'My goodness,' another girl said, 'what did you do about flies?'

"'Bless you, child, the flies, like the poor, we always had with us.'

"We were served cookies and milk, and the daughters told one of our girls that she must eat double to make up for the many cookies that her great-grandmother had given them when, as little girls at school, they always took the water pail over to be filled.

"After tea and many more reminiscences, we visited with 'Mother.' She talked to the girls and they sang hymns for her. She died a few weeks later, and our girls have a memory of an old settler which is still very vivid."

CREATIVE TYPE OF GROUP ACTIVITY

In a creative type of activity the leader is willing to give the group, or individual, time to make a definite plan; get the necessary equipment, information, or help; plan and carry out the necessary steps; and judge the results. The girls often think of these activities as the highlights of the year, because "we thought it up and did it all ourselves," or "it was our own good idea" or "we're so original!" When Scouts turn an attic or a barn loft into a meeting place because it was their

Two Types of Creative Activity: 1. Individual
2. Group

own good idea, they seem to work harder and are more interested than under any other circumstances.

The written Girl Scout program approaches the creative activity most nearly in what some leaders call "vague" or "less definite" activities. They say, "Number so-and-so is vague. I can't tell what you mean for us to do." Such activities have purposely been written that way so as to encourage the troop to think up their own reasons for doing what they do. For instance, in My Troop badge, number five— "Do something that will improve the appearance, comfort, or usefulness of your troop meeting place"—will require more original thinking than an activity that says, "Build a bookshelf for your troop meeting place,"—to say nothing of the probable accumulation of bookshelves if fifteen girls met such a requirement.

PROBLEM-SOLVING TYPE OF ACTIVITY

See section on group discussion in chapter "Developing Self-Government in a Troop," also leaders' records at the end of chapter "Group Control, or Discipline," for an interpretation and illustration of problem-solving activities.

SKILL TYPE OF ACTIVITY

Where repetition is necessary in learning an activity, achievement comes mostly through practice. In play and recreation, as elsewhere, there are many of these so-called skill type of activities. If a girl wants to swim, dance, paddle a canoe, ski, play the piano, build an outdoor fire, or bandage an ankle, she must be willing to practice before she can do these things with a sureness of touch and an ease that gives her pleasure in doing them. Even if a girl learns and practices in a group, each girl has to do her own practicing to keep up or to "get good at it," as the girls say. A girl never learns to build an outdoor fire, bandage an ankle, or paddle a canoe by just being along, merely watching other girls perform, or letting the others do it. She achieves and gains prestige in skills only as a result of her own efforts and practice over a period of time.

[197]

Good Teaching Methods for Skill Activities

The chief responsibility of the leader in a practice activity is to get the best possible attention. Practice alone does not insure excellent performance, but *correct practice with attention* will. A few good teaching methods to get this correct practice follow:

1. Girls should be given a correct idea of the amount of work to be done both for the whole project and at each step. Girls often want to get the First Aid badge, be in a play, or paddle a canoe until they realize that it means hours of work and practice. In order to perform well, they must know there is a price to pay, and only those who are willing to put in these hours of work can expect to reap the honors.

2. The leader should help the girls single out only those difficult parts that require repetition, and then pay special attention to those parts, letting the others go where possible.

3. Practice periods should not be too long. Fatigue, either physical or mental, is usually followed by inattention, boredom, or even rebellion.

4. Accuracy in early practice prevents formation of bad habits that have to be changed later. All of us have experienced this at some time or other, and wasted time as a result. Also, guarding against carelessness and lapses is necessary for time-saving and sustained interest.

5. Increased length of interval between practice is found effective in learning. For instance, two or three practices close together and then a longer interval before the next one net good results. It is hard for children to rehearse for a play or song at the last minute and then perform successfully, even when the total time is the same as if stretched out over a longer period.

There are other points that you can think of as you go along, but these are not too difficult for girls to grasp.

[198]

Tendency Toward Too Many Skill Activities

Since skills depend so much upon individual achievement, and success or failure is so apparent and so easily measured both by girls and leaders, there is a danger of filling the year's program too full of skill activities at the expense of other types, and measuring a troop's success and failure only in terms of these skills and activities. Because the business of everyday living properly demands skill, appreciation, problem-solving, and creative activities, a leader needs to include all of these in the year's program and help girls understand achievement in more intangible directions. It is extremely important that leaders lend the whole weight of their influence and personality at times to supporting appreciation, creative, and problem-solving activities.

When leaders teach activities requiring individual skill and practice, the groups should be small enough so leader can help each girl if necessary.

[199]

When Sally attempts to swim fifty yards, she either succeeds or has to be pulled out of the water. It is perfectly easy for her, her friends, and her leader to see how far she can swim. But, if the troop chooses to listen to Dvorak's "New World Symphony" over the radio, it is not so apparent whether Sally or Susie enjoyed the music the more, or even enough. The important thing is that Sally and Susie will want to listen to fine music again and enjoy it. There are no *exact* educational measurements whereby appreciation or feeling for art, music, poetry, one's country, or religion can be judged in terms of who passed and who did not pass, who succeeded or failed, who gets a first or second prize. Even so, we are sure that all are too fine for girls to miss. Problem-solving, appreciation, and creative activities are full of intangibles, but are still a necessary part and parcel of everyday living.

GIRL SCOUTS USE A SIMPLE DEMOCRATIC FORM OF TROOP GOVERNMENT

(See the entire chapter, "Developing Self-Government in a Troop")

LEADERS' RECORDS OF THEIR TROOP MEETINGS

The following leaders' records are good illustrations of what Girl Scout meetings are like. In all, Girl Scouts are learning by doing; having fun; taking responsibility in planning and carrying out their programs; developing habits of friendliness, cooperation, thrift, kindness. In all, leaders are sharing their hobbies and interests with their girls.

Notice especially the record form. This seemed to help new leaders plan their meetings more easily.

RECORD A—COOKING

LEADER'S PLAN TO PRESENT A PROGRAM ACTIVITY

1. What I hope to accomplish through this activity:
    a. Teach the girls to follow a recipe.
    b. Help them understand the use of a thermometer in cooking.

c. Make them responsible for a necessary part of an activity.

d. Teach them how to make good taffy and have a taffy pull.

2. I select a program of action to achieve these aims with this particular troop:

We discovered that only a few had ever made taffy. Recipes were compared, and needed ingredients were noted before we chose our recipe.

3. I select ways to carry out this program of action:

Each girl was made responsible for one ingredient or utensil to be used. Two were selected to assemble the recipe, one to watch the thermometer. A Saturday afternoon was selected for our taffy pull.

4. Estimated time I will need for various parts of the program:

Meeting, 2 to 4 P.M.

5. Cooperation I will need from the group and from individual members in the group:

All to contribute in bringing supplies.

The leader shares her hobbies and interests with her girls. Here the girls learn how to cook under the leader's watchful and encouraging eye.

Two responsible for assembling recipe; one to watch thermometer.

All the rest to join in a short game.

All to pull taffy and judge the results.

All to help wash dishes and put kitchen in order.

HOW THE PLAN WORKED OUT

1. *Attainment of objectives—both immediate and general:*

Each member remembered to bring her ingredient or tool. Keen interest in the value of the thermometer was noted. The recipe was followed accurately and the result was splendid. The girls decided that they wanted to explore the Homemaking program field in more detail.

2. *Command of the program material or subject:*

My own interest in homemaking, in correct procedures, and in use of helpful equipment in cooking made me able to direct this activity with confidence.

RECORD B—PUPPETRY

LEADER'S PLAN TO PRESENT A PROGRAM ACTIVITY

1. I hope to accomplish through this activity:
    a. An interest in dramatics.
    b. A knowledge of simple, well known children's stories.
    c. A common ground for working together—allowing for participation of whole patrol.
    d. A regard for detail—costume, scenery, character.
2. I select a program of action to achieve these aims with this particular troop:

    Make hand puppets and present a puppet show to other patrol in troop.
3. I select ways to carry out this program of action:
    a. Gain interest by leaving a model puppet on table and allow girls to play with it until meeting actually begins.

b. Joyce wanted to know what it was. (None of the girls had seen one before.)

c. Explanation of how puppets were used. (See the *Girl Scout Handbook*.)

d. Girls suggest we make a show.

e. What story? Decide on simple one we all know—"Little Red Riding Hood."

f. During the first week, collect pieces of cloth to make bodies and costumes. Dolls' heads of celluloid used for three characters. Wolf's head made of cotton cloth, stuffed.

g. Making four puppets.

h. Writing script.

i. Making stage—very simple.

j. Rehearsing for show.

k. Presenting "Little Red Riding Hood."

4. Estimated time I will need for various parts of program:

Thirty minutes for a, b, c, d, e. (See item 3.)

During work period we sewed. It took about forty-five minutes in each of three meetings to complete four dolls.

Marie and Viola worked on script one meeting.

While script was being made, Connie, Lois, Dorothy, and Jean made stage.

Two meetings—thirty minutes each—for rehearsal.

Show presented after patrol meetings for Pine Cone. Patrol to present it later when mothers will be present.

HOW THE PLAN WORKED OUT

1. *Attainment of objectives—both immediate and general:*

My girls knew nothing about puppets, and so I hoped to share with them the fun my sisters and I had with our shows. They were delighted with the little doll they could make do "tricks"—as they said. They all wanted one, and I guess, by general conversation, they all have several at home now.

I was also at a loss to understand why children here were so woefully ignorant of standard stories, myths, fairy tales, Bible stories. So we began telling stories. We've told many as we worked, and are planning the creation of more characters. We're even considering being in a play ourselves, something none have ever done. In fact, we may write our own play.

Somewhere the group was getting the idea that each girl was to work for her personal advancement, but we've discovered that it is fun to work together.

2. *Command of the program material or subject:*

I am an English teacher, graduate of the University of Maine, and am preparing for my Master's degree from Columbia through summer sessions. I have also studied dramatics since childhood, and besides my regular classroom teaching have taught storytelling and dramatics in summer assemblies.

3. *Applying specific methods:*

I think it best to take time to show the girls, and my girls are even younger than their years, how to do things. Cloth is scarce, so I try to help them plan to cut to the best advantage. But I try to respect their originality. I was really delighted with the drooping red tongue I discovered on Mr. Wolf in "Little Red Riding Hood."

We tell stories as we work—stories suggested by what we are doing. Sometimes I ask if they know such and such a story and character. Maybe I tell it to them; maybe I suggest that someone find it before next week.

I try to let individual differences take their course, but I think it unwise always to let the girl do as she likes. Many times I find that she doesn't like to do the task because she does not know how.

4. *Distribution of time according to importance of program parts and objectives:*

Our work period varies from thirty to forty-five minutes. We did not devote all this time to this project, as some girls are working on other badges. But in about five weeks we completed the work. We used one for discussion and explanation. The next three were necessary for sewing, designing stage, writing script. Two rehearsals for the well known story were sufficient.

[204]

5. *Securing cooperation of troop and certain individuals:*

This work was done without much outside help. We found, however, mothers and committee members only too glad to save scraps of cloth for our use. Our patrol's puppets aroused much curiosity in the other patrol, which made an excellent audience—both sympathetic and critical.

Our troop is new, but the town is vastly interested in our girls and will cooperate in any way possible, I know. In fact, the people say, "We will help in any way we can." This is encouraging, as money is scarce; but materials, examiners, pictures are all needed.

This is my first active experience with Girl Scouting, but I already love it, and our girls need it.

RECORD C—A PARTY

LEADER'S PLAN TO PRESENT A PROGRAM ACTIVITY

1. I hope to accomplish through this activity:
   a. A more friendly relationship between the "upper social" and the "non-social" groups of girls in my troop.
   b. A sense of responsibility in each girl in the troop for a certain activity and the feeling that her part is an important factor in the success of the troop's activity.
   c. Knowledge on the part of people in town that Girl Scouts can use public facilities without damaging them.
   d. An opportunity for the girls to have a good time with their friends and at the same time keep the expense of the activity at a minimum cost.

2. I select a program of action to achieve these aims with this particular troop:

   My troop is beginning to work on Second Class rank activities. As my special interests are music and dancing, I thought it best to start with an activity from this program field.

[205]

The requirements were read and explained to the girls.

They chose to know and dance the "Virginia Reel." After the dance was learned, they asked to have a party and invite their boy friends. We voted and agreed to this and to teach the "Virginia Reel" and other American dances to the guests at the party.

We had a Court of Honor and decided on the committees needed, committee chairmen, and members. We leaders were very careful, without saying anything, to place the "non-social" and "social" girls on the same committees, and in almost every case the "non-social" girl was given the chairmanship of the committee.

When these committee lists were read to the girls, they were all delighted with their responsibilities. I explained the major duties of each committee and the importance of each girl doing her share of the work. They were very free in adding to their own committee's lists of duties, and even suggested an entirely new committee—one for being responsible for borrowed musical recordings.

Each committee decided how much money it would need for its part of the program. The estimates were too high at first, but, after the second report to the troop, the costs were cut to almost half.

We decided to use the public library auditorium for the dance party, and each girl was asked, "Can you think of any special ways we can keep from doing damage to the property in the library?" Here are some of the suggestions: Don't bang on the piano. Be careful and not spill punch on the table and floor. Don't pull the Venetian blinds up and down too much. Don't run and slide across the floor. Be sure that no paper cups are left lying on the floor.

These children had had parties in the library before and had received much criticism from the public for leaving the auditorium "in a mess." This was the reason for the discussion.

The names of the committees and the cost of each committee's activities were as follows:

Invitation Committee .... $ .10
Refreshment Committee 3.55
Decoration Committee .... no cost
Music Committee .... no cost
Entertainment Committee .... no cost
Hostess Committee .... no cost

Total Cost .... $ 3.65

4. Estimated time I will need for various parts of program:

There were forty-five girls and boys present at the party.

We had three regular Scout meetings, at which time the party was planned in detail and the American dances were learned. We had one Court of Honor meeting.

The party was given on Friday evening from seven-thirty to ten o'clock.

5. Cooperation I will need from the group and from individual members of the group:

Girls' committees to carry out plans.

The assistant leader helped prepare the refreshments along with the committee members at the home of one of the troop committee members.

The other committee chairmen reported to me when they had completed their plans.

The troop committee members acted as chaperons for the party.

HOW THE PLAN WORKED OUT

1. *Attainment of objectives—both immediate and general:*

Frankly, this is the only activity I have ever planned that I thought was completely successful. All the girls, except one who was in a music recital, came to the party and entered into the dances and other activities with an enthusiasm that I've never seen before! The "dates" of the social group danced with many, if not all, of the girls

[207]

present. (I hate to keep referring to the "social" and "non-social" groups, but there is a decided feeling of "class distinction" not only in the troop but in the town as a whole; therefore, we leaders are conscious of the fact and are trying to help the situation without making an ado about it.) The auditorium was left in perfect order.

2. *Command of the program material or subject:*

My college work was all done in the field of health and physical education and recreation. Then, too, I have taught physical education for eight years and at a summer camp for the past five summers; so, with this training and experience, it was easy for me to help direct this program activity.

Chapter Seven

Girls' Interests and Needs

IF YOU WANT TO KNOW how to get the troop's program off to a good start with a sense of action and promise of going somewhere, scan this chapter. These familiar methods of stimulating an interest in new ideas might come under the heading of "influencing girls, aged ten to fourteen, for new adventures and experiences."

The material develops two main ideas and illustrates their practical application in troop meetings:

1. *Ways of finding interests girls already have, such as observation of youth activities in the community, use of interest check lists, discussion of badge activities, and listening to what girls say.*

2. *Ways of stimulating new interests, such as use of outside people, taking trips, bringing in new materials to troop meetings, seeing good movies, and listening to selected radio programs.*

W HAT ARE WE GOING TO DO FIRST?" "What are we going to do next?" "When do we go on a hike? I thought Scouts always hiked!" says Susie or Sally or any one else of a troop of enthusiastic Scouts. The leader who is caught in the midst of this bouncing energy and noisy enthusiasm knows that there are many different badges and Second Class activities in the *Girl Scout Handbook,* and she wonders how a leader ever helps twenty-four girls agree upon one or two program activities as starting points! Is it possible for these twenty-four eager young girls to be interested in the same thing? She has read that a Girl Scout leader builds a program based on "the interests and needs of the girls," and she wonders if that is not a bit "soft" for building character and citizenship—if Girl Scouts never do anything they do not want to do. Such are a few thoughts that confront a new leader and oftentimes a more experienced one.

It is unfortunate that we have too often hurried over the reasons why we are so concerned about "interests and needs of girls" and have sometimes given the impression that girls can do whatever they want to do and the "good leader" can make their dreams come true, so to speak—for it is erroneous to feel that there is anything sacred about a girl's interests or that they develop spontaneously. Girls get their interests from their environment just the way anybody else does, and these interests are always changing. These interests center around their home, school, friends, neighborhood, community. The leader is one of the most influential people in the environment of her girls. Thus, she has a large responsibility in helping them become aware of a variety of interests and choose worthy ones.

In simple truth, the leader's job in this area falls into two parts:

1. She *finds out* what *interests* the *girls* in her troop *already have,* and *adds to* or *widens these* with program activities in the same field.

2. She, out of her mature experience and judgment, sees that her *girls need* other *new ideas and experiences,* and *proceeds to stimulate an interest in them.*

To do this successfully, leaders must first recall the important part interest plays in learning, and know ways of finding and stimulating interests in a group as well as in an individual.

Finding or stimulating interests depends to a great degree upon what we call "set" or "mind set" or "mind set to an end," and "readiness" or "ready" to act or play a part. We have the same idea when we say of a friend or a member of the family, "She knows what she wants, and it isn't going to be easy to stop her"; or, "He's made up his mind." This "mind set" affects one's behavior in a highly significant manner—so much so that it is one of the recognized laws of learning. This is called the Law of Readiness. Educators feel that we do not learn very much until we are "set" and "ready," since "set" and "readiness" symbolize active interest and purpose.

As groups or individuals get a "mind set to an end," useful and appropriate ideas are likely to arise; they are unwilling to be distracted, or will say there is no time for the irrelevant; they concentrate their efforts upon finishing the job; they need little or no urging or prodding from leaders, teachers, parents. It is for these reasons that we are concerned about finding and stimulating children's interests. It is under such conditions that habits of self-discipline are best formed. It does not mean that a leader will stand by and let Mary deliberately kick Sally in a relay game, or allow unfair play between teams to go unchecked. It does not mean that every whim in a troop is satisfied, or even encouraged.

A FEW WAYS OF FINDING INTERESTS
GIRLS ALREADY HAVE

The following ways of finding interests are described and interpreted with leaders' records of troop practices:

Observation of girls at work and play in their own neighborhoods.
Use of interest check list.
Discussion of badge activities with girls.
Listening to girls' spontaneous questions, suggestions, and exclamations.

OBSERVATION OF GIRLS AT WORK AND PLAY IN THEIR OWN NEIGHBORHOOD

WHAT DO THEY CARE ABOUT MOST?

Since girls' interests center around their home, school, friends, neighborhood, and community, why not examine these interests, both as to kind and quality, and notice the ones the girls seem to enjoy and care about most. What do your Scouts do in their leisure time—after school hours, Saturdays and Sundays, and summer vacations? Do they sing in the church choir, take music lessons, take an active part in Sunday school and church affairs, go to the movies every Saturday regardless of what picture is on, earn money by doing various odd jobs or taking care of children, play games in the neighborhood, listen to the radio a lot, or what? What annual community holidays or festivals do girls take part in, such as: Christmas tree party, Fourth of July picnics, Memorial Day services, strawberry festival? Does the school have sports and games, music and dramatic clubs, or fine arts and crafts courses? If so, in how many do Girl Scouts participate or show ability or talent? Because of having or not having these more informal educational activities in school, do you find girls wanting to do more of these same activities, or others, in troop meetings? Do girls have few outside contacts with troops from other neighborhoods or towns? Do they camp in summer? Is too much, or too little, going on in your neighborhood for Scout-age girls? Do girls live at great distances from the center of things? The better a leader sees this community picture of youth's activities the less surprised or puzzled she will be when the girls respond wholeheartedly to one activity, reject or scorn another, or are indifferent to a third.

LEADERS' RECORDS: TWO OBSERVATIONS OF GIRLS AND PROGRAM ACTIVITIES THAT FOLLOWED

"The dearth of boy-girl entertainment or recreation in our neighborhood bothers the Scoutmaster and me. The parents try to be strict with them, but seem indifferent about opening their homes or planning the decent fun the boys and girls need. We are now teaching them dancing, and have found several people to help us."

"I am having a different patrol at my home for Saturday lunch each week as we work on the Cook and Hostess badges. I wanted them here in my home when I realized that several of my girls did not even know how to use a knife and fork. Some of the girls' parents are very ignorant and poor, and nearly all of my girls help with the housework. Perhaps some of these simple things they learn in Girl Scouting will be practiced at home. That is my hope."

The Interest Check List

USING THE CHECK LIST

The main reasons for using an interest check list are:

To find out which activities girls want to do first, and which activities they wish to do during the next one or two months.

To give new Scouts an idea of what they might do.

To see how different girls' interests vary.

To give every girl an equal chance to vote on the troop's program.

THE MAKE-UP OF THE CHECK LIST

Try to have each item on the check list present a clear picture to the girl as she reads it. Example—a moonlight hike in the snow; a skating party at Bear Lake; visit to pottery works in Greenville; making a first aid kit to use on hikes; having a radio party to hear Christmas carols from London. It is difficult for a girl, and most certainly a ten- to twelve-year-old girl, to check "community living" or "international field of interest" and know what she is doing. Psychologists say that it requires a minimum mental age of twelve for average children to make concrete application to their everyday living from abstract terms like *international friendship* or *justice*. Therefore, the items listed need to suggest to Sally and Susie a concrete, clear picture of what their troop may be doing.

It seems best to list about ten items and leave space to add at least one, two, or three other activities. When the list is too long, girls get inattentive and do not check the last ones carefully. The lists are made up in a variety of ways—sometimes entirely by the leader or with girls adding to the leader's list, or by the girls themselves.

As you select program activities, try to keep in mind your own talents and abilities and those of your friends and neighbors. Young

By using interest check lists, the leader sees what activities and ideas interest the majority of her girls; such lists also give her a picture of individual interests. The use of these lists also makes each Girl Scout realize that she has an opportunity and responsibility for making troop plans. The girl on the left is more interested in the way her friend is checking her list than in exercising her independent choice. You will find one or two girls like her in your troop, too!

[215]

ten- to fourteen-year-old girls have had so few experiences in club or group activities as compared with your maturity, you need not stand in awe of what they already can do or know. Most of the time, when girls show a mild interest, or no interest at all, in an activity, leaders find with a little questioning that the activity is so new or unfamiliar the girls' imaginations just cannot work unless they see or visit or hear more about it. It often helps to discuss the scope of activities suggested, and what the troop might do in case "everybody voted for this one" or "that one got the most votes." Such a discussion will help a new troop see what is ahead, and is apt to increase group morale as the girls look forward to their good times.

LEADERS' RECORD: USE OF AN INTEREST CHECK LIST AND
PROGRAM THAT FOLLOWED

Notice especially the girls' response to activities suggested and the way the leader often implies the use or purpose of program activities suggested. The leader does not report a response to every single activity, but do not let that worry you. An able leader always has more ideas than she can use, and most girls become restless after a twenty- or thirty-minute discussion.

The leader writes, "At our first meeting this fall, we decided upon an interest check list in order to plan our program for the winter. Our troop is made up of girls who are somewhat underprivileged, with the exception of possibly four girls. Hence, my assistant and I wished to list activities that our girls would miss if it were not for Scouting:

Make layette for Red Cross.
Hay ride, with outdoor cooking afterwards.
Party on Mrs. Low's birthday, inviting mothers.
Outdoor sketching.
Winter hikes, collecting plants for winter flower show.
Make quilts for hospital.
Bookbinding. (Very few girls have done bookbinding. It may

[216]

require a visit to an artist's or craftsman's shop for girls to see
how they could do this successfully.)

Make sports belts.

Make puppets and have puppet shows for other troops.

Assemble health charts.

Operate self-lending library, each girl contributing books and
lending them to troop members.

Dancing lessons—the gym teacher will find time to help us.

Visit various local industries, the dairies and hatcheries.

"The girls were enthusiastic about Red Cross work and anything
that savored of a party. They do not get much social enjoyment in
their homes. So we decided on sewing for Red Cross and tea for
Mrs. Low's birthday as our first projects. Outdoor sketching was not
popular, unfortunately. Yet, we are lucky enough to have a well
known artist to help us. However, the girls were nearly unanimous
in wanting to make sports belts. They have very little in the way of
personal adornment. Our artist friend very kindly helped with the
tiny drawings on wooden blocks which, when laced together with
leather thongs, form the belt. They were not particularly interested
in winter hiking to gather plants for a winter flower show, feeling
that this was a little babyish.

"The girls were interested in a puppet show, and that project is
now under way. They have been invited to give it at their school
assembly. We stimulated interest in the puppet show by a discussion
of costumes for the puppets and stage properties. We had directions
for carrying out a puppet show, and explained them to the girls, who,
until the explanation, had felt puppets might be too difficult for them
to construct.

"Health charts bored them, but the self-lending library has proved
to be popular. They were unanimous in wanting dancing lessons, so
we arranged for the gym teacher to come once a month to instruct
them. They are making nice progress, and through her help and
suggestions their poise and carriage are showing decided improvement."

DISCUSSION OF BADGE ACTIVITIES WITH GIRLS

ITS ADVANTAGES TO GIRLS AND LEADER

Before "doing a badge," as the girls express it, they would profit greatly from a good discussion of the activities. The obvious and desirable reason for this is that Sally and Susie, and all the others, need to see what they are to do and why they are doing it, what plans need to be made, and how they may use the skills and information they hope to gain. A good discussion lessens the chances of Sally and Susie wanting to change to something else after they get started, or going over to Mrs. ——'s house to start sewing without any thread, needles, or material.

Discussing badge activities with your troop also gives you a fine idea of what the girls have done, can do, want to do, dislike to do, are unaware of, and wherein they need a different point of view. It is such a simple and easy way to find out where to start. Yet, so many leaders hurry right over this step! (See section on group discussion in the chapter "Developing Self-Government in a Troop" for more detailed help on this.)

LEADER'S RECORD: DISCUSSION OF BADGE ACTIVITIES WITH GIRLS

A leader reports her group's reaction to the suggested activities in the badge My Community. She writes:

"1, 2. All were keen for getting up an exhibit of old-country things. Four girls were of Finnish descent, and the exhibit proved to be overwhelmingly Finnish. Each girl had a short story of her ancestry, and all seemed proud of their old-country heritage.

"3, 4. Ours is a rural community—everybody knows all about farming. We live a short distance from a world-famous cannery.

"5. Girls could not think of any interesting occupations in the neighborhood, so we started out with the question, 'How many different occupations can you find that are represented in our school district?' I offered a prize for the longest list and gave the girls two weeks to do their 'snooping around,' with the astonishing result that we found twenty-one distinct jobs represented. Very broadening for the girls who thought there were only farmers and millworkers!

"6. We have only one church. Most girls attend Sunday school somewhere else, but all have helped the community church with suppers and programs. They take it for granted that they should take an interest in church, school, and Grange affairs and are always willing to help.

"7. 'Why, we take care of ourselves,' said one girl. True, we have no fire protection—but all know the State Milk Inspector, and, I found out, do not like the idea of any kind of inspection. Somehow they seem to resent rather than appreciate what little has been done for them in this way. We have to make a study of this subject. They know too little about it.

"8. Girls checked up on this, and found most violations on highways. They wanted to put up more traffic signs by the schoolhouse; thought most drivers were too careless when children were around.

"9. Cannot do.

"10. Only two girls had library cards, but, when you consider that the nearest library is ten miles away and you have to pay a dollar and fifty cents for a card, that is not surprising. Girls want to get state library service for the troop, especially reference books on crafts. We are building up a troop library, but girls feel they cannot undertake anything for the community as a whole yet.

"11. 'Oh, we know all about that!' It seems the teacher—and all the girls from ten to fourteen have the same teacher!—gave them quite a talk on the subject. We talked about schools in other lands. Most girls have the mistaken idea that other boys and girls do not have the schooling the Americans have. They were surprised when I told them of my own schooldays in Europe.

"They wanted to stop here, and finish the discussion another time. Their interest was high, and they were eager to start."

LISTENING TO GIRLS' SPONTANEOUS QUESTIONS, SUGGESTIONS, OR EXCLAMATIONS

The most frequent opportunities for recognizing interests come to a leader as she watches her girls at work or play. Girls are constantly expressing their convictions, approval, desires, boredom, disapproval, and disgust by what they say, how they act, the way they look. An alert leader recognizes these signs of interest, seizes them as opportunities to lead on to larger fields of interest, or ignores or disapproves them. The following are typical indicators of interest or lack of interest and will remind you of others:

GIRLS' QUESTIONS

What do you mean by ....?
How is .... made?
Why can't we ....?
When may we ....?
Wouldn't it be fun ....?
Isn't it possible ....?
Where is ....?

GIRLS' SUGGESTIONS

Let's ....
The troop in .... does this.
We might try to ....
I wonder if we would be allowed to ....?
It would be fun to ....

GIRLS' EXCLAMATIONS—POSITIVE AND NEGATIVE

Gee, that's swell!
Look at that ....!
Let me see it!
Do we have to ....?

[220]

The Leader Builds Program

upon girls' interests

We do that in school!
May we go there instead of ....?

LEADERS' RECORD: LISTENING TO GIRLS' CONVERSATION
AND RESULTANT PROGRAM ACTIVITY

A leader gave this photographic account of her troop's interest in folk dancing. It is so well reported it is almost as good as a visit to the troop. Notice how the leader enters into the girls' conversation, picks up their interest in folk dancing, and puts it right into the troop's program. She writes:

"At the conclusion of a troop meeting, I was busy talking over some badge requirements with two girls when I heard several others discussing something with great interest and evidence of envy.

" 'Well, if the eighth grade can do it, I don't see why we can't.'

" 'She says it's because they're getting ready for the party.'

" 'Lucky!'

" 'Lots of the boys don't dance. . . .'

" 'Well, gee, you don't *have* to have boys!'

" 'We used to do it in sixth grade troop.'

" 'It's fun!'

" 'We never did. We didn't have any music.'

" 'Well, gee, I don't see why we can't if the eighth grade can!'

" 'What can the eighth grade do that you can't?' I asked.

"It developed that the eighth graders were being taught square dancing by the gym teacher during the noon play period.

"I learned that the principal, who knows all his students, realized that a rather large group of eighth grade boys were not particularly social. Many of them did not dance, did not care about it. Square dances were being taught the eighth graders in an effort to get these boys to participate. My Scouts are seventh graders and had been left out.

"The girls went on:

"Elaine: 'If Carla wants to learn, I can teach her!'

"Barbara: 'It's no fun with just two.'

"Myrtle: 'I want to learn, too.'

[222]

"Elaine: 'Mrs. _____, couldn't our whole troop do it?'

"Leader: 'It sounds like fun. How many know it?'

"Two hands went up. Two more, rather doubtfully. There must have been over a dozen girls still present.

"Leader: 'It should not be hard to learn. I used to know the figures. I'm afraid I've forgotten. . . .'

"Elaine: 'I know them all.'

"Barbara: 'Me, too. We could teach you.'

"Betsy: 'We haven't got a victrola.'

"Annabelle: 'At school Miss _____ plays the piano.'

"Nancy: 'We've got a piano, but nobody can play good enough.'

"Leader: 'We can all clap hands and hum!'

"Elaine: 'I know the words to "Turkey in the Straw."'

"Barbara: 'Betcha don't know all of them!'

"Elaine: 'I guess nobody knows all the verses!'

"Leader: 'I'd like to learn some of them.'

"Chorus of 'Me, too! Me, too!'

"Leader: 'We might see how many we can find. It's one of our real American folk songs, you know!'

" 'Yes, let's!'

"So we planned to try the 'Virginia Reel' at our next meeting. It was fun, if exhausting. (Did you ever try singing your own music for very active dancing for quite a while?) Elaine and Barbara came over to my house the following Saturday morning to give me further instructions, because the whole troop wants to learn how to 'do it right away.' We are collecting verses to 'Turkey in the Straw,' and are now planning to learn other American square dances and folk dances."

STIMULATING INTERESTS

"One of my girls said when she heard opera on the air she changed the dials."

"They passed up pottery on an interest check list just as if it had

The Leader Tries Different Methods

when stimulating girls' interests with new ideas

not been listed. We have a fine pottery works about two miles from here, and I had hoped they would want to do this."

"My girls seemed perfectly oblivious to wild plants and flowers. They don't even know poison ivy when they see it—a rather important thing, since the woods around here abound in the treacherous stuff."

"Unfortunately, my girls do not want to sketch, and we have a well known artist who is willing to help us."

"I don't know why my girls stick together so closely. We went to . . . . to a rally, and my girls would not enter the games and do what the other Scouts were doing. I wonder if there is something wrong with me."

The foregoing are typical responses a leader may get when she tries to introduce new ideas and experiences to her girls. The responses are not very different from those your grown-up friends make when they are introduced to a new idea or new situation, are they? But, just because girls say, "We don't want to!" or, "We don't like that!" or a leader gets a blank stare or an empty response to her efforts, it does not mean that she should not keep right on trying to widen her girls' horizons as much as she can. It is important not to let girls refuse a new idea or new experience too soon or too finally before learning more about it, seeing it work, or trying it out.

This attitude of open-mindedness and the fun and adventure that go with doing new things, seeing new places, meeting Girl Scouts in other troops, needs to be encouraged. We need not value a stray "I don't want to" so much that a child misses the chance to do bookbinding with a fine craftsman or sketching with a well known artist. We can work toward this open-mindedness more directly than we do. For instance, when using an interest check list, just say, "Girls, if you find an activity you feel you do not know much about, or one that seems vague, just write 'not sure' or 'don't know' by it and we will discuss it. That might turn out to be the most fun of all! Besides, it is much smarter to find out about a new idea before saying yes or no too quickly." Or, again, just ask them why they object. A leader may get just the clues she needs to launch this same activity later.

[225]

A Few Ways You Might Stimulate New Interests

During a new experience, we think, we feel, we have impulses, we move. One of these may be dominant, but the others are present also. It is for this reason a leader tries to reach a girl through any or all of her senses. She wants to get not only the idea over, but action, feeling, and emotion mixed with it. That is why trips, exhibits, radio, movies, are playing such an important role now in education. They are called visual and auditory aids in education. Nevertheless, it may be a jolt for some of us to change our "habit patterns" and seriously use the radio, movies, and trips as educational aids in our program activities. But they are effective. .

The following ways of stimulating new interests are included here:

Using outside people for discussions, demonstrations, or teaching an activity or course.

Seeing good movies, both educational and commercial.

Listening to selected radio programs.

Bringing in new material or exhibits, such as a bug, a flower, hiking equipment, a pet, a new dress, a book, or current newspaper or magazine articles.

Taking trips.

USING OUTSIDE PEOPLE FOR DISCUSSIONS, DEMONSTRATIONS, OR TEACHING AN ACTIVITY OR COURSE

A troop's program is so varied during the course of a year that it is almost necessary, as well as more interesting, to use the talents, hobbies, and abilities of the various people in your community. No one leader or person can possibly have all the various abilities needed, nor is it expected. Girls need to see many people of fine personality and accomplishment, to talk to them, to know them at their life's work. They should have an idea of what nurses, doctors, craftsmen, bakers, gardeners, singers can do. They need to enter into these same activities and develop similar ones themselves. (See the section on "Program Consultants" in the chapter, "Working with Your Community.")

Planning with Girls

The first few times a new leader uses an outsider it is best to plan with the girls and make careful arrangements. When the outsider must play the double role of guest and temporary leader, and girls must play the role of both hostess and gracious student, it takes more thought and preparation on the part of all than may be imagined. It is not a time when the leader takes a rest, but a time when she is particularly active and alert. The following suggestions may help you and the girls plan:

Shall we ask Mr. —— to help?

What information do we expect from him?

What use can we make of such information?

How soon do we need it?

What are our obligations when asking for help?

If Mr. —— comes, shall we list the questions we are concerned about and take them to him beforehand?

How many will he want to meet with at a time?

What days can he come, and how can we fit our time with his most easily?

What are some of the things we should remember not to do that would make him dislike helping us again? Being late? Not paying attention? Not taking part in either discussion or activity?

Planning with Outside People

The leader and girls should help an outsider see exactly how his time and talents are going to be used. A few suggestions follow.

Tell him:

How the troop became interested in his coming, and out of what in the girls' experience did the idea or plan arise.

What the girls have done up until now in this field of interest or badge, if anything.

What the girls hope to learn from him.

Time needed to carry out the activity.

Number of girls taking part. (Watch this carefully. Some people cannot manage a group of twenty-four girls but can work

[227]

successfully with six or eight, especially where girls come to
their homes.)

Ways to present activities to girls.

Equipment needed and who will be responsible for it.

Best place to have this meeting. (Often such a person prefers
meeting where he can use his equipment or exhibits.)

The only warning is not to let the person lecture to the girls more
than ten to fifteen minutes, unless he can hold them spellbound. The
girls get restless, inattentive; and a few of them, if not almost all of
them, may act rude according to adult standards—but perfectly normal by child standards.

Leader's Record: Use of Outside People

"The girls in our troop have been interested in camping, hiking,
and singing games, but have been indifferent to practically everything else. I did not like the narrow range of interests and thought,
surely, there must be a way out of this.

"Not long ago, a member of the Hobby Club asked me if there
was any way their members could help. They had four or five members who had collections of antique glass and would be glad to have
the girls come to see them. I did not bring this project up in troop
meeting, but asked one of the ladies who had a nice collection to
send the troop a written invitation; then she suggested making it
a tea.

"You should have seen their faces when the secretary read the
invitation for the troop to come to tea. They were thrilled and said,
'Of course, we have to accept the invitation.' I said, 'But you don't
know a thing about glass!' And I was informed, 'Well, we had better
study a little. Let's have a loose-leaf notebook, and anything we find
on antique glass will go in it.' So we were off! They read about glass,
wrote papers on it and put them in the book, which is now labeled
'Ye Notebook of Arts and Crafts.'

"By the time the five women had invited the girls to see their
collections, the girls were very glass conscious. Then they decided to
design and make a glass bracelet for each hostess, so we made bead

[228]

looms from cigar boxes and have finished the bracelets. They also sent for the article 'Glass Blowing for Beginners' in *The American Girl*. Glass bricks are being used in two new buildings downtown, so we went down to see them, and then went to the lumber yard to find out more about glass bricks.

"Soon the Glass badge will have been earned by twelve girls who were not interested in anything but camping and hiking!

"Oh, yes, the main thing—they have searched in their own cupboards and grandmother's, too, and have found two or three pieces of antique glassware, and were so surprised because, as they said, 'clear on the highest shelf—covered with dust, we found what people are buying in antique shops.'"

Seeing Good Movies, Both Educational and Commercial

One day we will find sound movies to be the greatest instrument for educating people that has been evolved since the invention of movable type. Nothing else has, so far, reproduced life settings so completely as the sound movie. When libraries of sound films are the order of the day, the efficiency of learning will probably be doubled. Educators have already found that certain subjects usually taught only in high school can be taught to fifth and sixth graders with use of movies.

Sources of Educational Movies

Upon investigation, leaders most frequently secure educational movies on safety from state highway police; movies on conservation, fire prevention, and park recreational facilities from the Forestry Service; movies on health from various county or state health agencies; movies on gardening, child care, homemaking from agricultural and home demonstration agents; and occasionally movies of sports or trips from amateur photographers in the community. There are free films, and films that can be rented for negligible costs. When troops have taken advantage of available educational movies, both leaders and girls have been most pleased with the results. They almost always invite the Boy Scouts, little brothers and sisters, parents, and teachers, and thereby arrange a fine evening of educational entertainment for their neighborhood.

[229]

Leader's Record: Use of Educational Movie

"Our troop was working on the Tree badge. One activity was to get someone interested in trees to talk to the group. Another activity was to invite someone to talk on conservation and tell us what the United States Government and Maryland are doing for tree conservation. I talked these matters over with the girls to see if they knew where to go for help. Most of them were too young to know; others recalled I had suggested calling the Anne Arundel County Agricultural Agent. I did this. I told him what we were studying, what we had been doing, what we had accomplished, and then read to him the activity we wished him to help us with. He was much pleased with our approach to the subject, and said he would get us a 'real tree talker' who would bring slides to illustrate his talk.

"Our county agent sent us a representative from the Forestry Department, University of Maryland. He brought slides showing how to tell the different trees in our state and gave us a great amount of information. The girls invited their parents, the school teachers, and school children, and I called by telephone a number of people interested in trees. They came, and we had a very delightful and successful meeting. The girls were delighted with the whole outcome. They had also invited other Girl Scouts and Boy Scouts, and quite a few came.

"When the activity concerning conservation came up, I got in touch with the President of our County Conservation Association. He immediately talked to our Assistant State Forester, who came with slides, and again we had a big, big meeting which was open to all and to which the Boy Scouts and all Girl Scouts were invited. This was one of the most enjoyable meetings I have ever attended. The speaker was a tree lover, a former Boy Scout, father of a Boy Scout and a Girl Scout, and a man full of wit."

Selecting Good Commercial Movies

Commercial films, or the movies, have a tremendous influence upon setting American standards in many ways. This is especially true where concerts, stage shows, amateur music, and dramatics clubs are few or non-existent. We have not used our imaginations nearly

[230]

enough in helping girls select good movies and enjoy the ones they do see more.

A troop might spend a few meetings on movie appreciation, and by use of critical judgment increase enjoyment of photography, the story, the setting, the dialogue, the music and sound effects, the acting, the direction, the accuracy, and appropriateness of the story.

Some of the following questions will help your girls judge the good and poor parts of a movie. There are other questions you will want to add, but these might start you off:

Is the movie like the book or play? If not, what are the changes?

Shall we read the book and find out if we are familiar with the story? Shall we read it before we see the movie, or after?

Does the actor fit his part, or is he miscast? In facial appearance, build, height, weight, voice, age, disposition, does he meet requirements? If special talents are needed for enacting the role, such as dancing, singing, riding, swimming, oratory, is he equipped with these abilities?

Does the player appear natural in his make-up and his costume, or is he ill at ease? Were the costumes correct for the time and place?

If the player has assumed a foreign accent, or a necessary mannerism of speech, does he seem to be "to the manner born," or are we conscious that the speech is assumed?

Does the player convince us that he has submerged his personality and is the character in the play? Are we conscious of the character or the actor only?

Does the movie make us laugh or weep? Does it excite us, thrill us, inspire us? Does it grip us, or deeply move us?

Does the player photograph well from many angles? Is his face expressive? Can he express with his eyes subtle shades of meaning?

Is the right tempo created for each scene? Do the fast motion and the slow motion effects keep in time with the music and action of characters in the play?

Is any of the music played familiar to you? Is it all jazz, or popular, or is there some classical music accompanying action in the picture?

Do you think the parts hang together?

GROUP LISTENING TO SELECTED RADIO AND TELEVISION PROGRAMS

A Rich Source of New Ideas and Program Material

Programs of music, dramatics, games, and foreign broadcasts are a certain and constant source of program material for a troop. A leader may not have a movie or a library in her town or be anywhere near an art gallery, concert hall, or the legitimate theatre, but she can find a radio or television set in the neighborhood.

In addition to supplying useful information on all phases of the Girl Scout program, radio itself has become so important that a special Radio badge has been developed in the Community Life field. Furthermore, radio is an excellent medium of Girl Scout public relations. No one dealing with youth can afford to dismiss or ignore it or discount its influence as a propaganda medium. In less than two decades, radio, which started as a leisure plaything, has become an educational medium for both children and adults. Many universities, such as Harvard, Ohio, and Wisconsin, have their own educational broadcasting stations and have added courses in radio and television to their curriculum. Even Girl Scout leaders have been given training courses by radio.

Two Leaders' Records: Group Listening to Radio Programs

One leader describes her first attempt in using radio in her troop program. Perhaps this will encourage you to give it a trial.

"At one o'clock Sunday the girls began arriving at my home to listen to 'March of Games.' Seventeen of the twenty girls came. We thought it would be fun to play the games along with those on the radio. So we started in. It proved to be even more fun than the girls had thought it would be. They tried hard to get their answers in ahead of the contestant on the radio and were quite successful. After the program on the radio was over, they stayed until four o'clock playing the same games, and now we very seldom have a meeting that one or more of these games are not played. They all listen at home every Sunday, and if a new game is played we play it at troop meeting."

[232]

Another leader tells about her troop's interest in gardening and how much help she and her girls get from radio on this.

"Most of the girls in our troop listen to 'National Farm and Home Hour' on Saturday. This program comes just before our Scout meeting. Nearly all our families have vegetable gardens, and our troop has a good flower garden at the Scout cabin. We get lots of good ideas about the preparation of soil, choice of seeds, spraying against bugs and blight, flower arrangement, and even canning and preserving. 'National Farm and Home Hour' programs help us remember a lot of our gardening ahead of time, since many of the programs are timely and come just before the proper season."

Group-Listening
One of the richest sources of new ideas and program material
comes to the leader and her girls by radio. Gardening, music,
dramatics, and great events in near and faraway lands are but a
few of the daily programs a leader might use to widen her girls'
horizons and stimulate an interest in new activities.

BRINGING IN NEW MATERIAL OR EXHIBITS, SUCH AS AN INSECT,
A FLOWER, HIKING EQUIPMENT, A PET, A NEW DRESS,
BOOKS, NEWSPAPER OR MAGAZINE ARTICLES

Focusing Girls' Attention on New Ideas

Girls as well as leaders could acquire the habit of bringing new materials to troop meetings. To see a thing first-hand is important for young girls, because so often they are seeing it for the first time. This is hard for most adults to remember. Girls have not had as many years to get about in the world and see things as their older leader. And they are so responsive and full of questions about the new things they do see!

There are many ways of focusing girls' attention and stirring their imagination about new things. Placing a craft, a puppet, or an attractive flower arrangement in a conspicuous place will bring such questions as: Who made it? How does it work? Can we do this, too? Again, the leader might be sewing on a costume or a garment for the Red Cross as girls arrive at troop meeting. Bulletin boards can be used to post new recipes for outdoor cooking—or news of Girl Scouts and Guides in faraway places. The leader might ask Sally to bring her stamp collection or a new birdhouse for others to see.

Once interest is aroused, the leader must be ready to follow through with action. The interest span of ten- to fourteen-year-old girls is much shorter than an adult's. If they are offered an attractive dessert to look at and smell, but are not allowed to taste it, they may not be so eager for it later.

Leader's Record: Arousing Girls' Interest Through an Exhibit

This leader did not deliberately wear her new dress and hat to troop meeting to start girls on a clothes-making project, but she could have. She writes:

"I had planned to play bridge after the meeting, so had dressed in my best bib and tucker before I left home. As soon as I took my coat off, some of the girls commented on my pretty dress. I thanked them and went on with the meeting. After our business was over, they

[234]

asked me to stand up and turn around. I did so, and when I told them I had made the dress and trimmed the hat to match, they at first refused to believe me. I let them examine both carefully, and the result was a general discussion on clothes planning. Most of the girls are very clothes conscious, and the possibility of being able to make something that would fit them and make them look smart as well pleased them.

"I told them how I plan and budget my wardrobe, and how, even though they may not be able to make all of their clothes, they could plan carefully before buying, so that their accessories, shoes, and hats blend with their coats and dresses. We also got onto the subject of dressing appropriately. They were quite eager for advice, and when we began suggesting the colors that seemed to compliment each girl, they were keenly interested. At each meeting since, someone has asked for advice on a clothes problem, and many of the girls are planning to make clothes—with me as their style consultant."

Girls might be encouraged and expected to help find ideas and plans. Even if only ten of the girls save clippings from newspapers or magazines about Girl Scout activities in other troops or towns, such as hikes, games, or crafts, it would add to the troop's source material and ideas. Some troops have folders for these clippings.

This leader tells how several of her girls initiated a brand new interest in their troop after seeing a newspaper clipping.

"A brand new interest for the girls is attending the joint Girl Scout and Camp Fire Girl program in a nearby city. Several thousand girls are taking part, it seems.

"Several girls came to me after school, very excited, with a clipping in regard to this program. They said, 'Why can't we go?' I told them I thought it a very good plan if we could get cars and permission from parents. The clipping included a picture of two of the girls of the organization with their addresses. The girls decided they would write these girls for more particulars. They are watching the post office for a reply to their letter. We hope their plans to attend may be carried out."

[235]

TAKING TRIPS

The idea of taking educational trips is based upon the old idea that seeing is believing, and the new method of educating a child through any one or all of his senses. Taking trips is not a frivolous idea or a lowering of standards or just going somewhere, but an effort to root the girls' learning in the realities of life.

The difference between "just going somewhere" and a fine new experience for girls depends a great deal upon how well the leader and girls have planned for their trip together.

Planning for a Trip

In preparing for a trip, leader and girls might consider the following:

List names of girls who are to go to each place

Make arrangements with manager or operator about convenient time and number of guests to expect.

Learn something about thing to be visited so girls will know what to look for. This is a very important step, since it adds to their reason for and interest in going.

List questions girls want answered

Send to the place to be visited a copy of questions, badges, or rank requirements related to visit. Say the purpose of the trip is to stimulate a new interest, add to an activity, or whatever.

Discuss suitable conduct with girls, such as staying together as a group, suitable clothes for occasion, taking part in discussion or asking questions to prove your interest, inconspicuous behavior in public.

Leader's Record: A Trip

A leader describes the trip her troop made to the First Settler's Cabin when they were working on My Community badge.

"At one of our meetings a committee member dropped in to visit the troop, and she mentioned the interesting time that she had had at Portage, where the first cabin was built in this state. The girls asked if it would not be possible to visit it themselves, and were so enthusiastic that I said I would find out. I find that girls are really very interested in pioneer history, which surprises me. They get so much enjoyment out of seeing the crude makeshifts that accompanied living long ago. This is an outline of our plan.

Program Plan	How to Carry Out Purpose of This Meeting	Who Will Be Responsible and Take Charge of This Activity?
Visit the cabin at Portage.	Trip.	Scout leader, assistant leader, committee members, and several parents.
	Look up settling of Wisconsin in library books.	Two Scouts to obtain reference books from library. Each girl responsible for bringing her own lunch.

Number Taking Part	Equipment Needed	Who Will Be Responsible for This Equipment?
Fourteen Scouts, leaders, and helpers.	Lunches; permission to examine cabin and relics.	Each girl for her own lunch. Leaders for permission to visit cabin.

"We met, as designated, at the Scout meeting place, and every girl was on time, with her lunch packed and ready to go. I had explained to them that promptness was essential, and that keeping a driver waiting when she had been kind enough to donate her car and time was just not done. We went to Portage and ate lunch in a park near the cabin before visiting it. As soon as the lunch was over and the containers burned, we began our trip through the little hut with the attendant explaining the various parts of the exhibit.

"Afterwards, we discussed it at a Scout meeting, and they all agreed that they had had a wonderful time. And now that I have seen how easily everything went, I think they can hike together more often.

"The girls enjoyed the whole project very much. One or two rather hung back when it came to cleaning up after lunch, but at a word from me they did their share. Two of the girls seemed rather bored

[237]

with the attendant's little talk, and began whispering to each other, but a look freighted with disapproval from me subdued them."

As you look back over this chapter, with its variety of methods for finding and stimulating interests, you may wonder how you can ever use them all. You may not, but it is important to be familiar with all of them and know when and when not to use each one. Each method has its advantages and limitations. These will help you find out what activities your girls are already interested in, and add new ideas and new experiences to the ones they already have.

Chapter Eight

Leader-Girl Program Planning

YES, we know you can plan a program, but we want you to teach the girls how to do so. This will be much easier than you think once you see what the leader does in relation to what girls can do as they pass through different stages of development.

The material develops two main ideas and illustrates their practical application in troop meetings:

1. *Teaching girls to make long-term plans at three different levels of ability.*
2. *Teaching girls to plan meetings in detail and how the leader judges their ability and progress.*

G IRL SCOUTS PLAN their own programs," we say with great pride and conviction. This statement has been misleading for many new leaders. Perhaps we should say, "Leaders teach Girl Scouts to plan their own programs," or, "Leaders and girls plan their programs together." This idea and method of program planning stems from a belief in educating young Americans to think and act as democratic members of a group. Girl Scout leaders, teachers, parents—many adults who work directly with American youth—believe firmly enough in the democratic way of planning, but they do not always translate this democratic way of planning to the ten-, twelve-, and fourteen-year-old level.

There is the tendency on the part of all adults, not just Girl Scout leaders, to postpone this teaching. Girl Scout leaders are quick to say, "My troop is new; my girls are so young; next year . . . ," or, "They are such little girls in that patrol; the older girls know how to telephone, but they . . . ," or, "When I asked them what they wanted in their troop meeting programs, they said, 'Oh, you decide for us!' " or, "They just looked blank when I asked the patrol leader to write out their patrol meeting plan." Leaders do get such responses from girls, especially in new troops and even in some troops of several years' standing. But, the whole point is to teach young Americans not to look blank or say, "You decide for us," when they are asked to do something or to think for themselves. "While they are so young," it may seem easier to decide for your Girl Scouts, but, in the long run, it will be very hard for them if they are to live in America. It may be easy or quick to tell one hundred fifty million Americans what to do, but, so far, Americans have had a way of taking destiny into their own hands. The nation does not always do what one person says: the people decide, vote, and act in the way that seems right for the greatest number. There is every indication that our young boys and girls will need every bit of ability to think and act as responsible members of a group that we can develop in them, and a Girl Scout troop is an excellent place for young girls to practice and learn this.

When teaching girls to plan and manage their troop programs, we must show them how to:

1. "Block out" long-term plans; and
2. Plan in detail the next one or two meetings; but always according to their age and ability.

Girls are not too young to start learning how to take the longer range view, be on the program-planning committee, or plan the details for new games equipment or a Saturday morning breakfast hike. This does not mean that we expect ten- to fourteen-year-olds to "decide everything for themselves." There are decisions adults must make; but most decisions centering around troop programs girls can make or should be taught to make. We are a youth organization, but we are not a young organization without adult leadership. The following leader's comments about health and safety, respect for parents' wishes, religious tolerance, community customs, and Girl Scout membership policies are typical decisions adults make, while, at the same time, they show girls how these larger ideas affect their troop programs.

"In our troop, my assistant and I postpone patrol ideas that are not suitable for several general reasons. For instance, several mothers absolutely refuse to let their girls go camping, or sleep on the ground overnight any months except June, July, and August. Again, we do not plan activities during examination week at school that would displease parents and teachers. Then, there are religious considerations. Our girls are Methodists, Baptists, Presbyterians, Catholics, and Universalists. We have all five churches in town, and all the girls belong to one or the other. If someone thoughtlessly suggests a party during Holy Week, for instance, you can see why it is advisable to set a later date, can't you? We have got to the courtesy stage on Friday night parties, thank goodness! The refreshment committees now plan to have cheese, tuna fish, or egg mixture sandwiches as well as meat-filled ones. As a result we are now interesting girls from the Catholic church.

"Then, if the suggestion is not in keeping with community standards and would be detrimental to the welfare of our girls, or would lower our troop character in the eyes of our community, we try to show the girls why we cannot carry it out. In a small town there are some things considered not just right that would be perfectly all right in a city. For instance, in a neighboring city troops can sponsor card parties if they wish, with parents and friends attending. Well, it just wouldn't 'go over' here.

TEACHING GIRLS TO MAKE LONG-TERM PLANS

Experienced leaders can look back and realize that their troops have grown through different phases of program planning. For the sake of pointing up these different stages of growth, we will describe and illustrate three, although there are few clear-cut lines in child development. Children change and develop so gradually and so unevenly they defy most attempts to measure them exactly; but the general direction is clear.

Early Stages of Program Planning: Almost Complete Dependence Upon Adult Leader for Suggestion, Stimulation, and Direction

WHAT TO EXPECT OF GIRLS AT THIS STAGE

In this stage Girl Scouting is new; program planning is a novelty. It may be the first time a grown-up has expected the girls to suggest ideas, plan a meeting, preside over a patrol meeting, or find a new game to play at the next meeting. Most of them expect adult control because they are used to it at home, school, and church.

One leader said, "I found that my girls belong to clubs in schools in which they are styled leaders, but where, in actual practice, their duties are perfunctory. This idea carried over to the troop, and it was only after repeated efforts, discussions, suggestions, that they actually realized that the responsibility for running the meetings, planning

[243]

the work beforehand, and getting cooperation from all the members was really dependent upon them."

Another leader points out the necessity for helping the youngest girls make practical suggestions. Only by being given the opportunity to make suggestions and plans can they learn how.

"We have four ten year olds, four eleven year olds, six twelve year olds, and five 'just turned' thirteen. The thirteen year olds are very good at planning, and the older twelve year olds are good, too. The ten year olds either say very little or offer rather fantastic suggestions! With a little suggestion from the leader, the ten year olds usually qualify their ideas so that they are workable. For instance, the troop was holding a Court of Honor to make plans for a bicycle hike. One enthusiastic ten year old said when distance was mentioned, 'Oh, let's go to the farm!'—a distance of seven long miles one way. We talked of the number who had never ridden more than a few blocks on a borrowed bike and had not yet trained their 'bicycle legs,' and she readily amended her suggestion to a two-mile destination."

If girls are not ready to take as much responsibility as the girls or leader, or both, thought they could, they usually hesitate about starting; do not make a plan that suits them or one that works; do not work together as a group; or choose a mediocre activity and present it without much imagination or idea. When any one of these signs appears, the leader must step in quickly and teach the girls how to proceed. It is very important that these first troop-planning responsibilities result in successful group action, and most, if not all, members of the group should feel a pride and success in their work.

LEADER'S RECORD: EARLY STAGES OF PROGRAM PLANNING

"Since this is a new troop of Girl Scouts, none of whom has had any experience in such a group, their ideas of what can be included in the Girl Scout program have been decidedly limited. So far, suggestions for activities have come more or less from me. By now, however, the girls are beginning to realize the number of things that

Girl Scouts can do, and are beginning to make useful and original contributions.

"Some of the troop objectives that were outlined in a recent Court of Honor were:

> To do community service and make the public more conscious of our willingness, as Girl Scouts, to help.
>
> To have the troop take part in at least four Second Class activities.
>
> To learn more of the out-of-doors, perhaps do the Foot Traveler badge later.
>
> To earn money for the immediate purpose of purchasing troop equipment, and for other purposes as occasion arises.
>
> To introduce two dramatics and crafts activities—puppetry and shadowgraphs suggested.
>
> To have one or two parties centering about the spring holidays.

"We started our Court of Honor by discussing what we considered our weaknesses in our own troop and what we could do about them. Included was a discussion of our place in the community and plans for making the public more conscious of us as Girl Scouts and our desire to give service.

"We then talked over the activities we did in the troop that we liked particularly well and wanted to do again. Among things mentioned by the girls were dramatizations, Juliette Low stories, singing games, hikes. We enjoyed the community service that we did with the Red Cross and wished to do more of the same thing.

"Then followed suggestions for new activities, with a request for puppetry and more shadowgraphs, which we have done just once or twice. With the approach of spring, we also anticipate more hikes and some outdoor cookery.

"We then considered what holidays we wished to observe. Here we mentioned Easter, Arbor Day, and Mother's Day—for which we considered a mother-daughter banquet.

"All these things settled, and our objectives for the next few months determined, we listed definite things we wished to do, set tentative or actual dates, and adjourned for a bit of fun."

[245]

The Leader Scales Down a Too Big Plan

NEW GIRL SCOUT: Let's go camp on the mountain for a week! My brother is packing right now to go today!

LEADER: Let's talk it over and see what we can do.

LEADER: You girls certainly are learning to be good outdoor cooks and hikers. Next summer, our troop will be able to go camping in the mountains.

Second Stage of Program Planning: Alternate Withdrawal and Support on Part of Leader as Girls Take Initiative and Responsibility

WHAT TO EXPECT OF GIRLS AT THIS STAGE

Whenever she possibly can, the leader will try to keep "hands off" and give the girls a chance to do their own planning; but their progress is not steady. It has a zig-zag line of direction. For instance, the leader starts the girls off; withdraws her support, allowing girls to go as far as they can alone; again gives them help just as soon as they can go no further, only to retreat again as soon as they are under way. This shift of method in leading a group is needed all the more if girls reach this stage of group organization and planning when they are about thirteen, a time when they act the part of a little girl one minute and are surprisingly grown-up the next.

LEADER'S RECORD: SECOND STAGE OF GIRLS' DEVELOPMENT IN PROGRAM PLANNING

The following illustration shows a long-term plan and reports on the way the first two meetings worked out in actual practice. This shows how much planning girls can do if given a chance. Also, notice how many small changes are being made along the way as they achieve their goals.

First Weekly Court of Honor Meeting

"The patrol leaders met with me on Friday afternoon to plan for the next meeting. There were so many things that needed to be done, the girls decided to make a long-term plan for the next four meetings. They divided a sheet of paper into fourths—four meetings on the sheet. Activities were jotted down in order of their importance. Room was left in each block for changes or left-over ideas. The girls could see plans ahead for the first and second meetings better than the third and fourth. This seemed to be all they could manage at the moment. The patrol leaders blocked out the following month's plan.

[247]

Score Yourself

on leader-girl program planning in several activities, such as first aid, cooking, hiking. Try to stay in Group 1 as consistently as possible.

	SAMPLE ACTIVITIES		
	First Aid	Cooking	Hike
GROUP 1 Helped girls decide by group discussion: a. What to do. and b. How to do it.	✓		
GROUP 2 Told girls: a. What to do. but b. Helped them to decide how to do it or vice versa.		✓	✓
GROUP 3 Told girls: a. What to do. and b. How to do it.			

Outline of Month's Plan

First Meeting

1. Count and store troop's canned food.

2. Put seeds in mouse-tight containers.

3. Determine what are excused absences.

4. Number of unexcused absences a girl can have.

5. Practice Christmas carols.

6. Troop transportation for next meeting.

7. Check attendance, collect dues, have good-bye wish.

Left-over ideas or changes:

. . . .

Second Meeting

1. List girls who are interested in becoming Girl Scouts.

2. Decide on color of neckerchiefs.

3. Plan for Juliette Low Fund.

4. Discuss what to do with our new *Girl Scout Handbooks*.

5. Practice Christmas carols.

6. Send cards to sick members.

Left-over ideas or changes:

. . . .
. . . .
. . . .
. . . .

Third Meeting

1. Penalty for unexcused absences.

2. Practice Christmas carols.

Left-over ideas or changes:

. . . .
. . . .
. . . .

Fourth Meeting

1. Practice Christmas carols.

2. List places to go caroling.

Left-over ideas or changes:

. . . .
. . . .
. . . .

"We tried to gauge the time needed for each part of the first meeting. Each patrol leader was responsible for asking members of patrol to bring a baking powder can or mayonnaise jar for storing seeds. We planned to sing one or two carols at each meeting so we would not have to do too much practicing at any one meeting.

"The troop scribe was to take charge of the next meeting and start promptly at 2:30 P.M. The troop committee was invited to attend the meeting and take part in the discussion.

[249]

"Checking attendance, collecting dues, and the good-bye wish were to be part of every meeting.

How Girls' First Troop Meeting Plan Worked Out

"The patrol leaders began by collecting dues and checking attendance. Then we sang carols. The discussion of troop transportation was then held, as the troop committee member who had offered the use of her car had to leave early. As the girls discussed the transportation of Scouts from each district, the new girls were mentioned. (This had been planned for the second meeting.) They decided that the old Scouts and new Scouts could gather at one place in each district to eliminate all but one stop for each car.

"The discussion of excused and unexcused absences was lengthy. The excused absences were practically the same as those the patrol leaders had discussed—death in the family, bad or stormy weather, lack of transportation, taking care of children for parents. The unexcused absences proved to be a problem. They tentatively decided upon one unexcused absence a month. The penalty for more than one was debated, but no satisfactory solution was reached. There was unwillingness on the part of several girls to set themselves a hard and fast rule for attendance. I helped discuss the reasons for having rules about absences. I explained that often the very thing we object to, and are often guilty of, is the one we can do something about if we try to correct it.

"The patrol leaders seem to be very wide awake and aware of their responsibility. They liked the group activity score cards. (See section "A Girl Scout Participates" in chapter "Developing Self-Government in a Troop.") They saw that several girls had valuable contributions to make but were too self-conscious to do so. They saw that there were two small groups who sat together and carried on a continuous conversation all during the meeting. They planned to study and help these two groups, and to make a special effort to help the shy girls feel at home. One of the girls plans to begin by asking one of the shy girls to accompany her home during the week. The patrol leaders confess that these girls have trouble making friends

[250]

quickly, and are timid about speaking up many times when they should. I feel fortunate in having them, though, because they show that with a little experience they will be a pride and joy to any leader.

"The troop enjoyed singing the carols. The girls have beautiful voices!

"The first and second activities were not carried out. The girls were quick to see that time was wasted and activities that go together should have been planned together.

"Observations made by the girls during the meeting were:

" 'We quibble too much over unimportant things.'

" 'Some of the girls didn't help with the discussion.'

" 'The girls didn't stick to the point.'

" 'Two of the girls giggled too much.'

" 'We planned too much for one meeting.'

" 'We could have finished everything if everybody had helped.'

Second Weekly Court of Honor Meeting

"The three patrol leaders, scribe, and treasurer carried on what I considered the best bit of thinking through of a program plan that I have ever seen. We discussed the chart 'Thinking a Program Plan Through' again in the light of happenings at the last troop meeting. They felt that our meetings were not organized, too much like school, and that there was no representation from the ten- and eleven-year-old group in the Court of Honor. One girl said that she believed the reason for these young girls' giggling and being uncooperative was because they did not feel any responsibility. She suggested the patrols be reorganized into three age groups—ten and eleven, twelve and thirteen, and fourteen. The other girls liked the idea immediately. Another girl said the younger age girl should have an opportunity to become a patrol leader and share other responsibilities. Another girl suggested a leader and assistant leader for each patrol.

"The girls spent a great deal of time discussing Sally. They felt the reason she did not come often was that she felt too out of place. 'Girls don't talk to her and make her feel welcome,' 'She probably feels self-conscious of her clothes—and because she is so poor.'

"The next troop meeting was outlined as follows:

[251]

Score Your Girls' Responses

to group planning in several activities, such as hiking, community service, giving a play. What percentage of your girls falls into the three groups below? Work toward getting as high a percentage as possible into Group 1. Rescore their responses from time to time.

		SAMPLE ACTIVITIES	
	Hike	Community Service	Play
GROUP 1 Girls prefer opportunities to help decide and plan. They enjoy managing troop affairs with my help.	90%	25%	80%
GROUP 2 Girls expect me to make plans and to tell them exactly how to carry them out.	5%	60%	20%
GROUP 3 Girls expect me to make plans and also to carry them out.	5%	15%	

1. Unfinished business of troop (20 minutes):
   a. Collect money for Juliette Low Fund.
   b. Ask if orange crates for bookcases have been brought.
   c. Sing carols.
   d. Store seeds.
2. Girls meet in old patrols for discussion (15 minutes):
   a. Change into age groups.
   b. Collect dues and check attendance.
3. Girls meet in new patrols to elect new patrol leaders and assistants (15 minutes).
4. Play games (15 minutes).
5. Practice Christmas carols (15 minutes).
6. Wishing Circle and Good-bye (3 minutes).

How Girls' Second Troop Meeting Plan Worked Out

"The scribe again took charge of meeting. The troop committee and I tried to keep hands off and see how far they could go without our help.

"The girls became so interested in their patrol organization they ran overtime. It looks as though the seeds are not going to be stored, but there is still plenty of time, I feel, for that; but something needed to be done to improve the individual's and troop's sense of responsibility, and the time was at hand.

"The giggling and lack of cooperation on the part of four girls were conspicuous by their absence. When the girls got in their new patrols, the patrol leaders and assistants were elected. One patrol chose its emblems; two patrols discussed presenting a Christmas play; one discussed making a library corner as a Christmas present to the troop. I visited each patrol and helped only when asked. One patrol wanted to raise a puppy to be a sentry dog for the Coast Guard. The girls liked the suggestion to send a card from the troop to girls who are sick.

"When the meeting adjourned, their remarks were still more convincing. 'We had fun today!' 'I like this way of having a meeting.' I feel we have made a great step forward. Although the details in

[253]

their plans were not always followed, the general plans were clear to all, and the girls have shown pride and responsibility in planning. I now know that I should have let them start doing this sooner rather than doing so much for them."

Third Stage of Program Planning: Girls' Ability to Set a Goal, Plan, Carry Through, and Judge Results with Leader Acting as Consultant

WHAT TO EXPECT OF GIRLS AT THIS STAGE

This stage is the reward the leader reaps from the first two. But the leader is as much a part of the group as ever. Her job here is to help girls get what they need for the fullest realization of their desires. Out of her maturity and wisdom of experience, she points the way to more grown-up goals. A leader of such a group no longer needs to check on the contents of the pack basket on a hike, but she probably starts the girls talking about a new hobby, or tells them about a troop camp they might have if they work hard enough for it.

The following example shows how capable young shoulders may become. You can easily imagine how much work a leader of a new troop would have to do to carry through a similar swimming party.

"All of the girls in our troop are eighth graders. I have had this same troop since they came into Scouts three years ago, so have been able to see how they have changed and developed. They have grown from the point of complete dependence upon the leader for planning and suggesting to the point where they now do the planning and suggesting themselves, with the leader sitting in as consultant. For instance, June was our last meeting and the girls had been told they could plan to do anything they wanted to for this last meeting. They planned a swimming party. Two of the girls had made arrangements at the pool (four miles distant); two more had arranged transportation; and the patrol leaders had made sure that all of the girls in their patrols knew of the plans. They also planned that we would swim from four to five o'clock, bring nose-bag lunches and eat them in the park after the swim. All of the plans worked out beautifully, and we had a grand time."

There follows a record of long-term planning where the troop has two experienced leaders and an active troop committee, is well organized, and has been going for three years—although there are some younger Scouts in the group. They planned for different patrol interests as well as troop interests. The three patrols show three different levels in their ability to plan. Patrol 1 has ten and eleven year olds; Patrol 2, twelve and thirteen year olds; Patrol 3, the oldest and most experienced Scouts.

Short Court of Honor the First Week in March

Leader: "Will leader of Patrol 1 check carefully with her patrol at the next meeting to see how many Second Class activities they have not yet done? All patrol leaders are to get suggestions from patrols for troop plans in April, May, and the first two weeks in June. Ask your patrols to vote on their first, second, and third choices for spring activities."

Long Court of Honor at Assistant Leader's Home Two Weeks Later

"Tea and cookies" . . . "school" . . . "Easter vacation" . . . then patrol reports, as follows:

Leader of Patrol 1: "Everybody wanted to do Second Class nature, outdoor cooking, clay modeling.

"Two girls had to stay after school the day we learned the American folk dances.

"Three girls were sick the day we started nature.

"Everybody wanted to go out to Cooper's Creek and have a hike like the one last fall."

Leader of Patrol 2. "Everybody wanted to start the Hostess badge if our patrol could give an Easter egg party for the Brownie troop.

[255]

The Court of Honor

The leader shows girls how successful group planning becomes the first step toward successful group action in a self-governing troop.

"We would like to go exploring up Black Bear Ravine next—a patrol trip.

"Other good ideas were a troop hike, an overnight hike, a style show."

Leader of Patrol 3: "We volunteered to take charge of June Court of Awards and will offer several ideas at the next meeting. We also want ideas from the other patrols.

"We would like to study flower arrangements so we can take part in the flower show in July.

"Could we have a patrol supper hike and invite some boys to help cook?

"We liked the sub-deb article in *Ladies Home Journal*, and thought

'Party Lines and Party Conversation' might be a good one to do next."

Leader: "Troop Number One in Larchmont wants us to join them at the camp site the second Saturday in May for a campers' reunion."

Assistant Leader: "The Troop Committee Chairman has invited the troop to have the June Court of Awards on her back-yard lawn. She thought it would not be too crowded if the girls did not invite more than two guests each."

"After much discussion as to time, number of troop committee helpers, others who had helped troops before, high school operetta plus other May school plans, the Court of Honor listed these things to take back to patrols:

1. Nobody would think of missing campers' reunion.

2. They would accept the Troop Committee Chairman's invitation for June Court of Awards. Patrol 3 ought to take charge, since they asked first, but every patrol should have some part.

3. Patrol 1 should complete Second Class; Patrol 2 should get their Hostess badges; and Patrol 3 must get ready for the Flower Show.

4. The troop should have a hike in April. Patrol 1 should practice outdoor cooking in Mrs. Carter's back yard before going on troop hike. Patrol 2 would have to choose between an Easter egg hunt and patrol hike. Patrol 3 could arrange with assistant leader about patrol supper hike and inviting boys.

5. The other ideas were good and would be saved until later—perhaps an overnight hike in summer and a style show late in May by Patrol 2 if they finish the Hostess badge and party in record time.

"Then the patrol leaders immediately called the following people to help them: the leader of Patrol 1 called a Girl Scout mother who had helped the troop with the Clothing badge and got her consent to help them two afternoons with sewing for the Red Cross. Then she called Mrs. Carter, the outdoor person on the troop committee, about practicing outdoor cooking in her back yard. Mrs. Carter named the day that suited her best. The leader of Patrol 2 called Mrs. Johnson, who always helped the girls with Cook and Hostess badges. She said she could not get started until after Easter.

"The leader of Patrol 3 called Mrs. Burroughs about Garden

Flower project. She was delighted, wanted to know if they were starting this week. 'Any time, dear, just come over to my garden.'

"All the business being attended to, the patrol leaders thanked the assistant leader again for the tea and cookies and left."

TEACHING GIRLS TO PLAN THE NEXT MEETING IN DETAIL

There follow three records of leaders who taught their girls to plan the next meeting in detail. Each illustration has two parts:

1. What the leader and girls planned.
2. Leader's comments on girls' abilities to plan, carry out, and judge a program activity.

Note especially the chart "Thinking a Program Plan Through." Most leaders who used this planning chart said it was simple and workable enough for new ten-year-old Scouts to use successfully. Obvious advantages of writing out a program plan for a troop of twenty-four girls are these: *all* girls can see the work that goes into a well planned program and not expect leaders to do this for them; all girls can see for themselves what the general plan and its parts are without depending upon the leader to tell them; the written plan can be posted on troop bulletin board so girls can refer to it from time to time if they forget; individual girls who have special responsibilities can copy it without asking the leader to review it with them; looking forward to troop events, both large and small, is part of a troop's fun. Even with adult groups we usually find that program plans and schedules that affect a number of people must be written out so all can see what is going to happen and how and when each person takes part.

It is very hard to record in the printed word the complex human relationships that take place in good group planning and action, but, since we cannot take you to a troop meeting to see this firsthand, these records are good substitutes. Also, read the leaders' records at the end of the chapter "What Are Troop Meetings Like?" where girls are more dependent upon leader's help than is illustrated in the following three records.

[258]

LEADER'S RECORD A: TEACHING GIRLS TO PLAN A PROGRAM ACTIVITY IN DETAIL

THINKING A PROGRAM PLAN THROUGH

1. *Aim of Activity:* To do some kind of community service; to finish whatever we start.
2. *Program Activity and the way it is to be carried out:*

Program, or what we do in our meeting.	How can we best present these activities to carry out the aim?	Who will be responsible or take the lead or be "in charge"?	Approximate time needed to carry out the activity.	Number taking part.	Equipment needed	Who will be responsible for this equipment?
Sew for Red Cross	Send Representatives from the troop to find out what we can do, what we need to bring, whether we are to go to sewing room or bring the materials to our meeting place, or work in small groups in girls' homes.	Troop president asked, "Who would like to go to the Red Cross Sewing Room and find out these things for us? She got plenty of volunteers and finally decided to send the patrol leaders, one girl from each patrol.	The group decided to devote two whole meetings to it, and more if tasks were not finished. The committee visited the sewing room on Monday before our regular meeting on Wednesday. We will have to use three meetings.	The entire troop, leader, and assistant leader. (Three of the girls were ill and did not go the first time.)	The Supervisor of the Sewing Room said no equipment would be needed; however, the girls discovered a "shortage" in scissors, so they brought scissors the second time.	Patrol leaders got large boxes and the girls placed their unfinished garments in the boxes with their names written on paper and fastened with pins. Girls left the sewing room in perfect order.

3. *Judging Results:* Five girls chose to make skirts; four sorted buttons; three pulled threads for cutting diapers; seven cut bootees from outing material; three sewed diapers; six chose to piece and line a blanket. The machines were old and "strange" to the girls—they had a difficult time in learning to thread the machines; the girls refused to be discouraged, though, and finally learned to use the machines. Next time the Supervisor will not have to spend so much of her time with the group.

Young Citizens at Work

Since service is a basic part of every Girl Scout's code, it should be included in every troop's program. Since leaders and troop committee members usually take an active part in community affairs themselves, they can be alert to service jobs suitable to Girl Scout age and experience. Here the girls are sewing at the community Red Cross rooms. They feel far more grown-up when they wear Red Cross caps.

LEADER'S COMMENTS ON GIRLS' ABILITIES TO PLAN, CARRY OUT, AND JUDGE THIS PROGRAM ACTIVITY

Girls' Planning and Preparation for This Activity

"The girls understood what they were trying to do, but they were so eager to 'just go on to the sewing room and sew' that I had to step in and ask questions similar to these: Do you think we ought to go to the sewing room on Wednesday without finding out first if we are really needed there? Then, too, aren't the clubs in town going to the room on certain days; and we wouldn't want all of us to go on the same day, would we? The girls then decided that we should send a committee to investigate. A list of things for the committee to find out was then decided. The committee did not tell the sewing room supervisor how many girls there were in the troop; and this was a mistake, as we did not have as many pairs of scissors as we needed.

Girls' Performance of Activity

"The activity went off beautifully! The assistant leader and I spent almost all our time with the girls who were not skillful and talented in sewing and helped these girls find things to do, such as sorting buttons and cutting diapers. The troop enjoyed the activity so much that the Red Cross Supervisor had to make us stop sewing so she could close the room. Many of the girls are still enthusiastic about the activity and are going to the room for about an hour after school one or two days a week.

"I do feel the activity is a good choice, and the girls feel as though they even thought of having a Red Cross sewing room in our town.

Girls' Ability to Judge Their Planning and Performance Afterwards

"We are going to the sewing room once more to complete the garments we started. The girls are proud of the things they have already made and are eager to finish what they have started.

"The girls who are cutting the outing material decided they might be wasting some cloth, so they pooled their sewing knowledge and found ways to get more bootees from the outing. Two of the girls learned to operate the old machines with a great deal of skill, so they devoted almost all of their time helping with this.

"The three girls who were absent the first meeting were taken in on the blanket making."

LEADER'S RECORD B: TEACHING GIRLS TO PLAN A PROGRAM ACTIVITY IN DETAIL

"There were two successful patrol activities that I had no part in planning. One was a Christmas play (original with the girls) which the patrol put on for the troop's entertainment. It was well written, bringing in some Girl Scout activities (handcraft demonstration) and community services. It was well presented.

"The other patrol's activity was in handcraft, when the girls planned to carve wooden pins and continued this activity as a patrol project, obtaining material and equipment without leader's help.

"These two patrols carried on these two activities while I worked with two other patrols.

"My reaction to both these activities was surprise at abilities shown and used when girls are left to themselves. Although I have known many of these girls for years through acquaintance with their parents, I had not quite realized their own individual personalities until our Girl Scouting brought us more closely together in the last few months.

"I asked the patrol leader to fill out the chart 'Thinking a Program Plan Through.' As you can see, she answered the suggestions in her own way—which I thought well done for a seventh grade pupil of twelve years."

PATROL LEADER'S REPORT OF CRAFT ACTIVITY

"*Patrol Project:* To accomplish skill in using tools, as we are carving pins out of wood. By demonstration and actual work, I, as patrol leader, will take charge of the leadership of this activity. As it only takes a few minutes, we are able to make our pins and exhibit them. My patrol, number one, has seven Scouts, and each one paid five cents for equipment. We had to have cedar wood, knives, safety pins, shellac, and plastic wood.

"*Explanation:* The wood is what we carve. The safety pins are what we use to pin the pins on to our clothing. We shellacked the wood to make it look shiny. And the plastic wood is a sticky-like substance which we used to hold the safety pins on to the wood.

"*Result:* The results of our patrol project, as I face them, were fairly good for the first time. If we were to do that again, I think the carving would look quite neat beside the first ones we made. We worked at three meetings for about thirty minutes."

Girls' Planning and Preparation for These Activities

"My girls seem to live up to a responsibility and, from appearance, like being in charge—almost never fail if it is up to them. When they occasionally make mistakes, other girls generally point them out; and sometimes I feel they are too critical. Then I smooth things over and at the first opportunity give the fault-finders a chance to bear some responsibility. This just happens without apparent forethought; and only we adult leaders know how much is planned, how carefully we do our guiding, and how often we watch results and take our cues when we are busy doing something else across the room.

"Girls in Patrol 1, reporting their craft project, planned time for a special activities period covering three meetings (about thirty minutes each). It seemed well planned, with the patrol leader consulting her father on some matters, and, I think, through his obtaining some material and equipment. I also heard through her mother that the girl had experimented considerably at home, so she was well able to help her patrol members in the work.

Girls' Performance of Activity

"Handwork project went along nicely, and, as I watched the progress of the work, I realize that I could not have done better work for all my experience in handcraft.

"The Christmas play needed an extra costume that the girls could not get. This was the only time Patrol 2 asked for any help. I had repeatedly warned both patrols that, unless I was notified, I would take it for granted that they could look after their own equipment and activity.

Girls' Ability to Judge Their Planning and Performance

"Girls in Patrol 3 want to put on a playlet for a patriotic program in February, and look to experiences of Patrol 2. I have heard such remarks as, 'Don't make up a play with too much costuming'; 'Don't have too many properties for girls to bring'; 'use things easy to get.' The girls show through their experience they have learned much toward their next performance and are willing to share the knowledge with others.

"Patrol 2 put in a bid for being hostess at our Valentine party, so we realize these girls are willing to be in charge again, although in a different way from their last party.

"I think that only a very few of my ten- to twelve-year-old girls are afraid of responsibility. They know we are there to help them when they need us, even though many times their need is only a bit of encouragement or praise, or a friendly pat on a girl's shoulder as I say, 'That's fine. Go ahead!'"

LEADER'S RECORD C: TEACHING GIRLS TO PLAN A PROGRAM ACTIVITY IN DETAIL

"We have a new Girl Scout House, which is appreciated by many of the girls but taken for granted by too many. Inside, it is easy to keep attractive, and the girls do this well. But the lawn is something else again. It has been impossible to plant permanent grass, which is very expensive in these parts because seeding (except for Italian rye, which is temporary) is out of the question here. You get your lawn by planting grass plants.

"In the meantime, two things soon became apparent:

1. Great crops of weeds and ferns sprang up through the rye.
2. The lot is so large that the Girl Scout House looks a bit lonely and could stand more landscaping, although the few shrubs we have are satisfactory as far as they go.

"At troop meeting I mentioned these needs quite casually, not knowing whether they would strike a responsive note or not. There was silence for a minute. Then one girl said, 'There must be something we can do.' The leader of the troop said, 'Suppose we take a few minutes to discuss it. Would you like to?' One or two girls pouted, but a majority of the hands went up. Then the leader indicated that I, the assistant leader, was to steer the discussion, and the plan worked out as indicated on the opposite page:

[264]

1. *Aim of Activity:* We want to make the lawn look better for the sake of the Girl Scout House and to let the community know we are trying to be neat.

2. *Program Activity and the way it is to be carried out:*

Program, or what we do in our meeting.	How can we best present these activities to carry out the aim of this meeting?	Who will be responsible or take the lead or be "in charge"?	Approximate time needed to carry out the activity.	Number taking part.	Equipment needed.	Who will be responsible for this equipment?
Weeding lawn and making preparations for a garden.	First-hand observation. Discussion in troop meeting.	Special committee for outdoor work. Homemakers on luncheon.	Three to four hours, if all work (more, if fewer work). Saturday morning best opportunity.	11 girls 2 leaders 1 consultant	Trowels Clippers Rakes Baskets Sandwiches Makings for salad and cocoa Cookies	Each girl for implements and sandwiches. Homemakers for material for salad and cocoa—all contribute equally. Leaders for cookies as a treat.

3. *Judging Results by Girls:* (See page 266)

....

....

....

....

....

LEADER'S COMMENTS ON GIRLS' ABILITIES TO PLAN, CARRY OUT,
AND JUDGE A PROGRAM ACTIVITY

Girls' Planning and Preparation for This Activity

"The record 'Thinking the Program Plan Through' is the combined effort of one of the girls and myself. The aim is hers, but my aim was larger. It was not merely to make the lawn look better, but to develop pride in community property and to get across certain facts about grass, soil, and weeds.

"The girls had no difficulty about understanding the objectives. They liked the idea of a definite plan like 'Thinking a Program Plan Through.' Those who had any special responsibility entered into things wholeheartedly. Nothing was forgotten. One patrol leader, to whom most of the girls instinctively looked as the one in charge, not only worked harder than any of the others but thought of new steps to be taken later, some of which can be carried out.

Girls' Performance of Activity

"The activity went off successfully. Three girls failed to appear. Two of these were accounted for by illness. There were three types evident in the group: those who tired quickly, finding the sun too hot, or wondering whether there were red bugs, or feeling pangs of hunger early in the game; those who could work well only when there was a pleasurable atmosphere, in the company of a best friend or that of a leader, or when the weeds came up easily; those who worked for the satisfaction of accomplishment. In the main, however, all but one really enjoyed it. There was an enthusiastic vote that we take up the next crop of weeds also.

Girls' Ability to Judge Their Planning and Performance Afterwards

"The improved appearance of the lawn gave the girls much satisfaction. The fact that certain tools were unsuited to the work came out in checking up. The girls felt that a more efficient plan of digging weeds could be worked out next time to avoid the hottest time of day and enable the girls to get to the Saturday movie.

[266]

"The report of plans for a troop garden was disappointing. The difficulties involved in building up the poor soil, watching the garden daily, and producing vegetables in the short time left in the Florida spring season, took the edge off any enthusiasm. This part of the project will require more thorough study. Perhaps we shall find that our wisest plan is to begin building the soil now and leave the garden until fall, which is the time to plant a garden around here.

"The homemakers' part in the project was completely successful. Leaders as well as the girls were proud of the luncheon and the way it was cleared up without policing on the part of anyone."

Chapter Nine

Group Control, or Discipline

You MAY NOT TURN to this chapter until you have a "discipline problem." Perhaps you thought you would escape the unpleasantness of discipline, but it is needed in the best of families and troops. Every leader must exercise various degrees of group control. Over a period of time, this ranges all the way from positive suggestion and encouraging praise right through to an occasional and firm NO! The trick is in knowing your girls well enough to decide what kind and amount of group discipline the group needs at various times.

The material develops five main ideas and illustrates their practical application in troop meetings:

1. *What is group control?*
2. *What kind do you want and expect?*
3. *What type of leader are you?*
4. *Upon what does a leader's control depend?*
5. *What are frequent causes of a need for discipline?*

 "Don't Miss This"

W HAT IS GROUP CONTROL? group discipline? Is this control in a Girl Scout troop the same as in any other group? Every group has, and needs, some elements of control to get things done. Every group demands certain standards of behavior and performance from its members.

If you look in your dictionary you will find that the word *discipline* means *to teach, to instruct, to strengthen, to mold.* If a group is well disciplined in a certain way, it means it has learned. We, as leaders, err most with discipline in thinking that girls have learned when they have not. We often think they have learned when we have only punished them or shushed them up. But, if we approach all so-called discipline problems in the teaching spirit, young Girl Scouts can learn much when in conflict with troopmates, customs, or community opinion.

These conflicts will occur to some degree in every leader's troop. They stem from the fact that youth demands freedom, on the one hand, and the community demands discipline in hundreds of ways, on the other. Youth is inexperienced, eager, impulsive to act; and, in spite of adult warnings, often must learn by trial and error before understanding the natural punishments that come when running counter to group law or custom. Unless there is serious risk, or the price for girls to pay seems too big, we need not regard these experiences as unfortunate if out of them girls become well disciplined and they learn.

If every group demands certain standards of performance or behavior, what do Girl Scouts demand of its members? If ten- to fourteen-year-old girls' code of group behavior is partially formed (and we know it is), what is a Girl Scout leader's responsibility? The Girl Scout code of group behavior is in the Girl Scout Laws; each girl's personal code is in her Girl Scout Promise—"On my honor, I will *try* . . . to obey the Girl Scout Laws." One of the greatest contributions Girl Scout leaders can make is to reenforce this fine and courageous code of behavior at a time (1) when adolescents are breaking away from parental discipline and must take more responsibility for forming their own code of behavior; and (2) when we know our Scouts must become world citizens—and these young world citizens' honor, friendliness, and kindness will be put to a test in ways we, ourselves, have never experienced. Yes, we are talking about Sally, Susie, Arabella, and all the other Scouts in your very own troop—and in all the other thousands of troops. In this sense, group discipline in a Girl Scout troop is and should be the same as that of family, school, community, or nations of free men.

WHAT KIND OF GROUP DISCIPLINE DO YOU WANT?

What kind of control do you want, that of a boss or a friendly counselor? First, think of the people who had real influence upon you, so much so that their wishes concerning you really influenced, or controlled, your conduct. Some people take it upon themselves to order you about. Others respect your personality and express their wishes in forms of suggestions, advice, or friendly counsel.

Second, how do you feel about doing things that are taboo? Activities that of themselves have little attraction are often indulged in because they are supposed to be naughty. You can probably remember several silly and harmless episodes of your childhood that stand out in your memory as highlights of deviltry.

Third, recall occasions when you were punished. Did the punishment make the deed less desirable or only make you more cautious next time? How did you feel toward the person who punished you? Do you think punishments help your girls very much? More often girls learn other things that are undesirable. Different girls react differently to punishment. Some girls stay away from troop meetings, or retaliate with, "I've quit the Scouts!" Some drop out entirely, even though they may need the companionship of girls their own age very much. Some girls hide things they do, or lie to conceal their actions. Some girls become afraid of or dislike their leader, or believe all adults are a nuisance or cannot be trusted. Some become angry, have bad tempers, get sulky or nervous.

Fourth, what do you think about people who work upon others' feelings with such appeals as, "Be a good girl for my sake," or, "You

IF YOU WANT GROUP CONTROL—

never appreciate what I do for you," or, "I won't love you if you do that." Some girls feel that such an adult is silly and unreasonable, and they will not be motivated by such "baby stuff." Some feel guilty, or worried, or unhappy. Some children cannot grow up when an adult controls them by their emotions and does their thinking for them.

Fifth, what kind of behavior habits do you think adults encourage in children with prizes and bribes? Even when given by well-meaning individuals, girls tend to measure working success by the prize standard, often narrow in scope, at a time in life when they need to recognize various abilities in themselves and others as a preparation for the working world. Some girls will always expect to be paid or bribed to do what is right. Many girls who actually make real progress are disappointed, or feel they have failed, if they are not prize winners. Most girls need to practice cooperation more and competition less, especially in their recreational hours when the chance to give voluntary community service is greatest.

The control that is based upon request, confidence, and giving girls a chance to face issues as they arise in their troop experience is a goal for any leader dealing with youth. The leader who gets mad; acts hurt; commands; or uses physical prowess, size, knowledge, position, or vested authority to impress her girls will never build or strengthen their personalities. There may be times when she has to dismiss the group to keep them from annoying other people, destroying property, or developing habits of unwholesome conduct. She will expect them to "try her out" if she is a new leader.

WHAT DEGREE OF ORDER OR DISCIPLINE
DO YOU EXPECT?

What degree of order or discipline do you want in your Girl Scout troop where both activities and relationships are voluntary and where girls come for fun and recreation in their after-school hours?

First, consider how much moving around should and can occur.

Surely, they are ready for physical activity and relaxation after sitting in school all day.

What about your meeting place? Is there room to play games, dance, cook, put on plays without disturbing other people or their property? Is there plenty of outdoor space? More and more educators are stressing the importance of attractive rooms and play space for children in influencing not only kind and quality of program but, also, attitudes and behavior. One leader said: "Since we have painted our room, the girls are so careful to clean up after themselves. Before, I was always reminding and coaxing them. I had no idea a little paint would save me from this petty discipline."

Secondly, how much communication should be expected between members of troops? Are there times when this is to be encouraged and times when it is prevented? If so, by whom? Do you ever find yourself talking too loud or yelling to make yourself heard? If so, stop it. Agree with the troop upon some kind of signal, such as raising your hand, whereby you can get prompt attention and quiet and be heard. Girls may enjoy yelling for a while, but they soon tire of it. Often the ones responsible for noise complain because of that same noise. Do they have businesslike patrol meetings? If there is silence, let it come when they are absorbed in doing quiet things. If they are gay and noisy, let it be because games, singing, or dancing demand it. Let them see for themselves that moving and running about will defeat their own ends if a businesslike patrol meeting is needed.

It will take time, but it is possible to realize a condition where girls may discuss plans, respect patrol and troop meetings and presiding officers, share the joys of cooperative thinking, and respect one another's opinions. But don't expect it too soon, or too long at one time!

Thirdly, how much individual thinking and initiative can be expressed without destroying the troop's life? Does it annoy you when the girls do things without your help or even asking you, find new ways of doing old things, get new ideas? Or, do you encourage it? How do we get individual thinking without having a circus ring for each individual? Review the section on "A Leader's Progress" in the chapter, "Ranks, Badges, and Progression."

WHAT TYPE OF LEADER ARE YOU

Master and Educator Types of Leader

A psychologist* made a study of "master" and "educator" types of Boy and Girl Scout adult leaders. In this study he reports this about adults' attitudes towards individual thinking and initiative of boys and girls.

"The 'master' does not encourage difference of opinion. Any boy or girl who cannot adjust to the leader's idea is allowed to drop out. One leader quaintly put it, 'I prefer independent followers who realize that my way of doing things is right.' If the troop as a whole ceases to be in sympathy with her plans, the master type no longer finds it worth her while to attempt leadership. Her remedy is simply one of changing her group, but usually she seeks another field of action, unless she can convince them she is right or make them see why her point is better than theirs. For instance, one explained, 'If my girls are not in sympathy with me, I try to find some way to bring them around to my point of view. Otherwise, I drop them or quit myself.' If only a few of the members are out of sympathy, the master type simply recommends that they drop out.

"Since the 'educator' is more interested in character development of her followers than in putting over any particular ideas of her own, differences of opinion between herself and her followers do not disqualify them in her mind for membership. In her role as interpreter, she regards misunderstanding as a challenge and an opportunity, not as a personal insult. She is willing to adapt her own opinion if necessary. This appears very clearly in the reactions of the educator to the question, 'What do you do when you find your followers not in sympathy with you?' Instead of dropping the group as the 'master' type is inclined to do, the 'educator' attempts to discover the reason for the difficulty. Answers to this question are significant. 'Find the reason for disagreement and remove the cause.' 'Try to gain their confidence and find out reasons for disagreement.' 'Accept the difference of opinion

---

* "Types of Leader in Group Work" by Paul Pigors, in the September-October, 1936, issue of *Sociology and Social Research.*

as a challenge and try to understand the girls better.' This last statement is particularly characteristic of the educator. Almost without exception, this type answers in the affirmative the question, 'Is it worth
while to attempt leadership when your followers are not in sympathy
with you?' Thus, 'By all means. This is the true test of leadership.'
And again, 'This is when leadership is most needed.'"

Two Leaders' Evaluations of Their Group Control

In the following report, the leader stressed the necessity for girls
doing their own thinking. She also tells how much she is doing as a
community citizen along with this. Perhaps because of her many civic
responsibilities she realizes all the more the difference between the
"master" and "educator" types in community leadership, and the necessity for developing leadership in young people. It seems particularly
significant that this leader is on the school board in her town. She is
certainly an active citizen. She says:

"I do have control of my troop, when I am with the girls at least—
you can never be perfectly sure of any group when its members are
not under direct supervision. I do not mean to imply a lack of trust in
my girls, but even grown-ups do silly, unreasonable things sometimes
when feeling independent.

"When I am disappointed in something the girls do, I speak about
it *once*. I state my reason for feeling disappointed, and let it drop. If
the girls involved ask what I would suggest another time, I give as
good a suggestion, or suggestions, as I have been able to figure out.
But more often they have thought it through themselves and come to
talk it over. I do not forbid any plan unless I feel it may make for
unwholesome conduct. Consequently, when I do say no, there is no
argument. The girls feel that since I do understand them and respect
their opinions, they must respect those few and far-between ulti-
matums. I think that individual thinking should be encouraged to
the limit. Girls who herd together, willing to follow one girl's idea, are
not growing in initiative at all. Of course, we are not all gifted in the
same degree to do creative thinking, but it is possible, at least, to make
your own decisions, and there is no sense in not doing it.

"My assistant is often able to give me valuable information or suggestions, as she has two nieces who just naturally tell her all the news. I keep strictly out of things that the girls are working out for themselves, ready to suggest when the girls ask for suggestions, to praise if everything is intelligently carried out. I have given a lot of time and work—mental and physical—to my Girl Scout work, but I have profited in it in becoming more tolerant and broadminded, keeping young in spirit. I am, at thirty, much less sophisticated than I promised to be when I was teaching. I had only one-third of the third grade in a large city school where the foreign population predominated and 'paddle-rule' was expected. I was young, and thought I was pretty smart. I felt very superior to this little town when I came home weekends. Now I live here again, perfectly contented, and I wouldn't trade my Girl Scout troop, my Sunday school class, or my place on the school board for life in any city. My Scouts call me by my first name, but in a perfectly natural way, and I feel sure they respect me much more than if I were bossy or insisted on a formal title."

Another leader talks about the group control in her troop. It is interesting to see the variables and likenesses in leaders' ways of work and attitudes. She says, "We seem to have little difficulty with ordinary discipline. If so, I do not think of it as such. My method of control developed from advice to me when I was just out of school. My first position was under the direction of a fine woman who had been my teacher here in town only a few years before, and I was paid to help her in a season when her health was poor. Her advice to be just a little bit deaf, dumb, and blind to many things that go on, unless they had a direct bearing on a subject or would affect character growth, has proved invaluable, for I can understand now that a teacher or leader can wear herself out with minor details and not have strength enough left to give to essentials.

"When I see undesirable things developing and confusion or noise when there should be a moderate order or quiet, I think it might be time to change the activity. My hand raised brings quiet; generally followed by a question such as, 'Wouldn't you like to play a game or dance a bit?' or 'Have the patrol leaders any suggestions as to what their patrols would like?' One favorite is the privilege of dramatizing

[276]

a song while the rest of us sing it, a patrol doing the stunts with very short preparation. Usually something different to do or think about brings order without mentioning it. 'Let us . . .' or, 'We can . . . ,' seems to be the best way of presenting my ideas. Sometimes I secretly wonder what would happen if I issued such orders as, 'You gotta . . . !' I know others get results this way, but it would be entirely out of keeping with my personality, and I do not believe my girls would appreciate the change in me, although they do not seem to mind others giving orders in that tone. So I continue to use a method of substitution and try to give them a happy time. If I notice disorder, I try to give them enough to do; and, if a ringleader is found in the troubled area, I find an extra job for her.

"Recently our minister, in discussing the problem of discipline with our Board of Religious Education, of which I am also a member, said that he had noticed that my group meetings were generally very orderly, and yet he never heard me tell them to be quiet, or say sh-h, or ring a bell for silence; that some people by their manner of bearing and attitude command respect and attention. I did not think this all applied to me, but seldom does a group of children that I join seem self-conscious or aloof, or stop discussing a subject when I join them. More likely, they ask me to join them and tell me about it, and ask what I think about it; yet if I start to express an opinion they are always ready for it, and I think it is really because they do not want to miss anything. I do try to *make even a minor detail as interesting as possible,* and the way a subject is put to them makes a difference in their attitude toward it. The same idea can be presented as fun or as a real task or as just ordinary so that it has little effect on their minds."

UPON WHAT DOES A LEADER'S CONTROL DEPEND?

The leader's contact with the girls is an intimate, face-to-face relationship. Her control of them depends upon experience, knowledge of girls, and attitudes toward them. Leaders actually become accepted members of the group. They have two fields: (1) group activity, where they set the example and encourage by doing; (2) defining and forming attitudes through discussion and personal contacts. They are skillful in the use of the four principles for creating desire:

1. *Positive Suggestion.* This is the art of hinting, stating directly, discussing, or offering choices for the desired way of action. Making direct commands, prohibitions, or don'ts are then rarely ever necessary.

Example: One leader said, "A Girl Scout leader has many opportunities to say a word or two to help girls make the right decision. Already I have been asked about the 'white lie and the black lie'; whether one should say she had a good time at a party when she was bored. A child ought to know at least one honorable way out of every situation. There are many times when one virtue is in conflict with another and discrimination must be made. Children must be taught where to draw the line. Mark May deals with this in his article 'What Is Character Education?' by saying, 'A white lie is all right when it does not destroy mutual trust and confidence; when it does, it is harmful.'"

Another example: "I read a magazine article, 'Nobody Loves an Ingrate,' to my troop, and they were concerned and full of questions about the way they acted. I am sure it was a better way than my telling them directly."

2. *Comradeship.* Everything that tends to break down formality between leader and girl is desirable. The leader sets the example and encourages by doing. She toasts her kabob over the fire alongside of Susie. The next minute she may show Jane how to select and make a toasting fork. She is part of the troop but always remains an adult. She uses such significant expressions as "our troop" or "we" when she is explaining ways of doing things.

3. *Compelling Faith.* This is compelling expectation that a girl will do her best. This is sincere respect for girls' ability and their desire to do what is right, or seems best.

Example: "A much used expression of mine when discussing something with the older girls is, 'Now, this is a pretty stiff problem, but I don't hesitate to give it to you. I know what you can do, and I haven't a dream that you won't do it beautifully. I never cease to marvel at the tricky things you girls can do. If I overestimate some day, just

The Group Law at Work

SYLVIA (new Girl Scout, stamping her foot): If I can't be the Princess, I won't be in the play!

OTHER GIRLS: In OUR TROOP we always try out for parts. It's the only fair way. Everybody else wants to be Princess, too!

RESULT: When the girls tried out for parts, Susie did the best acting as Princess. Sylvia was chosen as one of the Spear Bearers. She was disappointed at first, but soon realized that all the girls had been judged upon performance and that demanding to be Princess had not helped.

speak up and say, "Stop."' But not one of them has ever said, 'Stop!' They have to have something difficult to prove their ability to me and themselves."

4. *Recognition and Commendation.* This is approval of the activity, which should be practiced.

Example: "Our older girls have many and varied interests, and we try to show them how happy we are with each successful venture. They do these things mostly on the side—often with outside people directing them, and their leader and her assistant merely two of an audience of interested adults. We are trying unnoticeably to bridge the gap between doing things as a Girl Scout requirement (as the younger ones do faithfully) and doing them in the community as a good citizen—an individual who likes to do things to make her community better because she is a member of it. For instance, several of the older girls help both the school and Woman's Club librarian in many ways. They repair books, file articles and books, rearrange shelves—just all sorts of little things. Often a note comes from the librarian saying how valuable the girls' help is and how splendidly they work. *I always read these notes to the troop and everyone is pleased.*"

WHAT ARE FREQUENT CAUSES OF THE NEED FOR DISCIPLINE?

Most leaders feel they have very few disciplinary problems. This is generally true, since the very nature of Girl Scout volunteer membership for both leader and girls is very disarming in itself. It appears that the following causes upset harmony in troop meetings or troop morale most often. It may help you to see them summarized:

1. The leader expecting perfect performance or behavior from all, or from "one or two girls who . . ." that just did not know what to do in new or strange experiences.

Adults often forget how strange and wonderful the world is for young people, that youth's continuous stream of questions is due to this constant discovery. An experienced leader expects to have at least one or two girls who vary from the sixteen to thirty others in practically every activity undertaken. People who cannot accept individual differences to this degree probably will never be able to teach or enjoy leading a group of children.

2. Conflict of wills between a single girl, sometimes a small clique, and the rest of the troop or patrol.

This is where the leader needs to teach girls about individual differences and reenforce their personal and group code of behavior.

3. Poorly planned meetings, especially too inactive meetings where the classroom lecture rather than recreational approach to activity program was used.

Girls who come directly to troop meetings from school, where they have been sitting still most of the day, may need and want physical activity and fun at the beginning of the meeting.

4. Unawareness on part of leaders of girls' fatigue when school, family, or seasonal activities have been strenuous or very exciting.

Leaders may have a discouraging time trying to get girls to enter into or take part in the very activities they said they wanted to do previously. December and the last month of the school year are two times when leaders need to be particularly aware of girls' full schedules and offset them with relaxing activities and a minimum amount of responsibility to outside groups or audiences.

5. Lack of equipment for an activity so that all cannot be busy at the same time.

Girls do not like to look on and wait patiently while others have the fun of using the tools, even if they "forgot" to bring what was needed.

6. Mixed troops with wide age range without different programs for each group.

High school girls should not be expected to have the same interests ten year olds have. They need program activities geared to their age and ability.

7. Too big troops.

Thirty girls is about the top number for a troop. Not many leaders attempt too large troops, but some do. The size troop a leader can best handle depends upon a variety and combination of variables, such as: experience in group leadership, assistant leadership, helpful troop committee and parents, the way girls have learned to work together, and kind of meeting place and equipment.

Again, one cannot emphasize too strongly the importance of a well thought out philosophy of discipline or control. Read as extensively as you can. But, before this philosophy and reading can take on vital meaning, a leader must play a part herself in some experience that she recognizes as bringing about a change in herself and in her troop. Do not be too sure that only the girl or the group needs changing; you may be leaning more toward the "master" than "educator" type yourself.

LEADERS' RECORDS OF GROUP DISCIPLINE

The leaders' best opportunities for teaching better group conduct arise as they show girls how to manage their troop affairs. The Girl Scout Laws, the democratic way of living, and "the greatest good for the greatest number" may seem idealistic and intangible, but, in practice, a leader comes face to face with such issues as: "Our patrol leader didn't tell us, so we missed the fun"; "They all talk at once— I can't hear my ears"; "Susie won't pay her dues, but she spends plenty on candy and the movies"; "That patrol is late every time—we always have to wait for them." These are symptoms of larger troop responsibilities. Every one of them is an important starting point for sharpening individual and group responsibility, for strengthening the group code, for teaching "the greatest good for the greatest number."

The following five leaders' records illustrate the true meaning of group discipline—*to teach, to instruct, to strengthen, to mold.* Note particularly the parts and procedure of this record form. This seemed to be an easy and helpful guide for leaders when solving their disciplinary problems.

ILLUSTRATION A. *"We Forgot."*

LEADER'S RECORD

1. *How this disciplinary problem is labeled in your mind, the girls', or others' if affected:*
[282]

"Some of the girls were not accepting little responsibilities as they should, especially bringing to troop meetings materials that we had agreed were necessary to do our work. They forgot."

2. *Brief description of how this problem came about:*

"At Christmastime, when we were preparing a play, the girls were very careful about bringing in needed materials, but soon after this I noticed a decided change. At one meeting we decided to work on rainy-day boxes at next meeting. The girls divided into three groups. Each group was to make a box. It was voted that the groups would bring the necessary material for their own boxes. They seemed very enthusiastic. At the next meeting only one girl had brought her materials."

3. *Translate the difficulty into a problem that can be solved:*

"Some of the questions that immediately came to my mind were:
"Aren't you interested in this activity?
"Didn't you understand what we were to do?
"Why didn't you come to me if you were not interested or did not understand?
"What should we do when we find out we cannot carry out the plans that have been made?
"You were eager to do this at the last meeting. Did you give it enough thought and plan carefully?"

4. *Leader's discussion of problems with troop:*

Leader: "We had planned to work on our rainy-day boxes at this meeting. Now that you have not brought your materials, what do you suggest that we do at this meeting?"
One girl (not especially interested in Scouting): "Let's go home."
Leader: "Do you think it quite fair to ask me to give up my afternoon and have it wasted?"
Chorus: "No!"
Leader: "What suggestion do you have for people who forget things they are supposed to do?"
One girl: "We could play games at this meeting."

[283]

Another girl: "We could have group singing."

Another girl (very active and interested in Scouting): "I think that when we forget things and neglect our duties we should take time right away and do what we promised. I think we should all go home right now and get our materials. Then I think we should come back and get to work as soon as possible."

5. *Girls' plan of action and how it seems to be working:*

"The girls decided that the last girl's suggestion was a good idea for the moment and would also be a good rule to follow for future meetings. It has seemed to work out well. The meeting I referred to above was one of the best we have ever had. The girls seemed a little conscience-stricken to think that they had been inconsiderate of my time. They worked like beavers. Since that meeting I have not been confronted with the same problem."

COMMENT ON LEADER'S RECORD

"We forgot," like being late, can become a habit. It is just as well to meet this the first time it begins to appear.

The leader conducted a good discussion and took time to get at the reasons the troop forgot to bring materials. Through this discussion the group decided what to do, and "one girl" taught them where their duty and responsibility lay. Her suggestion was excellent since it was a natural punishment, i.e., when we neglect things and forget our duties we should take time right away and do what we promised. These disciplines, or learnings, are simple in themselves most of the time. They get big if we allow them to accumulate.

The leader was also in her own right in reminding the girls that they were wasting her afternoon as well as theirs. Leaders need to do this now and then when girls are thoughtless of their leader's time or energy.

ILLUSTRATION B. *Starting Troop Meetings on Time*

LEADER'S RECORD

1. *How this disciplinary problem is labeled in your mind, the girls, or others' if affected:*

[284]

"The problem is starting troop meetings on time. And it is really a bigger problem than some realize. Naturally, there are always those who are on time no matter what the occasion. My usual plea at each meeting was, 'Let's all be on time at the next meeting so we can start promptly and have more time for our activities.'"

2. *Brief description of how this problem came about:*

"It is characteristic of the whole town to start meetings late. PTA meetings scheduled to start at eight start at nine. Troop meetings started at four-fifteen instead of four, and it was getting to be a habit. No matter who or what, they strolled in late. Naturally, we did not want to begin the meeting without all present, and it was not always easy to start group activities when only a few were there."

3. *Translate the difficulty into a problem that can be solved:*

"My plans were simple. The first thing was to start the meeting promptly at four. They enjoyed the formal opening and did hate to miss it. That made a few of them hurry a little bit. When that did not turn the trick altogether, I had to think of something else. So I asked the girls what they would do if I did not come until four-thirty. They were astonished that I would even consider coming late, so I was equally astonished that they would come late. But that did not get us very far either. They still came late.

"My last effort brought results. I did not announce anything at all for the next meeting. Thursday, at four, my faithful few were there. Four-fifteen came and we were all gone, except those who were late. I had taken the rest to my house for a party. Those who were late did not know where we had gone. The rest of the girls had a grand time and told the others what they had missed. It was to be expected that some of them got mad. What I did not expect was one of the mothers 'flying down my neck,' but I got in a few good points to her about everything around here being late and all that. Actually, I nearly fainted when she saw my point of view and calmed down. At the next meeting of her sewing club she suggested that the parents were to blame for tardiness and caused quite a discussion. Needless to say, I enjoyed that very much."

[285]

4. *Leader's discussion of problem with troop:*

"The next meeting was spent in discussion of what to do with girls who come late. The following are a few suggestions the girls made:

" 'Let's fine them.'

" 'They can't hold office.'

" 'Tardiness should count up as absences do. Being late three times should equal one absence.' "

5. *Girls' plan of action and how it seems to be working:*

"They decided that a girl could not hold office if she were late and that tardiness equals absence. It is working quite well in most cases, and particularly in the case of a patrol leader who was always late."

COMMENT ON LEADER'S RECORD

This leader had to break a poor troop habit that was a poor community habit also. This is a fine illustration of a natural punishment or "paying the price through the situation." In this instance it simply meant if you were late you missed the fun. Leaders will save themselves a lot of trouble if they deliberately set the stage and punish through the situation, as well as discipline girls more effectively who have not responded to positive suggestions and milder forms of guidance. As girls grow up, we treat them more and more as adults. We teach them to see relation between cause and effect, to take responsibility for their own actions. In this case, too, one girl in the troop was over-protected and had a mother who was unwilling for her to be punished. She was the mother who "flew down the leader's neck." If this leader had played upon the child's feelings with, "Now, be a good girl and be on time to please me," or threatened or scolded her, or shown favoritism, she would have had a much harder time answering the mother's complaint. Most adults and children understand natural punishments better than any other kind, accept them with less resentment, and learn more as a result.

[286]

ILLUSTRATION C. *"She ruins our singing."*

LEADER'S RECORD

1. *How this disciplinary problem is labeled in your mind, the girls', or others' if affected:*

"We have twenty-seven girls in our troop, and I can truthfully say all the girls have been vitally interested in Girl Scouting since the troop was organized, with the exception of two, and now there is a third one. Betty Ann and Nina, the half-interested ones, have been regular in attendance, however, with each one having missed only two meetings the entire year, but I think the main reason they continue to come is so they will not be left out of things. Betty Ann takes an active part in helping to plan the troop's activities, but she does not help carry the plans out. The girls feel this, but they have just been putting up with her and saying nothing about it. Then, too, she ruins the singing in the troop, and the girls resent this more than anything else she does or does not do."

2. *Brief description of how this problem came about:*

"Betty Ann, Nina, and Mary were not present at the meeting two weeks ago and one of the girls said, 'They have gone to town.' I did not make any remarks then, as I want the girls to want to come to the meetings rather than have them feel they have to come, and too, we have not had any trouble with attendance and tardiness thus far.

"After we finished our first song, which Betty Ann had practically ruined at the meeting before with her loud off-key alto, Vivian said 'I'm glad Betty Ann isn't here to sing alto!'

"Everybody joined in at once with, 'Me, too!'—'So am I!'

"And I asked, 'Why, what's wrong with her alto?'

"Well, that sentence was a bomb!

"Marion spoke up with, 'She just can't sing alto, and, because Nina does, she wants to, too. She always ruins our songs in the auditorium, glee club, and everywhere.'

"I said, 'Well, wouldn't we rather have her enjoy singing even though she might not sing exactly right than for her not to even try?

[287]

"'Yes'm, but somebody ought to tell her not to sing alto,' was the reply.

"This was a serious problem in the group, and one we could not dismiss lightly. Finally I said, 'Well, I don't know much about singing either, but how could we teach her to sing alto?'"

3. *Translate the difficulty into a problem that can be solved:*

"Celeste, who sings beautifully, is well liked by all, and is very modest about her many talents and abilities, said, 'Let's let the ones who sing alto go in another room and practice one song together. Then we could come back and sing it with the others.'

"Everyone thought this was a good suggestion and one we would try at our next meeting. It worked like a charm! Celeste was careful to sit by Betty Ann and asked Doris, another strong alto, to sit on the other side of her. The Scouts were delighted with their results and felt they had accomplished something big—and they had!"

COMMENT ON LEADER'S RECORD

This record is a stern test in the skill and art of leadership. Here the leader is forced by the girls' disapproving conversation to take a stand against gang opinion, change the group's attitude, and help them choose a "high road" to action when they are eager to take the "lower road." Creating sympathy and understanding toward others in the group is a very subtle thing. But, in a recent study of sympathy of children toward their classmates, it was found that the most sympathetic classes received from their teachers (1) positive suggestions to help one another, (2) help in correcting their own mistakes.

ILLUSTRATION D. *"We never get anything done."*

LEADER'S RECORD

1. *How this disciplinary problem is labeled in your mind, the girls', or others' if affected:*

"To me, the unrest that girls show in Scout meetings that are held after school is a natural physical reaction from many hours of quiet during school. To offset this, we dance the 'Virginia Reel,' gather around the piano for an informal sing-song, or play active games. Being a new troop, we had to learn that this was necessary at the beginning of our meeting, and we had to provide some time for planning and deciding things at each meeting."

2. *Brief description of how this problem came about:*

"At first, our meetings were informal and we accomplished some things, but, as our troop began to grow in number, this procedure soon became obnoxious not only to me but to the girls as well. The girls began to realize they were not finishing their Second Class work. After our troop membership grew beyond eleven, so much informality was out of place. We had to accomplish more business in less time. One girl said, 'We need more order so we can get our new patrols worked out, decide how many, and get our patrol leaders.' A few others agreed with her, and I agreed with them."

3. *Translate the difficulty into a problem that can be solved:*

One girl: "Why don't we ever get the right ones on committees? I mean somebody who'll do what they are s'posed to do?"

Leader: "Your committees have been selected at the last possible moment without the troop's deciding what is expected of the committees and which girls can best do the job."

Another girl: "When are we going to elect new officers?"

Leader: "You have not allotted time for business and have not helped me plan the meetings so you can include these things you do want."

Another girl: "Seems like we should have a president—or somebody to sit at a table."

Leader: "You will have to choose between having a president, secretary, treasurer, and committees and having patrols and Court of Honor. You don't need both."

Another girl: "What about our patrols? That's what Scouts have! Why don't we get new patrol leaders? Elect some who will do what should be done, but how?"

Leader: "Again, time should be allotted for discussion of duties of patrol leaders. We need to select leaders carefully, and support them once they are selected. The whole troop has to help decide what the patrol leader's job is, and then select the most able girls. You were in too big a hurry before. It is as much the troop's fault as the patrol leaders'."

4. *Leader's discussion of problems with troop:*

"After we had decided that we must arrange our programs, or plan our meetings in order to accomplish something, I started in this way. I called a Court of Honor meeting, and the three patrol leaders and I had an informal discussion of our troubles.

"One girl suggested, 'Let's make everyone be quiet, and let them raise their hands when they want to talk.'

"I then asked her, 'Raise your hands to whom? I don't want to be before the troop constantly. I'm not to be your teacher.'

"Two girls chimed in, 'No, we don't want that. It would be just like another class, and soon no one would stay.'

"One girl suggested, 'Let's have a president!'

"Another girl, 'Girl Scouts don't have presidents!'

"At this point I suggested we might decide on an officer Girl Scouts do have and let her take charge of the entire meeting or business part of it. All three girls said that would be all right, but they would let the troop decide which girl should preside and for how long—and not for long, because all would want to take turns being in charge.

"One patrol leader said, 'Let's have a few minutes every meeting to decide things.'

"At the next troop meeting I made a report to the troop of our patrol leaders' meeting. I explained in a simple way how grown-ups organize and keep their meetings moving along in a smooth manner."

5. *Girls' plan of action and how it seems to be working:*

"Briefly, the girls decided on the following schedule for their troop meetings—

a. Some kind of physical activity and fun—games, music, folk dancing, and so forth.

b. Patrol meeting—Roll call; old business; new business.

c. Other Girl Scout work.

d. Taps.

"For our troop, this has solved the problems of never getting to things that must be decided by group discussion and of including active fun at beginning of meetings."

COMMENT ON LEADER'S RECORD

This new leader recorded what frequently happens in new troops. There are two important parts:

1. The leader recognizes that physically active fun and play is a very important safety valve and protection against disciplinary problems. Read the section "Girl Scouting Is Fun" in the chapter, "What Are Troop Meetings Like?"

2. The leader must teach girls how to manage and plan their troop meetings. Good troop organization really *develops over a period of time.*

A felt need for troop organization is apt to come gradually, since most Girl Scouts come into a troop without any experience or information in this area, even though they may be fascinated with the idea of being elected to an office. Most troops grope for this order and unity in much the same way as illustrated in this record. Many times the leader warns them against haste, but they want to elect patrol leaders today—not next time, or appoint a committee to do something for troop without deciding just what the job is. They are often unfamiliar with the simplest mechanics of group meetings even to the most commonly used words, such as agenda or names of offices. Leaders of new troops truly do a teaching job in this area. See chapter "Developing Self-Government in a Troop" for more help.

Notice the brief outline of the troop meetings. Many new troops seem to organize their meetings roughly in three parts after they get over the first pains of experimentation. They seem to feel a need for (1) physical activity and fun; (2) time to plan and decide things, using either the town meeting or representative type of troop organization; (3) "Girl Scout work" of a more serious nature. New leaders have a tendency to concentrate on part three until the girls teach them better.

ILLUSTRATION E. *"The patrol leaders lead the wrong way."*

LEADER'S RECORD

1. *How this disciplinary problem is labeled in your mind, the girls', and others' if affected:*

"How can we plan and conduct our meetings in an orderly manner and without wasting so much time? The school discipline is extremely lax here; thus the girls do not understand good group behavior, and say, 'We behave like this at school and home, why not here?' And, frankly, it is true. Likewise, in their Sunday school class I think it sometimes is as good as a three-ring circus."

2. *Brief description of how this problem came about:*

"Troop disorder was caused mostly by two girls, not particularly good friends, who were trying to outdo one another in both mischief and attention getting. Mother would not believe it of them because they could be 'Mother's angel-pie' when Mother—socially prominent —was around. This was ticklish for me to handle."

3. *Translate the difficulty into a problem that can be solved:*

Leader: "Why, as patrol leaders, can't you get these girls to be quiet and help do what the patrol planned to do?"
One girl: "Let's make them pay a fine."
Another girl: "Let's tattle to their mothers."
Sally: "I know gum makes noise, but it's fun!"
Susie: "You wouldn't dare to make me leave!"
Sally: "I laugh loud and talk in school without raising my hand."
Susie: "This isn't school. You can't make me keep still or behave!"

4. *Leader's discussion of problems with troop, and girls' plan of action and how it seems to be working:*

"Frankly, the two mischief makers are the two best 'brain girls' in the troop, and really the best leaders, if I can tone them down. That's why I wanted them elected to office."

Leader: "Shall we make Susie and Sally officers so they can preside with me and I can make them behave?"

One girl: "I'll say that's an idea!"

Another girl: "Then I'll make faces at her like she did me when I was president!"

Another girl: "As chairman, she has to learn to be better because she must be an example."

Another girl: "As chairman, she can't chew gum or pull anybody's hair."

Another girl: "I'll say good riddance! Put her up there. Maybe the rest of us can behave."

"Sally was made chairman. She is becoming an excellent chairman and is thinking and planning for her troop. She is very hard and exacting with the girls and is trying—really trying, but, thank Heaven, it's a sweet way, not bossy. The girls do listen to her and mind her, to a certain degree of course. I know she's going to be tops.

"The other little rascal met with the same sort of remarks and discussion from the troop that Sally did. She was elected treasurer. The outgoing treasurer was a meek girl and did not make an effort to see that the girls kept up with their dues. Susie is outspoken and spares no one's feelings. Children can be so hard and cruel. She would count up back dues and say, 'Why, Alice, you owe seventy-five cents back dues!' Next week Alice would pay in full. Then she would take another one: 'Why, Grace, you owe fifty cents back dues!' The next week Grace would pay in full.

"Frankly, this method of collecting dues worked like a charm, and I let it go, for there isn't one girl in my troop who cannot afford to pay her dues or who doesn't go to the movies at least twice a week. I maintain that any girl who has money for the movies and ice cream sodas can pay her dues. As we become more orderly, I will need to be less strict. I hope to show them how to speak and act more kindly toward each other, and perhaps convince them in time that we can get things done and be nice to each other at the same time."

[294]

When discipline is lax in school, home, and church you must expect to be tried out under the same system in troop meeting. Until you can teach girls over a period of time that planning, law, and order are more profitable ways, you must play the role of educator and not be shocked or indignant at children's daring, mischief, and cruel remarks. You must also keep a firm hand and not let girls "decide everything" or "do just what they want." We know that responsibility as well as freedom and privilege is a necesary part of democratic troop government.

Here the leader started with the two mischief makers and stated her terms. She recognized their ability and put them to work. Ordinarily we would not suggest that troop officers be decided upon in this way, but the troop was willing and the trouble cleared up. Not all mischief makers are potential leaders. Some are attention getters, flighty, noisy, without being smart enough to lead others in the group.

This leader is starting with girls as she finds them and moving rapidly toward better troop organization. If we really teach or discipline, we must be willing to start with girls as they are and show them how to correct their mistakes. We must try to be the "educator" type of leader.

Chapter Ten

Character Education

In the preceding chapter the emphasis was on working with the behavior of the group. This chapter shows you how to reinforce the Girl Scout's personal code of conduct—"On my honor, I will try . . . to obey the Girl Scout Laws." The need for this chapter is brought home most forcefully when a leader says, "I have one or two girls who . . . !"

The material develops three main ideas and illustrates their practical application in troop meetings:

1. *Why character training of the individual Girl Scout is so important.*
2. *Why the relationship between leader and individual girl must be friendly and trustful.*
3. *The methods considered most effective in character training of children.*

THE CHIEF SCOUT, Lord Baden-Powell, when asked how large a Scout troop should be, replied, "So far as my own experience goes, I cannot train individually more than sixteen boys—but allowing for my having only half the capacity of the experienced boy worker, I would allow for his taking on thirty-two."

He went on to say, "Why worry about individual training? Because it is the only way you can educate. You can instruct any number of boys if you have a loud voice and attractive methods of discipline. But that is not training. It is not education. Education is the thing that counts in character building and in making men.

"It is not the slightest use to preach the Scout Laws or to give them out as orders: each mind requires its special exposition of them and the ambition to carry them out.

"That is where the personality and ability of the Scoutmaster comes in."

THE LEADER'S PERSONALITY AND ABILITY

What part is played by personality and what part by activity or program in a character-developing experience for leader and girl? Who is it that builds one's character? Is it built from the outside by others, or is it built by one's self? Is it built partly by one's self and partly by others?

See if you can list those fine personalities that you feel had something to do with making you the person you are today. Choose persons outside your family whose influence you felt when you were Girl Scout age. This relation is comparable to your Girl Scout leadership.

Names and relationships	Why I accepted their influence	What they did for me

The average adult can recall not more than five or six persons who in her childhood had any influence upon her. Why do you remember these persons vividly while others you have forgotten or find difficult to remember?

Here are some of the most frequent answers Girl Scout leaders give to this question:

"She seemed to like me."

"He asked me to help him do something, and did it in such a way that I felt he thought I amounted to something."

"She told me that I ought to prepare for something big, that I must get a good education."

"She told me that I could do better than I was doing—that I was not measuring up to myself."

"He praised me for what I had done."

HOW THE GIRL RESPONDS TO THE LEADER'S PERSONALITY

One leader said, "I find that any girl I want to influence has to like and trust *me* before I can do anything with her."

We enjoy the persons we like and are annoyed by persons we dislike. These feelings are even stronger with teen-age girls, and sometimes amount to worship and hatred.

The chart below was worked out after observing children's responses to other people. It may help you in observing their relations with you.

CHILDREN'S RESPONSES TO

LIKED PERSONALITIES		DISLIKED PERSONALITIES	
Positive Response	Negative Response	Positive Response	Negative Response
1. Seek to be with.	1. Avoid being kept away from.	1. Seek to stay away from.	1. Avoid being with.
2. Seek to please.	2. Avoid displeasing.	2. Seek to displease.	2. Avoid pleasing.
3. Seek to reveal virtues.	3. Avoid revealing faults.	3. Frequently seek to reveal faults.	3. Frequently avoid revealing virtues.
4. Seek to be like.	4. Avoid being unlike.	4. Seek to be unlike.	4. Avoid being like.

[298]

HOW THE LEADER RESPONDS TO THE GIRL'S PERSONALITY

Score yourself in your relations with one of your Betty Jos, Genevieves, or Adelaides, and size up your chances for influencing her:

1. Do I really like Betty Jo when she brags, boasts, giggles, or wiggles, and do I understand how she "got that way"? . . . . Do the expression on my face, tone of my voice, and nature of my contacts with her prove to Betty Jo that I really like her? . . . .

2. Do I have faith in her desire to do the right thing? . . . . in her capacity to make suggestions? . . . . and carry out plans? . . . .

3. Can I share her interests? . . . . Or am I on my dignity and above listening to tales of 'rithmetic, roller skates, baby brother? . . . .

4. Have I any interests of my own that I can share with her? . . . . Does she know how well I can bake a good chocolate cake, knit ski mittens, and grow the best tulips in town? . . . .

If you can answer yes to all these questions, except the second part of question 3, you are well along the way toward gaining Betty Jo's confidence and faith in your leadership.

A FEW METHODS CONSIDERED MOST EFFECTIVE IN CHARACTER TRAINING OF CHILDREN

Studies have been made in the educational field to learn more about what, specifically, character education is, and what teaching methods are most effective. The *what* and *how* of character education are still complex, and few people, if any, know any quick, easy, or exact answers. Character education is as complex as life itself, because it is life and ever challenging to leadership.

Descriptions of several effective methods and their significance follow.

I. PROGRAMS AIMED AT CHANGING SPECIFIC ACTS OF BEHAVIOR ARE MORE LIKELY TO SUCCEED THAN BROAD GENERALIZED PROGRAMS

This bears out the old saying, "It's the little things we do that count most." The many little things we do are the units of behavior that help form our habits.

For instance, in teaching honor in one of the school projects, the specific everyday experiences that the children faced in and out of school were listed by children with their teachers. They considered (1) just how dishonesty was practiced and whether or not it was a serious matter, and (2) if so, what could be done about it. First on their list was honor at school, involving honesty or truthfulness with regard to tests, homework, grading one's own paper and grading a classmate's paper, borrowing in class and gymnasium, and excuses for absences.

Then they listed what they could do about honor on tests and named it "Ways of keeping from being suspected of dishonesty in a test."

1. Do not look around during a test.
2. Do not sit sidewise on your seat. Sit straight up in your seat.
3. Do not change seats and give the impression that you want to sit beside a pupil who knows more about the test than you do.
4. Keep your textbook out of sight. Never open it on a pretense of getting a piece of paper out of it.
5. Do not ask to borrow things or leave the room during a test.

Such simplicity! Any child can understand this. Yes he can, but does he?

Everyday living is made up of a continuous stream of these "little things that count," these specific acts of behavior. It is for this reason adults must teach children what is right, what is appropriate, in many different situations. When we can count upon children acting in a certain way in a familiar situation, then we believe a habit is established.

When thinking of habit, we must think of habit of thought, habit of feeling, habit of judging, as well as outward behavior. If we think of habit in all its possible ways of conduct we may then say the

[300]

unit element of character is habit—and habit, of course, is something learned.

II. To the children, character education must not appear to be planned or direct, but the leader deliberately plans for it

Children resent any obvious effort on the part of adults to improve their character or to be made "good." But they are ready and willing to solve their own problems and little worries that rise naturally in their everyday living and do their part in helping others. Attention is then centered outwardly, on helping the Red Cross for instance, instead of inwardly on their own goodness.

One leader mentioned "courtesy classes." "I tried courtesy classes twice, but saw they wouldn't work—especially since two goody-goody girls liked them so well. Now I teach courtesy and good manners every opportunity I have. The Boy and Girl Scouts have a party once a month. The girls need so desperately to know what to do and say in the 'nicest and politest way,' I feel they are learning a great deal. The Scoutmaster says the boys are just as concerned about their manners."

Another leader's report shows the vast difference in a girl's response when a leader gives her specific jobs and everyday responsibilities (as shown in the second and third months' records) rather than scolding her about her Girl Scout Laws (as shown in the first month's record in the chart that follows). This typical contrast comes through in hundreds of leaders' records as they shift from a direct to an indirect method of character training. Also, note in the chart the shift from a program of broad, generalized terms in the first month to simple specific ones in the second and third months.

Sylvia's moral code is not yet formed in abstract terms but in concrete terms. Can you imagine Sylvia's mother saying, "Sylvia, dear, I want you to realize how necessary it is for you to cooperate with the household. The family functions as a unit. Remember the Ten Commandments that you learned in Sunday school," if she wanted Sylvia to pick up her pajamas. She simply (1) says, "Sylvia, will you pick up your pajamas," and (2) sees to it that Sylvia does pick up her pajamas.

[301]

WHAT THE LEADER TRIED TO DO	SYLVIA'S RESPONSE

First Month

Reminded her with the others about Girl Scout Laws, their meaning, and obedience, indirectly by giving examples of others.	No results that I could see.
Reminded her directly of Girl Scout Laws and obedience.	Reacted the same way.
Encouraged her to perform with others in a program.	Took it entirely too lightly; did nothing but giggle.
Encouraged her to take on a lone responsibility.	Refused with embarrassment.

Second Month

I appointed her chairman of a committee for finding a suitable location for our bake sale.	She was highly pleased to accept such a responsibility. She worked diligently and did find a suitable location.
I introduced block printing to the troop.	She was most enthusiastic. I was surprised. It seemed to quiet her nervousness, and she settled down to many an evening of quiet pleasure.

Third Month

In the block-printing experiment, I urged her to show some of the younger girls how it was done.	Responded very well. Felt a sense of duty, and was pleased to be of some help.
On a recent hike I put her in charge of first aid treatment.	She was happy to do this, as we had some skinned knees and a cut finger.

III. THE EXPERIENCE-PLUS-DISCUSSION METHOD IS DEFINITELY SUPERIOR TO EXPERIENCE OR DISCUSSION BY ITSELF

Three methods were compared in a study. It was found that "talking it over" started the girls thinking, but it failed to provide the drive necessary for putting into practice the very same things it was so easy to think and talk about. On the other hand, when activities were planned and carried out without any discussion of the habits or principles that they were designed to teach, the character growth was again meager. A combination of the experience and discussion methods proved to be best.

Example: In the library unit the purpose was to teach respect for property and rights of others when using a library.

In the discussion groups, the work centered around a lecture given to them by a librarian. The lecture was cleverly organized and presented, and proved popular with the girls. It covered the origin of the central library and the branches in their town, and the method of support; how to receive the benefits of the library; types of books available for girls; rules of the library and the reasons for the rules; and how to take care of books. Free discussions were conducted during several periods on the points emphasized in the lecture and on the application of these points to care for library books.

In the "experience-plus-discussion" groups the same lecture was given, with experience added. This group developed a small library of its own and administered it for the remainder of the year. This project provided the group with first-hand experience in some of the problems that librarians face and gave a number of children their first taste of borrowing books from a library.

THE FRAMEWORK OF OUR MORAL CODE

Let us review briefly, as leaders, the permanent framework out of which our moral code has evolved, and out of which each person's moral code is evolving continually.

1. All human beings have wants and needs. As soon as the power of thought develops in a child, needs and wants cease to be blind. A

[303]

child begins to look ahead, plan, and foresee results. As this happens, parents, teachers, and leaders step in and guide this thinking, planning, choosing—which is the intellectual phase of character out of which develops what we call "inner conscience." As children grow up, adults try, and do succeed for the most part, to teach children to want what is right and to fulfill their wants and desires in an honest, cheerful, kind way. In doing this through thousands of everyday acts—i.e., choosing between what is right and wrong, between what does and does not give the most enduring satisfaction or what is best in the long run, children gradually learn moral ways of satisfying their needs and desires, and most of them eventually acquire wisdom and prudence in their more mature years.

2. Then, we all live together—in companionship and competition; in relations of cooperation and subordination. These relations are expressed in demands, claims, expectations. One person has a conviction that fulfillment of his demands by others is his right; to these others it comes as an obligation, something owed, due, to those who assert the claim. What are these rights and duties for a Girl Scout in relation to members of her family, school classroom, Scout troop, community, Scouts and Guides in other nations? Out of the interplay of these claims and obligations comes our concept of Law, Duty, Right, Moral Authority, not only for ten-year-old Sally but for everybody.

3. Human beings approve and disapprove, sympathize and resent, as certainly and naturally as they seek what they want, or impose claims or respond to them. Thus the moral good emerges out of the general ideas of virtue and moral excellence that regulate praise and blame. This approval or disapproval can run counter to or break written laws, change customs, set the fashion in big and small ways. In children, this is often referred to as "age-grade standards," the "gang opinion," or "the crowd's ideas." In a neighborhood or nation it is called public opinion. A Girl Scout leader must be "accepted" by girls in a troop before her influence can be strong enough to change or mold the group opinion or standards. Leadership often meets its sternest tests in this area. Too often parents, teachers, and leaders waste their energy trying to discipline a group of ten to

[304]

THE LEADER COPES WITH HUMAN NATURE—I

Sally and Susie go to the movies, while their troop mates
get ready to entertain seventy-five guests at their annual
Parent-Daughter supper.

The girls were so indignant about Sally and Susie "coming
only for supper, and not doing one bit of work!" that the
leader had to settle the issue at the next meeting. Here
the girls are eagerly voting for the rule: *Every Scout
must do her share of the work if she is to enjoy the fun,*

fourteen year olds when they should be changing age-grade standards, molding group opinion, or emphasizing the positive rather than the negative way of action. This fact is one of the hardest things for adults who work directly with children to remember and face realistically.

In reviewing the above, we realize that human needs, desires, purposes; society's demand and law; sympathetic approval and hostile disapproval *are constant*. We cannot imagine them disappearing as long as human nature remains what it is. As young Girl Scouts develop habits of kindness, helpfulness, thrift, and obedience they should realize that these are the *best guides civilization has to give them*, not only for their troop but also for Girl Guides and Girl Scouts throughout the world.

LEADERS' RECORDS OF THEIR SYLVIAS

The following records show development of individual Girl Scouts in a troop. These leaders selected one girl in the troop who seemed to need extra help and worked with her over a period of two or three months. Such extra help—whether it is called guidance or coaching or tutoring—is usually given with the idea of helping a girl catch up or learn enough to keep up with her group, whether it is her arithmetic class in fifth grade or the Girl Scout troop. A leader cannot give every girl in her troop a lot of individual help nor should she try, but she can work with one girl at a time. About 90 per cent of the leaders who kept these records for two or three months, and did at least one thing a week to help Sylvia, saw a "big difference for the better." Many leaders said "straightening out Sylvia" was the most satisfactory job they had done as a leader during the year.

These leaders seemed to feel they had no specific formula or easy key to understanding Sylvia. They felt as did Dr. J. Edgar Park, former President of Wheaton College, who once said at one of our national conventions, "You get nearest the truth about people when you approach them not merely as an organizer or as a scientist but as an *artist*; still more when you forget yourself in the process and begin to enjoy the common touch of the everyday friend. Analyze all you

[306]

will, but do not forget that you know nothing of truth until you yourself are shaken out of your superior pose by the mystery and beauty that is Sylvia's. Try to understand her all you can, but remember that if you could fully understand anyone else, you would have to take a place above the throne of God in Heaven, for one of the few recorded instances where God is said to have spoken directly to man, He spoke in the form of a question asking him why he was acting as he was."

But we catch something of the truthful reflection of Sylvia and the art of leadership in the records that follow. Perhaps reading them will help you. Note the friendly and sincere ways these leaders worked with their Sylvias, and particularly the record form and teaching methods used.

Now, a word or two about who is and who is not a "problem child"—a much overworked label and a poor one.

When a leader says, "I don't have any problems; my girls are wonderful," the answer is, "She is lucky, because many leaders do have one or two girls who need special help beyond what a volunteer Girl Scout leader can give. Such girls need help right now while they are young and their defects can be most easily corrected by social workers, child guidance people, doctors, and others. As long as a certain per cent of American children have broken homes—parents not living or divorced; too indulgent parents who cannot help their children form a passable code of behavior; failure in school; speech, sight, or hearing defects; too little food to eat; and so forth, these same children will appear in our troop. If we are interested in children, we will do all we can to correct these conditions in society, and help the Sylvias in our troops more directly. And Sylvia is an excellent starting point!

With thousands of troops, averaging from sixteen to thirty Girl Scouts, we must expect some serious problems. For instance, it is estimated that 4 per cent of all school children have speech defects. This does not mean that every Girl Scout leader will have a girl in her troop with a speech defect, but some leaders certainly will. If the leader's troop is in a city, county, or state with speech clinics, Sylvia may be going to a clinic already. If so, the leader's responsiblity will be small, perhaps only to encourage other Scouts to be sympathetic and patient with Sylvia's efforts to speak steadily and slowly in troop meetings. If nothing is being done, the leader may "refer" Sylvia to the clinic or encourage her parents to take her there. Leaders need not be afraid they will be accused of meddling. Most parents are pathetically grateful for such aid and interest in their children. A few may be too negligent or ignorant to care. The latter reason is still not good enough for a child to go through life with a speech defect if it can be corrected at an early age, and society cares enough to pay the bill. Leaders must also face the fact that some towns will not have clinics or doctors near enough to correct speech defects, and there are some speech defects that cannot be corrected. But, whatever the circumstances or the variety of problems, we do not stand idly by and say, "It can't happen in a Girl Scout troop."

Record A—Sylvia

Age: 12. *School grade:* 7th.

Health: Seems easily fatigued; has some foot trouble which makes physical activity hard for her at times.

Status in Group: Is accepted; since she has an active younger sister who ridicules her a great deal, her own group feels sorry for her.

Attitude Toward Whatever She Is Doing: Follows suggestions of others; rather lazy.

New Interests Acquired in Troop: Rather keen interest in handwork; we have been working in weaving, and although her work is rather careless and shoddy, she carries it through to completion and is very proud of her efforts.

Things of Importance to Her Right Now: Her own physical appearance, the interest she arouses in the boys of her class, new things in her home, such as modernized kitchen equipment.

Attitude Toward and Influence of Leader: Yes, she seems to be personally fond of me and anxious for my praise—wants to handle me a great deal; also has a great fondness for my daughter who is a member of her group; her mother seems to think a great deal of any attention I pay her; her people are Italian and do not mingle with others in town, and I have been careful to show them every courtesy; I was instrumental in getting her sister to camp for a week and they were very grateful.

WHAT THE LEADER TRIED TO DO	SYLVIA'S RESPONSE

First Month

I have tried to get her to be outstanding in her group through her handwork, which I found out she likes and feels more equal to the others in. She is behind in her school work and feels inferior, even admits it—says she cannot play games or work as the others do. I have tried to encourage her in thinking there isn't anything she cannot do if she wants to badly enough to work for it.

In our weaving project, she has completed three different baskets and mats. She is extremely proud of them, and seems to have greater confidence of her place in the group.

Have praised her for her appearance. Her little sister who is so far beyond her in activity and pushes herself forward is not very neat.

She seems to be trying to "dress up" more, keeps her hair neat, and so forth. Thus she seems to be feeling she can go beyond her sister in some things. I believe she is gaining in self-confidence.

I have also tried to lead the other girls in her group toward helping her as much as possible unobtrusively. They have, without any pressure from me, made her assistant patrol leader.

This seems to be helping her get over her inferior feeling, even to the extent of beginning to be a little "bossy," which I take as a good sign.

Second Month

I have tried particularly to hold her to finishing the weaving project, a newly found interest in handwork—to show her that she,

She finally became interested in finding pictures of the use of weaving in our homes, and was very critical of others in their arrange-

[309]

too, can do well if she tries. She has, as I reported, a feeling that she just can't do well what others can do. I tried to help her particularly over the hard places. She doesn't seem to be a bit interested when it comes to working with her head, thinking things out, or reporting on reading matter.

I turned over the section of the scrapbook on the picture work to her.

I couldn't go any further. She could not copy out patterns on graph paper or do any of the reference work on history. I could feel her withdraw at any mention of that type of work. I did not press it or require it for her badge, fearing to lose all I had gained.

I found in making the definition of terms graphic, by using their own works and discussion of looms, all the girls seemed to be more interested in their part of it. I asked her just to sit down and listen.

When we had a tea, I especially asked her and her sister to bring their mother. She is a very attractive young Italian woman, unable to speak much English, and she has never attended any gatherings in the town through her unusual shyness. I feel, however, through my slight acquaintance with her, that she is not so shy in my presence.

[310]

ment of pictures in our scrapbook.

She developed a very *big* feeling and was a regular tyrant, over-fussy about the placing of the pictures, cleanliness of the pages, and their relation one with another. This I took as a sign of development—in her respect for her own ability and in her correlation in thinking.

Here was something familiar to her. At first she just listened. Then she put in a few suggestions until she had such a ridiculous one they all laughed. I found a loophole for her, and we all enjoyed it. She did not blush and withdraw as she had on one other such occasion, I noticed.

The child dashed home from school, dressed herself neatly, and brought her mother so proudly to the meeting. The younger sister could hardly wait for her mother. It was like a picnic for them. And the mother was so pretty and tastefully dressed. Sylvia did not expect her badge, and was delighted and proud that her mother could see her get it.

I did not succeed in getting her to take any part in the girls' program.

I am going to try through music and dancing to help her even further. I think maybe I can get her to take a more active part next time.

She served tea and took care of her little brother, I think less shyly.

Third Month

Having finished our weaving project, our young lady had dropped back slightly into her old rut. She likes to work with her hands, and we have turned from handwork for the moment.

I must now try to get her to enter into games. She consistently develops trouble with her arches, or pain in her side or sore throat, when it comes to games of any kind, mental or physical. This I find to be her usual habit in her gymnasium classes, apparently quite successful in insuring her against unwanted participation. I quietly joked with her in an aside at the last meeting, letting her think I was in on her little secret but would not let the others know. I was amazed when she grinned and gave me a broad wink. I let it

Yet there is a decided advance in the part she takes in group activity. When we had a Valentine party after school and the girls could not assemble the necessary things, our assistant leader and I took everything in a large basket— food, snappers, napkins, and chose a few to set up the party for all. Sylvia was the first to step forward to arrange the table, and caused much merry bickering by her arranging and rearranging. She fussed over the table through all the games.

I found, however, when we came to dancing that Sylvia has quite an opinion of her own dancing. She does carry herself well and seems to have a natural swing. When I saw that she was in tune with her partner, I asked the others to watch her, and pointed out how she held her partner so that she could really guide her.

She was very proud, and I've noticed when it comes to dancing she has no sore feet and no pains in her side. This, too, will some day give me an opening, at least a place to work from. She evidently

Two suddenly grow up—!

Help with good grooming!

drop right there, deeming it the wrong time for a lecture. Some time I shall have to work in a game or story of some such activity and start a discussion of just who gains, just what is strict honesty in such dealings, and see if she will take part in any such discussion. She probably will not even recognize herself, but I may get another wink!

I must tell you. Sylvia took the part of Handel's mother in a play today, was pretty as a picture and knew her part perfectly. She conducted herself with an ease and a conscious pleasure in herself that was a delight to see.

feels so very inadequate when it comes to her part in games, and I shall continue to try to help her find joy in them. I'm sure it will help her in everything she does to overcome this queer reaction.

"This completes my three months' record with my special Sylvia. I am very proud to report that putting this down on paper in concrete form has been of great help to me with all the other girls. I have since had another youngster who is a great deal of trouble at home, in school, everywhere, and this conscious effort on the part of working with one girl enabled me very quickly to hit upon a device which has made that child a real asset to our troop, almost pitifully anxious to please, instead of a sulky, unyielding thorn in our sides as she was for several months. She is an only child, about to have a little brother or sister to take much of her attention, and this discovery may be very helpful in the future. She seems to need very badly to feel that someone likes her, that someone thinks she can do things, instead of getting all her attention by being disagreeable.

"And, thus, I find now that every girl is a fascinating Sylvia needing a little different treatment. This is a fascinating thing to watch and study."

Record B—Sylvia

Age: 13. *School grade:* 7-B.

Health: Vitality excellent, has more energy and pep than any other girl in the troop, probably as much as any two put together.

[313]

Status in Group: A leader; the girls like her, yet despair over her disruption of any Scout meeting; out-of-doors they will follow Sylvia anywhere because she knows so many things to do and see.

Attitude Toward Whatever She Is Doing: Out-of-doors she makes suggestions and helps carry out plans, also follows suggestions well. Sylvia is a tomboy if ever there was one. Indoors she is uncomfortable and cannot settle down to quiet activities. Out-of-doors she is a grand person.

New Interests Acquired in Troop: Greater interest in trails, nature lore, and sports; none in sissy things.

Things of Importance to Her Right Now: Being able to climb a taller tree, throw harder paper wads more accurately, and have some excitement around her all the time, and to "beat the boys."

Attitude Toward the Influence of Leader: We are on friendly terms. Although she makes troop meetings exceedingly difficult sometimes, I like her very much and she seems to return the liking. On hikes she is usually with me, and once in a while we really have a good talk. She is always ready to help me in any way. Our big troubles are "these Scout meetings" and the "sissy" activities.

WHAT THE LEADER TRIED TO DO	SYLVIA'S RESPONSE
First Month	
First week: Talked to her about the noise and disturbance in troop; asked her to help keep order.	She really helped for half the meeting, but the rest of the time was as usual.
Second week: Had her help me teach some handicraft.	She showed ability but was restless and did not stick it out very well.
Third week: Had several girls visit my home, her among them, to talk over our troop difficulties, and make suggestions.	Sylvia contributed many valuable ideas to the discussion and really tried hard at the next meeting.
Fourth week: Sylvia was elected	At the next meeting she fairly

a patrol leader to help work out a new plan for the troop.

glowed, and asked me to come to her patrol and help her get started. She was suddenly dignified and serious, taking her responsibility seriously. The girls were all a bit surprised at Sylvia, but liked her as a leader.

Second Month

First week: We had a Court of Awards to which mothers were invited. Sylvia helped with one handicraft group.

Everything was fine at first. Then, when I had to leave the troop room to help the other group, she started the wildest disturbance. It all seemed no use, she was the same trouble maker again.

Second week: Last meeting discussed this at Court of Honor. Sylvia told on herself and was sorry. Would be a better leader the next time.

Was a good leader again. Peace reigned.

Third week: Different program introduced at troop meeting. Patrol leaders given more responsibility.

She helped greatly at this meeting, and we had the best order and accomplished more than we had for many months.

Fourth week: Sylvia's patrol was put on clean-up for the meeting.

The girls, under Sylvia's guidance, did a beautiful job of cleaning up the troop room, and Sylvia herself was a real leader and help.

Third Month

First week: Sylvia was given another chance to help with handicraft.

She did much better this time, and has real possibilities at this work. She is especially interested in making and learning to play a shepherd's pipe, so we will try that soon.

[315]

Second week: I asked her to help keep a discussion going when we had a speaker, and asked that she and the other patrol leaders be examples to their patrols.

Sylvia did very well at this meeting and was a real leader, asking intelligent questions and getting response from her patrol.

Third week: Sylvia was one of the Color guards for two meetings.

She did this task well, too, and has gained much dignity and poise.

Fourth week: She was absent because of illness.

Missed her first meeting, but had her patrol so well organized that they could go on very well in her absence.

Record C—Sylvia

"My Sylvia is twelve years and four months old, and is in the sixth grade, which is about where she should be in school. Her teacher tells me that she is in the upper third of her class. Her father and mother are divorced.

"Sylvia's health is quite good. She seems to have a lot of vitality, although she is very high-strung and nervous.

"Sylvia spends her weekends going with her mother, who has a rather questionable reputation in the community, to shows, dances, parties—staying out until the wee small hours of the morning. She has done this since she was old enough to walk, I guess.

"She is a rather attractive little girl, having very blond hair and a nice complexion. She is very conscious of her appearance, and is always fixed up. She has her hair done elaborately, or does it herself, and always wears some make-up and very bright fingernail polish. She seems to have lots of rather 'cute' clothes. She knows all the latest song hits and dance steps.

"Sylvia is accepted by some of the girls in the group but not by others. She would like very much to be a leader, but is very bossy, selfish, and irresponsible. Consequently, she has never been elected to an office in the group. She likes to be in the limelight, and often achieves this by having temper tantrums or acting silly.

"She always is ready to make suggestions, and worries about what other people are doing and how they are doing it. Her suggestions are seldom practical and not ones that the other girls are apt to support. She isn't very good about helping to carry out plans, even those she has had a share in making. She always forgets at the last minute and has to be reminded a number of times by the girls and myself. Her favorite comments to me are: 'Oh, Mrs. . . . . . ., I forgot all about it!' 'Nobody told me about it!' 'I didn't know anything about it!'

"This girl seems to enjoy a number of our activities, although she goes in more for fun, and will get out of the work if she can. She seems especially to enjoy the games and singing. She enjoyed our troop camp last year.

"I'm not too sure that I am on friendly enough terms to have much influence with her. I have talked with her a lot, and she has been to my home a number of times, since she lives in the same neighborhood. However, I have the feeling that, while she is nice to me to my face and seems to want to please me, she may not be that way behind my back. I have no proof of this, however, and I could be wrong about it. I have had several little run-ins with her about trouble she has made in troop meetings."

WHAT THE LEADER TRIED TO DO	SYLVIA'S RESPONSE

First Month

First week: Sylvia was very unruly in meeting—upset her patrol meeting by giggling and acting silly. After the patrol leader had tried to quiet her, without success, I stepped in and asked her in a nice way to please stop giggling, and tried to point out to her that she was spoiling the meeting with her foolishness.

Sylvia replied, "Oh, they're getting a kick out of it." However, some of the girls said with disgust, "We're not, either!"

I finally decided that she was enjoying the attention and would be better off if left alone. So I told the girls to try to go ahead with their meeting anyway.

Second week: Sylvia again was partly to blame for upsetting the patrol meeting. This time she and her cousin, who is in the same patrol, got into a quarrel. When I arrived on the scene, they both started tattling on one another. This made me a bit angry, since they are always doing that. I sent them both out of the room until they could behave themselves. After some time, I went out to tell them they might return if they were good.

I found Susie pouting but ready to go back. Sylvia was not in sight. I later found her in the girls' room in tears. She does love a scene! I tried to talk with her and reason with her, but she only cried harder and argued unreasonably. She said she would not go back to the meeting (wanted to be coaxed, I decided), so I decided the best thing for her to do was to go home, which I told her to do. She went sobbing home to her mother, who called me in on my way home from meeting.

The next two meetings I tried to be as pleasant as possible to Sylvia, and help and encourage her with her work.

I'm still having trouble with her forgetting.

[318]

She still continued to "act" until the patrol meeting was over.

I told Sylvia's mother what had happened and why I had sent her home. Sylvia was right there taking it all in, of course. I told her mother the same things I had told Sylvia about this quarreling over nothing. Sylvia braced up a little and seemed to listen to what I was saying. I was able to kid her into smiling before I left. She seemed to realize the trouble it had caused the other girls and me.

Sylvia really made an effort to be on good behavior and not make herself conspicuous by being silly or quarreling.

She seemed to realize she had caused work and worry for me and

the other girls. I don't know how long this will last.

Second Month

First week: Sylvia did not start any quarrels, but tried to "amuse" the patrol by sitting in the waste basket and pretending she could not get out. I heard the laughter, and, on going in to see what it was about, found her thus. I laughed it off, too, saying that maybe that was a good place for her to stay out of mischief.

She, of course, enjoyed the attention she got from this little act, but for once didn't go to such extremes that everyone got tired of her. They soon quieted down and went ahead with their meeting.

Second week: The girls had been taking turns teaching new games at each meeting. Sylvia asked to do this for the next meeting and was given *Games for Girl Scouts*. Later, in her patrol meeting, the girls got into an argument over program planning. During this Sylvia got quite indignant, and after the meeting handed her patrol leader the game book and said she wasn't coming to Scouts any more because they never did anything. The patrol leader came to me about it and was quite concerned. I told her not to say anything more to Sylvia and Sylvia would probably forget it, too.

Sylvia turned up at the next meeting as though nothing had ever happened. Nothing was said to her about it. She had apparently forgotten all about it, including the games—which were taken care of by someone else.

Third week: Sylvia's patrol's meeting went smoother, much to my relief, and I was able to give some attention to another patrol that needed my help.

Sylvia seemed to be cooperating with what was going on. At least, for once, I couldn't hear her arguing and "laying down the law" to the rest.

"Two things happened during the month outside of weekly meetings which were encouraging to me. One was Sylvia's vegetable garden. She asked me to stop and see it. I was very pleased with what she had done and told her so. She seemed very proud, and I am hoping she will keep up her interest all summer and earn her Home Gardener badge.

"The other was her part in the program we put on for the PTA meeting. Sylvia and another girl dressed in costume and sang 'The Keeper.' She was very interested in this, and worked hard on her costume. It went over very well and the audience seemed to enjoy it.

"I really believe Sylvia has some nice qualities if they can be brought out and encouraged, and her selfish, bossy traits discouraged. However, I feel rather helpless at this when I get unfavorable responses. Reading back over the past two months' report does give me a longer view, and helps me to see some encouraging signs in retrospect."

Chapter Eleven

Working With Your Community

You WILL FIND many people glad to help your troop in all sorts of ways. Just tell them what you need. The purpose of this chapter is to show you how the different groups in your community may enrich your troop program and at the same time give your girls an opportunity to demonstrate their ability as useful young citizens.

The material includes:

> *Suggestions on how to work with—*
> *Troop Committees.*
> *Sponsoring Groups.*
> *Parents.*
> *Program Consultants.*
> *The Girl Scout Council.*
> *Leaders' Associations or Clubs.*
> *Civic Organizations interested in Girl Scouting.*
> *Hints for selecting effective community service.*

YOU AND YOUR COMMUNITY are embarked on a cooperative enterprise when you take over a Girl Scout troop. You are giving your
time and energy to helping a group of girls develop into good citizens.
Your community is furnishing you with many things: a meeting
place, backing in your efforts, people with hobbies to share, facilities
that you may use. For, admirable as the mental and muscular powers
of Girl Scout leaders are, they still need help from their neighbors,
friends, troop committees, and local councils for the very simple reason
that they cannot possibly know all parts of the Girl Scout program
nor accomplish all the things the troop will be clamoring to do. Nor
should they try!

Aside from using community help as a means of sheer self-protec-
tion, the citizenship goal requires that every Girl Scout leader keep
her troop in contact with the community. Any leader who tries to
do everything herself, never uses the community's resources to enrich
the program, or does not set the stage for greater participation in
current community activities, just misses the whole point of citizenship
training.

Perhaps the last attitude a leader should take is that she is asking
a personal favor when asking for help with the troop. It is always a bit
surprising to find a leader acting like a parent with one lone child to
protect, since she is courageous enough to do a leadership job with
twenty to twenty-five children, all of whom usually belong to other
people. Unless you are convinced that a Girl Scout troop is a part of
the community and exists to help make the community a better place
to live in, you probably cannot convince other people. Judging from
what other leaders say, the best way to get help is to ask for it and let
the community know exactly what you need. It is just as simple and
direct as that. While there are many jobs to be done, they are not difficult ones and can be easily accomplished with joint effort.

The problem of recruiting help really breaks up into two parts: (1)
You must decide who is qualified to do what the troop needs. Almost
every individual in town could help you in some way if you were well
enough acquainted with each person's interests. (2) You or your girls
must approach your prospects in such a way that they will want to
say yes. This means that you must show each prospect how a specific

[323]

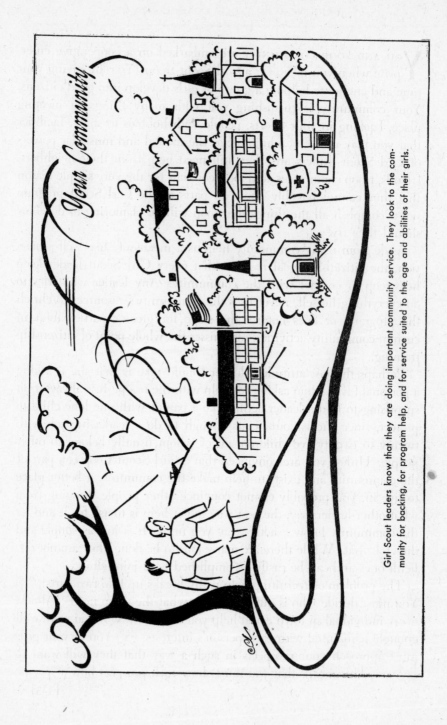

Your Community

Girl Scout leaders know that they are doing important community service. They look to the community for backing, for program help, and for service suited to the age and abilities of their girls.

experience with a Girl Scout troop would relate to other phases of her own everyday living. For instance, a Girl Scout mother would see that being an assistant leader or program consultant in your Girl Scout troop would help her understand her own daughter better and become acquainted with her daughter's friends. The law of readiness is easier. The interest here is strong and waiting. When people are ready they say yes immediately. An engineer whose hobby is geology is apt to be so pleased to find Girl Scouts interested in his hobby that he wants them to see a certain rock on Bear Mountain and takes them there to see it. A Girl Scout father who wants his daughter to go camping will work untiringly to get a troop camp established.

DEMOCRATIC COOPERATION IS THE KEYNOTE

Cooperation literally means working together, but the motives that cause people to work together vary all the way from force to love. Compulsion, compromise, exploitation, bargaining, leadership, and comradeship represent different levels of cooperation. All of us have experienced them at one time or another. They tell the story of man's upward struggle for control in terms of might to democracy based upon mutual respect and understanding. In our nation, and in Girl Scouting, we are continually aiming for cooperation of a democratic type.

Democratic cooperation means participation all along the line. There are three steps to be taken, whether it is in the Senate, the PTA, or the Girl Scout troop: (1) deciding what shall be attempted and how it shall be done; (2) putting the plan into effect; and (3) determining the success of what has been done so that mistakes need not be repeated. For instance, in Girl Scouting the troop committee members may help the troop plan a camping trip to a national park. They will (1) read and study about camping trips, plan for staff, menus, equipment, transportation, and dozens of other things in a very careful way; (2) carry out many of their plans alone; and (3) talk over their successes and failures afterward with the idea that "we will know more next year."

Working together in this way would mean participation all along the line. However, there may be some jobs that troop committee mem-

[325]

bers cannot do, so they ask others to share in carrying out their plans. The Boy Scouts may lend them tents, fathers may make arrangements with park authorities, the mothers may make out the menus with the girls and get the groceries together—all cooperating in a splendid way but actually carrying out the troop's plans. This is the type of cooperation involving action.

Some people are able to help a troop without much guidance from the leader, while others need to study their job a little before they get under full sail. Either way a leader has to believe in people's abilities and fit their work into the Girl Scout picture.

Whether your community is a small town or a neighborhood in a big city, there are many groups with whom you will want to work. They are taken up separately in the following pages. Only by a series of experiences in practicing cooperation will you eventually establish a cooperative feeling between your troop and the community. It is never attained by lip service or wishful thinking. Tell your troop committee members, nature lovers, outdoor hikers, garden club members, or civic groups specific ways in which they can assist. Bring them face to face with problems that can be solved only by their helping and working with the troop.

TROOP COMMITTEES

We cannot overemphasize the importance of a troop committee. Some leaders inherit a troop committee when they take over an established troop and have a group to depend on from the start. Some leaders are found by the troop committee that was organized preparatory to forming the troop. Other leaders start with their girls, because girls are there eagerly waiting, and then are confronted with getting the committee. In any case, the leaders are responsible for the troop program; the committee supplements and assists. It is a cooperative relationship rather than a supervisory one. If a new leader is chosen by a troop committee, it is reasonable to suppose that as she becomes acquainted with her troop she might suggest occasional new members.

[326]

GETTING A TROOP COMMITTEE TOGETHER

One leader tells us how she got her committee: "In my community I had a difficult time getting community backing. Girl Scouting was something new and people were a bit shy of it. No one wanted to serve on the troop committee. Finally I went to see the principal of the elementary school. She is a middle-aged lady who has been in the teaching business for years and recognizes the true value of things. She has a great deal of influence here, and, after I talked with her, she asked if she might be chairman of the committee. She gave as her reason for her interest this: that she has one nephew who had been a Boy Scout and two young nieces who are approaching Girl Scout age. She is very anxious to have a troop organized here and, because she is interested, others are!"

Another leader approached a civic club: "I inherited my troop without any troop committee. The grade school PTA had sponsored the troop in the beginning, but now that the girls are all in junior and senior high school, the PTA is sponsoring a younger troop. I went to a meeting of the Community Service Department of the Woman's Club. I told them how I needed their community help—the possible duties of a troop committee—the idea of Girl Scouting as I saw it— and the joy and privilege of learning to know twent-two lovely young girls in our community. I have a troop committee in the fullest sense of the meaning now."

Troop committee members are often chosen on the following bases:

They may represent a group of people interested in your particular girls, such as a Girl Scout father or mother; a person who is connected with the troop meeting place or the organization that is sponsoring your troop; a professional person who actively works with child education or welfare, such as a teacher, dean of girls, doctor, social worker, public health nurse, and so on.

They may be chosen because of their interest and ability in related Girl Scout program activities, such as camping, nature, crafts, music, troop budgets, transportation problems.

They may be chosen because of their loyalty and understanding of Girl Scouting that enables them to interpret the larger aims of the

[327]

organization and the activities of girls to parents and community. They can find concrete ways that the troop and other community groups can help each other.

What a Troop Committee Does

A few general things are listed below that troop committees might do to assist a troop. Some of them may remind you that you have a similar job to be done in your own troop. *No list is as good as the one you make up yourself, since all jobs to be done arise out of your very own troop for your very own troop committee.*

To assist the leaders the troop committee may:

Help to get assistant leaders, assistants for hikes and troop projects.

Provide a substitute for the leaders in case of absence.

Assist in acquiring helpful equipment.

Secure a suitable meeting place for the troop.

Assist with registration and record keeping.

Suggest attractive spots to which troop may hike.

Help and encourage leaders to take training.

Share the responsibility of overnight, weekend, and troop camping with the leaders.

Arrange for opportunities for community service and for other special activities.

Give encouragement to the leaders.

Help with making and balancing the troop budget.

Assist the Girl Scouts to earn money for special equipment, camp, and membership dues.

See that, if possible, every member of the troop has an opportunity to go to camp.

Interpret Girl Scouting to the community.

Interest the parents.

[328]

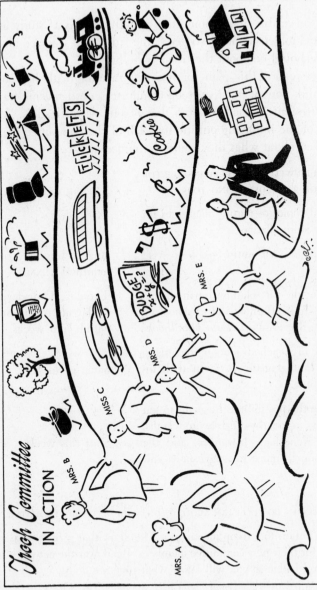

Troop Committee IN ACTION

MRS. B

MRS. A

MISS C

TICKETS

BUDGET x+y=?

MRS. D

Cookie

MRS. E

TROOP COMMITTEE MEMBERS assume various responsibilities.

MRS. A is the CHAIRMAN and sees that things get done. She takes over troop meetings occasionally, talks to parents, and helps in different ways. MRS. B (or it might be MR. B) helps with the outdoor program, troop camping, and hikes. MISS C is good at getting transportation and chaperonage for all kinds of troop expeditions. MRS. D keeps a kindly eye on the budget, understands figures, and takes care of money-raising activities. MRS. E finds persons and places to help with the troop program.

Launch a "Study and Work Program" for New Troop Committees

The most successful troop committees usually launch a "study and work program" to get members started. The study and work go along together and should be about the troop to be helped.

One leader reports this plan for her first meeting with her committee: "I think new or inactive troop committees need specific training not so different in method from that of our patrol leaders. We made copies of the following outline for each of the committee members and talked about what they could do immediately":

COULD YOU HELP WITH OR BE RESPONSIBLE FOR SOME OF THE FOLLOWING JOBS?	TIME TO BE DONE
1. Collect old copies of nature magazines for our nature study library.	By April 15.
2. Get permission for entire troop to visit . . . . Mills.	Any Thursday next month at 4 P.M.
3. Get instructor for Handywoman badge (six girls) four afternoons after school (4 to 6 P.M.). See the *Girl Scout Handbook*.	Tuesday, Thursday, or Friday afternoon. Start within four weeks.
4. Secure use of somebody's home for girls to practice Handywoman—to fit in with instructor's time.	Same as No. 3.
5. Investigate the possibilities for eight to ten girls going to nearby Girl Scout camps. Write to Kenosha, Milwaukee, and the national branch office for suggestions and camp folders.	Start this week.

THINGS YOU CAN DO TO LEARN ABOUT OUR TROOP AND GIRL SCOUTING

1. Accept invitation to a troop meeting on March 25 that girls are having especially for their new committee members. Read over the activities for the Minstrel badge so you will know what they are doing.
2. Read one story in *The American Girl,* an article in *The Girl Scout Leader,* and the first two chapters in the *Girl Scout Handbook.*

[330]

"This has worked well so far with my new committee. Everybody chose the job she thought she could do and has finished it. Several of them called me over the telephone to ask questions, but that was all the additional help I gave after the committee meeting. They are so pleased with themselves! I shall have another list next month before they have a chance to develop any idle habits."

In this plan, note especially:

1. The clear and definite information given about jobs to be done.

2. The short and simple jobs to be done. Is not the accumulation of so many small jobs, rather than the difficulty of one big job, the thing that "swamps you" as a leader much of the time? One or two of these jobs will require further follow-up and observation, such as summer camp and Handywoman badge.

3. The reading about Minstrel badge as preparation for a troop meeting, thereby increasing chances for new committee members to fit in and to be able to talk to girls about what they were doing.

4. The kind of publications and amount of reading of a general nature. *The American Girl* and *The Girl Scout Leader* articles and the *Girl Scout Handbook* are all stimulating and easily read. People new in Girl Scouting need to get some vision of what Girl Scouting can mean to girls in their town.

STRUCTURAL ORGANIZATION OF A TROOP COMMITTEE

NUMBER OF MEMBERS

Usually from three to five members. But if you need and can use more, then have more.

TERM OF OFFICE

Members are usually asked to serve for one year and are asked for a second year, if they are interested and are doing a good job. It is a wise plan to have some changes each year and to make it clear that appointments are annual. This saves difficulties and hurt feelings when it seems advisable to remove "dead wood," or when the needs of the troop have changed. The chairman may be either elected by the committee or appointed by the leader, or by a group interested in forming a troop. Her term of office should also be for one year, with a possibility for re-election or reappointment, if advisable.

MEMBERSHIP IN GIRL SCOUTING

The troop committee members pay the same national membership dues as the leader, and register with the troop.

NUMBER OF MEETINGS

Troop committee meetings may be monthly, sometimes oftener, sometimes less often. In general the frequency of meetings depends on the needs of the troop. For example, a troop committee that was helping the troop with a play or a weekend camping trip might meet weekly for several weeks preceding and immediately following the event and then not meet again for two or three months. Telephone calls or individual conferences often save an extra meeting. One meeting during the year should be designated as an "annual" meeting with a definite plan for reviewing the year's work. This meeting would be the appropriate time for terminating office and having new appointments or elections.

AGENDA FOR MEETINGS

Like any other meeting where business is to be transacted, better results are obtained if plans are made in advance and an order of business decided. The chairman of the committee and the troop leaders usually consult together in drawing up an agenda. The meeting may be very informal, but since its purpose is to get something done or decided upon, it is well to have a form to follow.

SPONSORING GROUPS

Many organizations in a community are interested in sponsoring a proved youth program such as Girl Scouting. Churches, men's service clubs, women's clubs, American Legion Auxiliaries, Parent-Teacher

Associations, and the Junior League, for instance, are all interested in the welfare of young people. We have a popular and up-to-date program for girls to offer them, and they have much to offer us. As troop sponsors they can be of invaluable assistance to you and your troop committee. They may help provide meeting places, equipment, financial aid, assistant leaders or program consultants, camping opportunities, community prestige, and community service projects. The Girl Scouts in return express their appreciation and sense of responsibility by offering to be of service when possible, by taking good care of any facilities offered, by thanking persons who have assisted the troop in any way.

When an organization is interested in sponsoring a troop, it must first get in touch with the local council, if there is one, in order to acquaint itself with Girl Scout objectives and ways in which the troop can be served best.

RELATION TO TROOP COMMITTEE

If a troop is sponsored by any organization, one of two things happens in relation to the troop committee.

1. One member of the sponsoring group should serve on the troop committee in order to keep in touch with the needs of the troop and ways in which the sponsoring organization could assist. This happens most often where a men's club or civic group is acting as sponsor.

2. The troop committee may be composed entirely of members of the sponsoring organization. It has a special responsibility for seeing that objectives of Girl Scouting and of the sponsoring organization are in accord with each other and maintained with mutual satisfaction. This happens most often when a church or PTA acts as sponsor.

The sponsoring group does not assume authority in directing troop activities, but cooperates with the leader and troop committee in helping to carry on a more successful troop program.

PARENTS

Parents are a group with whom every leader will want to have active cooperation. To begin with, unless parents understand something

[333]

about Girl Scouting and what your troop is trying to do, they may not encourage their daughters in regular attendance at meetings, prompt payment of dues, getting uniforms or other equipment. They may not give daughter a chance to practice some of her Girl Scout skills, or be understanding about her attempts to be of service at home, or even lend a sympathetic ear to troop affairs. Even if they are wholeheartedly with you in spirit, you may often need specific and concrete assistance from them.

The best way to secure parental understanding is to become acquainted with them as rapidly as you can. Meeting with the parents before you start a troop, or during the first months, is always a wise plan. The parent consent blank is a good first contact. Inviting parents to troop occasions, such as an investiture, Court of Awards, mother-daughter teas, father-daughter banquets, has been suggested earlier as part of troop program planning. Undoubtedly you will have some parents on your troop committee, and they serve as a link with other parents.

Believing that participation makes for active cooperation, many leaders have used the following check sheet, which is given out at a parents' meeting and collected at the door, so that everyone has a chance to "sign on the dotted line" before going home. Vary this to suit your own situation.

Ways that Parents Can Help Girl Scout Troops

. . . . . 1. Lend kitchen, living room, back yard, attic, or basement for an occasional troop meeting or to store troop equipment.

. . . . . 2. Provide chaperonage or transportation or both for a picnic or excursion.

. . . . . 3. Provide hospitality for troop (simple food and something to do) once or twice during the year if the leader has a sudden emergency.

. . . . . 4. Provide "telephone help."

. . . . . 5. Become "headquarters" and take over all responsibility for a troop's share of a cookie sale or other money-raising device.

. . . . . 6. Provide a "market" for the things that the girls would like to sell.

.....7. Help get all members of a troop in uniform.

.....8. Collect for the troop such materials as tin cans, bits of wood, cloth, paper, pictures to cut out, felt hats, candle ends, scraps of yarn.

.....9. Help leader with records, registration procedures, shopping for supplies.

....10. Share a hobby with leader or girls.

....11. Help with a party for mothers to talk over the ways they might help.

....12. Know what Girl Scouting stands for and help to interpret it.

....13. Consider giving Girl Scout equipment for Christmas or birthday presents.

....14. Be willing to provide simple refreshments for an occasional troop meeting.

....15. Help more girls have a camp experience.

....16. Assist in a Girl Scout troop.

....17. Be a member of the troop committee or become an associate member of the organization by paying the annual membership dues.

                                    Date.................

Name ....

Address ....

.... *Telephone* ....

Cooperation works both ways of course. So, in planning with your troop take care not to make life more difficult for the parents. For example, remember to get parents' consent for hikes or special expeditions away from the troop meeting place. Do not plan for meetings or parties on week nights unless you are sure the parents approve and make quite certain their daughters get home when expected. Be careful about not conflicting with school work, school events, or other

[335]

responsibilities such as music lessons. If your girls have home duties on Saturday mornings, take this into consideration in deciding on what time to meet for the hike. Remember, parents are trying to develop character and successful young citizens too, and expect you to co-operate with home, church, and school.

PROGRAM CONSULTANTS

Program consultant is the name given to a man or woman who is willing to share his or her interests and special program abilities with young people. They are to be found at large in every community, and ways of finding them are discussed a little later. You might first like to know how and when to use them effectively. Not everyone who comes to your meetings to help you occasionally needs to be given this title. In general it refers to the persons who are willing to set aside enough of their time to help your girls with badge projects, or who are available to leaders for informal training and conferences in a special subject. As a troop program develops, or as girls grow older, consultants become of increasing importance to leaders.

In using program consultants, the leader keeps right on watching her girls for growth in self-reliance, for cooperative effort, and for the development of individual interests. The consultant is often more concerned with the program material, good standards of workmanship, and demonstrated skill. Hence the leader and consultant should work together on planning and carrying out any program.

How to Know When a Program Consultant Is Needed

Maybe you as a leader have been uncertain about when to turn to a program consultant. We have all known groups of girls who loudly expressed great enthusiasm for something, but whose interest petered out as they went to work on it. That is disappointing and discourteous to the consultants who are helping you. Do not blame your girls for not knowing their own minds, or discipline them by making them go on regardless. Such misfortunes will not happen if you have taken time beforehand to explore the subject sufficiently. The passing fancy has a real place in every troop program also; for the Girl Scout troop is an ideal place to experiment, to sample, and to reject. It is probably

Fathers and older brothers make fine program consultants.

one of the subtlest skills in group leadership to know which fancies should pass and which ones should be caught and coaxed into abiding interests.

There are three good signposts to help you know when it is time to call for outside assistance.

The first is when you feel you have taken your girls as far as you can in a subject in which they are interested. This may be when you have reached the limit of your troop resources and equipment, or when groups of girls are at different stages, and it is impossible for you and your assistant to be in three places at once.

The second sign is when you feel the interest in the subject is deep enough to warrant the attention of a specialist and the contribution that can be made by an outside person. Often older girls need this form of community contact to help them discover permanent avocations, or even vocations.

[337]

A third sign is when you feel it beyond your ability to set the stage or to acquire the skill necessary to getting off to a good start. This might be especially true where health, safety, or special techniques are involved. Winter sports, first aid, and campcraft, for instance, are subjects where expert assistance would be advisable from the beginning.

Whatever sign tells you it is time for a program consultant, your next step is to consider the three main ways of using one and decide on the right way for your troop.

The Leader Goes to the Program Consultant

We have already said that it is a wise plan for you to guide and develop as much of the troop program as you can, and here is an opportunity for you to get advice on your plans and hints on source material and equipment. You may take a course from a program consultant and have the fun of learning for yourself; or you may get the help you need through individual conferences, leaders' association meetings, or even over the telephone. Thus you gain confidence to go ahead with the troop plans and have backing from an expert.

Whenever practical and possible, this method of going to the consultant is a fine way for leaders to develop their leadership ability and enrich their troop program. If a troop is planning to major in outdoor activities, for example, it is a wise leader who fortifies herself with additional knowledge about first aid or nature or trail cookery.

The Program Consultant Comes to the Troop

Having the consultant come to the troop is a very common practice. It has many advantages and some dangers, unless carefully watched. The advantages are those of a fresh point of view and the stimulation provided by greater information on a given subject. If the troop has been prepared for this special help, this plan makes possible more rapid progression in skill; it helps the leader who has girls with diversified needs, if she can turn one group over to someone who can develop their interest to a high point of satisfaction. The dangers lie in letting a troop program get broken into unrelated pieces, in letting the activity become more important than what is happening to individual girls, and in the possible breakdown of the leader's relationship with those girls. The dangers may be avoided if the leader and consultant plan together, ahead of time, and discuss after each meeting what happened in terms of girls' attitudes and program skills. *Do not ever* turn over your troop, or any girls within your troop, to a consultant without making sure she knows something about Girl Scouting, something about your general troop program, and something about the abilities and background of your particular girls.

The Girls Go to the Program Consultant

There are times when having the girls go to the consultant appears the sensible thing to do, and under certain circumstances it is. But take care that this plan does not drop into the realm of having girls go to unrelated classes just to gather information. In no time at all this can destroy the unity of the troop program, and may remove the girl from the guidance she deserves to have.

Swimmers and life savers must go to the pool or waterfront for their instructions; nature enthusiasts go on bird walks and into their outdoor laboratory; girls interested in the cultural arts often go to studios, museums, workshops, where the needed material is at hand. If you are going to use this plan, make doubly sure the consultant knows Girl Scouting and your girls. Perhaps she would appreciate some help in understanding our Girl Scout method of doing things. Visit the group if you can; at troop meetings ask for reports of progress; and have part of the information gained used in connection with troop programs.

Where to Find a Consultant

All of the foregoing statements rather assume that a leader has only to indicate a need and a consultant is at hand! We know this is often not the case, but neither should it be difficult to get one. A troop committee member often acts as program consultant or can locate men and women in the community who would be glad to share their enthusiasms. A leader may know someone amongst her friends and acquaintances who could give her just the help she needs. This is a very pleasant and profitable way to introduce one's friends to the importance of Girl Scouting. If you are working under a council, get in touch with the program committee, since it is interested in having a complete list of active program consultants. Many program committees give special help to consultants in the form of a letter, mimeographed material, or informal interviews. This help enables the consultants to understand Girl Scouting, the local ways of work for maintaining program standards, and available community resources that might be new to them. If neither you nor your troop committee are able to locate a consultant in a special field, the council program committee should be able to help you very quickly. It is part of its job to be familiar with all the local program resources. It can suggest to you either persons or places where you and your girls could go for help, or it will put you in touch with a program consultant who might come to your troop meetings.

Ask someone who has lived in another country to share her knowledge and interests with your girls.

How Some Leaders Have Used Consultants

In the following four examples note what the various leaders did to make their experience with program consultants successful.

1. "Both my assistant and I need help with singing and dancing. My assistant is fine at all homemaking activities, and I like the games and outdoor things. But we have a great many girls of foreign parentage who sing beautifully and who love to dance. Finally I persuaded a friend of mine who is much interested in music and folk dancing to help us out. She was scared to death, since she claimed she knew nothing about how to manage twelve- to fourteen-year-old girls. We worked out the meetings quite carefully in advance so she knew just what was expected of her, and I discussed the fifth Girl Scout Law in detail with the troop before she came. The girls were enchanted with her and she felt at ease with them because they responded so spontaneously to what she knew. After earning the Minstrel and Folk Dancer badges the girls' manners and ability to cooperate as a group have improved so much we are about to branch out into ballroom dancing and boy-girl parties."

2. "One day I was going up to the city on a bus and met an old acquaintance whom I had not seen for several years. I found that she was now a widow and to occupy her time had been studying astronomy. This woman had been a teacher for many years. I could see from our conversation that she would be glad to have something to do, so I impulsively asked her to come to troop meeting and tell us about some of her studies. She replied that she knew too little, but when I told her the group was made up of ten- and eleven-year-old girls who knew nothing about her subject, she thought it over. A few days later she wrote that she would come. In the meantime, I asked the girls if they would like to hear her. They seemed eager, so arrangements were made and she came. I sent her a list of the simplest requirements in the Star badge so she would have some idea of what would be interesting and helpful to the group. The girls loved it and are eager for her second visit. She wrote and asked the troop to come to her home and bring our suppers when the weather permits. From her home we can go on a hike up the mountain, and I assure you we can hardly wait."

[341]

3. "One mother would love to teach handicraft, but preferred to have the girls come to her house where she could keep an eye on Jackie. At meetings, we work on the badge activities as a troop. This makes a varied and elastic program because we may be doing dramatics, playing games, singing, folk dancing, or taking a short hike.

"The girls who wish crafts go to Mrs. S's house each Tuesday after school and work for an hour or so. This helps us with our group work and helps Mrs. S. get acquainted with the girls. I am properly enthusiastic when the girls rush into the library on their way home to show me their work."

4. "At the beginning of the winter we had the game warden speak on winter birds. He brought a feeding station that he had made from an orange crate in three minutes. He showed pictures of birds that stay during the winter and told stories about them . . . He came to our troop camp and brought two conservationists with him . . . He has since helped with various troop activities and is going to help us with a tree project this spring."

THE GIRL SCOUT COUNCIL

In most communities where Girl Scouting has been established, the troops have the backing of a council composed of men and women interested in the welfare of young people. There are two forms of council structure. One form is called a traditional council. Persons serving on the council represent the social, religious, educational, business, and civic points of view of the community as well as various geographical areas.

The other form is called an association council. It is composed of all the adult registered members of the Girl Scout organization in the community. This entire group elects a board of directors that administers the work of the council. It is important that you as a leader attend the association meetings because your point of view and vote are needed.

The concern of the council is to keep the wheels of Girl Scouting turning through such activities as organizing troops; selecting, placing, and training adult volunteer workers; maintaining program standards in troops; carrying on a publicity and public relations program;

financing the local work; and cooperating with the community all along the line.

Where there are a good many troops in a community and the administrative work is heavy, a central office or headquarters is usually established where you may turn for help. There may be one or more professional workers who assist the council in its work, and help the leaders directly through training, troop visits, and informal conferences.

The council's work has many aspects, all of which help the leader directly or indirectly. The various parts of their work that relate most directly to troops are described briefly so that you may see your job in relationship to theirs, and ways in which you may cooperate. Each part may be handled by one or two persons or by a committee, depending on the size of the city and the complexity of the job. There are councils that cover one city only, and those that bring together a number of towns, cities, and even counties.

The Troop Organization Job

Those concerned with troop organization have the task of forming new troops, helping old troops to keep running, selecting and placing new leaders, making initial contacts with affiliated groups, finding meeting places for troops, and getting troops to reregister on time.

The Program Job

The program job is concerned with maintaining program standards and policies, enriching the program for the troop leaders of the community, relating the program to local conditions, finding suitable community service activities, making program consultants available to leaders, maintaining a year-round program on three age levels, and setting up program centers for special city-wide activities, summer and winter.

Girl planning boards and girl participation in local and national affairs fall under the supervision of those concerned with this program job.

[343]

THE CAMP JOB

Those concerned with the camping job have the task of offering a year-round camping experience to girls of all ages. They are responsible for all types of camping: established camping (where girls from many troops live for two weeks or more under the leadership of a resident staff); day camping (where girls from many troops spend a day at camp, returning to their homes at night); troop camping (where a single group of girls and their own leaders go to continue their activities in a camp for a weekend or longer); and trip camping (in which experienced older groups travel and camp in a different spot each night). They are also concerned with maintaining standards of health and safety and administering a camp program consistent with the goals and methods of Girl Scouting. Where there is an established camp or camping cabin for troop camping, these persons are responsible for the physical property and for maintaining the site at a high point of efficiency.

THE TRAINING JOB

Those concerned with training have the task of making plans that insure the training of each volunteer leader, council, and committee member—training that is designed to help her do her Girl Scout job. This training is given before and after going on the job in various ways: through training courses, round tables, informal education groups, in regional and national conferences, through supervision, self-training, apprenticeship, and publications.

THE FINANCE JOB

Those concerned with financing the local Girl Scout work have the task of: analyzing the needs of the organization; analyzing the needs and financial resources of the community; making out the budget for the year; appealing for funds to the community, either through the community chest or independently; spending the money wisely and in compliance with the budget; accounting for income and expense at appropriate intervals; giving advice to troops on troop budgets and money-raising projects.

[344]

THE PUBLIC RELATIONS JOB

Those concerned with publicity and public relations help leaders, girls, and committee members to be aware of the public relations aspects of everything they do. With the cooperation of all members of the organization, they carry out a publicity program to maintain public confidence in the value of Girl Scouting and to win support for the extension of Girl Scouting. The public relations committee uses newspapers, magazines, movies, radio, exhibits, speeches, and all other contacts with the public to accomplish this.

LEADERS' CLUBS

In a community with a number of troops, there are occasional meetings for all leaders in order to get acquainted, to discuss successful practices, common problems, and to arrange for training. These meetings are most often planned by a leaders' club, composed of all the leaders and assistant leaders in the community. Sometimes there are regular monthly meetings, sometimes quarterly, sometimes only as a need arises. Find out when these meetings are held in your community or neighborhood, and go whenever possible. A new leader gets great stimulation from talking with other leaders, definite help from their discussions, and practical advice on troop problems. Many leaders like to visit other troops once in a while, or offer each other a helping hand, and these appointments can be made at leaders' meetings. Often community-wide or inter-troop activities that will be of tremendous interest to your troop are planned at these meetings.

In traditional councils, the leaders' point of view, so necessary to council planning, can be obtained: (1) by cooperation of the commissioner and the president of the leaders' club; (2) by asking persons with recent leadership experience to serve on the council or on council committees. In an association council, leaders are official members of the council and have a direct share in making policies and plans.

[345]

OTHER GROUPS IN THE COMMUNITY

One of our national policies is that the Girl Scout organization co-operates with educational and other groups whose ideals and procedures are in accord with its own. There are certain organizations that are especially close to the life of a Girl Scout troop.

THE SCHOOLS

Girl Scouting has always cooperated with the schools, since the school programs and troop programs supplement each other for the common good of the girl. Troop furnish a medium through which things learned in school can be practiced or used in connection with community service. Schools furnish us with meetings places, volunteers to help with program, opportunities to promote and practice Girl Scouting. They lend equipment, include Girl Scout publications in the library, and serve as Girl Scout sponsors. They recognize in our movement an educational agency of real value. Girl Scouts in turn can serve the schools by volunteering promptly when teachers ask for help with a job; by taking care of school property; by assisting with younger children in the building and on the playground; by taking over special responsibilities, such as Color guard, messenger service; by serving in lunchroom and cafeteria. It is an excellent plan for the leader to work with some designated member of the school faculty who could suggest or open up all the program and guidance resources of the school that the leader might use.

The Parent-Teacher Associations are especially helpful in working out a joint relationship with home, schools, and Girl Scouting.

CHURCHES AND SYNAGOGUES

Since the first part of the Girl Scout Promise indicates a girl's desire to do her duty to God, the religious affiliation of our individual girls, or of the group as a whole, is of concern to us. The church or synagogue is responsible for the religious education of its Girl Scouts and each girl is encouraged to be a better member of her own religious group as part of her Girl Scouting.

All religious groups—Catholic, Protestant, and Jewish—have been

[346]

very generous in sponsoring Girl Scouting. They provide leadership, meeting places, and help us win the confidence of the community. As leaders of Girl Scout troops, we should avoid planning activities that conflict with religious activities or services to which girls should go. If a troop meets in a church or synagogue, the leader should find ways in which the troop may be of service either in caring for the property or by assisting in functions. If girls of another denomination wish to join a church or synagogue troop, they must have the written consent of their parents. On weekend hikes or camping trips arrangements must include an opportunity for each girl to attend the religious services of her own faith.

PUBLIC LIBRARIES

Libraries are always cooperative with Girl Scout leaders and are a great source of help. By all means, visit your public library, talk to the librarian, and give her some idea about what your girls need. Ask her help in developing a good reading program or advice on ways in which your girls could be of service. Librarians suggest book lists, arrange a Girl Scout reading shelf, obtain program books that you and your girls need, arrange exhibits, lend books for a camp library. You will notice throughout the badge activities the suggestion that girls consult the local librarian for resource material to help them meet the badge requirements.

It is almost impossible to keep an up-to-date reading list in the basic handbooks for each badge or field of interest. Good new books on a given subject come out every year or so, others go out of print. Often one library has an excellent book on a subject, while another library has a different book that is equally good. Nature books vary according to the section of the country. Different troops and individuals have special needs, so one general reading list is seldom satisfactory for everyone.

If your library does not have up-to-date copies of the basic Girl Scout books, perhaps your council or your leaders' club would give it some copies so that all girls in your community might benefit.

In smaller towns where there is no public library, get in touch with the state library extension service for help or advice. Address

[347]

your letter to the State Library Service in care of your State Department of Education. Explain your needs and inquire what help could be available for your girls in your community.

OTHER CIVIC ORGANIZATIONS

Many other civic organizations in the community help us with our program, such as the American Red Cross, the police and fire departments, museums, hospitals, and public health services.

These organizations furnish us with program consultants, or an occasional visitor to our troop. They provide us with places where girls may learn or practice parts of their badge work, because of their facilities or equipment. Girls in turn give service to these organizations as needed. They might sew for the Red Cross, cooperate with protection rules of the fire and police departments, provide scrapbooks, games, or flowers for the hospitals, prepare material needed by public health nurses, assist in museums with any tasks suited to their age and ability.

STANDARDS FOR EFFECTIVE COMMUNITY SERVICE

Since every troop does some form of community service, a leader will need to check any proposed project against the national and local policies set up for the protection of every girl. The following points will help you judge the value or wisdom of any service project.

1. It should have value in terms of character development and citizenship training. Girls should have some share in choosing, planning, and evaluating the service they want to give. They should go prepared to serve intelligently.

2. The girl should understand her particular task in relation to the total piece of service; i.e., when a girl stuffs envelopes or helps with a routine office job, she should understand the service that organization is giving the community and why her share helps its work. She should feel approval of her effort and a sense that her service is significant enough to make her want to do it again.

3. Parents' consent should be obtained for all service that is given outside the troop meeting.

[348]

4. The service should be non-remunerative, non-political, and non-commercial.

Service to one's community is part of Girl Scouting. It is not paid for. It should not be used for political purposes or for the benefit of any commercial enterprise.

Service should not be confused with legitimate money-raising projects. For example, a girl gives service by taking care of a neighbor's child for a few hours, freeing that neighbor to attend a civic meeting or to do an adult piece of community work. If qualified Girl Scouts take care of neighbors' children for remuneration, when the neighbor wishes to make this arrangement in order to have more free time for her own affairs, it is not Girl Scout service. It is a private arrangement between the neighbor, the Girl Scout, and her parents.

5. Service projects involving money raising by Girl Scouts should be carefully checked with the finance committee of the council or with the lone troop committee, to make sure that they conform to local regulations and to the national Girl Scout policies.

6. Interference with school or home duties should be avoided.

7. The service should be under the supervision of some adult in Girl Scouting or some designated person in the agency, experienced in working with girls.

8. The environment in which the girls are placed should be in no way detrimental to the health, safety, and moral development of the girl.

Neighborhoods, especially in large cities, should be known to the leader as ones suitable for girls to be in. Overfatigue, strain from large public gatherings, or long hours must be guarded against, especially with younger girls.

9. The service should represent the kind of public relations that is in keeping with the dignity of the Girl Scout organization. Any publicity that might be harmful to the girl by exaggerating her importance or making her unduly conspicuous as an individual should·be avoided.

10. Girls should wear uniforms whenever possible.

Chapter Twelve

Your National Organization

ITS HISTORY AND PRESENT SERVICES
TO ITS MEMBERSHIP

You WILL KNOW by the time you have reached this chapter that you are a part of a great movement that reaches into every corner of the world. Scouting is carried on by public spirited citizens who care deeply about the welfare and happiness of young people. When you have read this chapter you will have gained a better understanding of Girl Scouting and your relation to it in this country.

The material includes:

The development of Girl Scouting.
The national organization.
Services to local groups.
National policies every leader should know.

Don't Miss This!

HISTORY OF GIRL SCOUTING

THE EARLY HISTORY of Girl Scouting under the guidance of Lord Robert Baden-Powell of England, Founder of the whole Scouting movement, and Mrs. Juliette Low, who introduced Girl Scouting to this country in 1912, would make a book in itself. Most of it is delightfully told in the book called *Juliette Low and the Girl Scouts.**

The history of our growth in the United States is a tribute to the vision of the American women who gave so generously of their time to serve American girlhood. From the very beginning the Founder of this new movement realized that while the essential spirit and purpose of Scouting had great appeal for all youth, each country had to adapt the program to its own needs and that boys and girls should have different programs and separate organizations, even while sharing similar aims and enjoying some of the same activities. For that reason, when the girls in England tried to copy their brothers, after the publication of *Scouting for Boys* in 1908, Lord Baden-Powell enlisted the aid of his sister Miss Agnes Baden-Powell and other English women to launch the plan for Girl Guides—a program based on Scouting ideals but developed especially for girls. He said, "The girls are the important people, because when the mothers of the nation are good citizens and women of character, they will see to it that their sons are not deficient in these points. As things are, the training is needed for both sexes, and is imparted through the Boy Scout and Girl Guide movements. The principles are the same for both. It is only in the details that they vary."

From the beginning Lord Baden-Powell proclaimed the purpose of the Scouting movement as a way of developing an individual into an efficient, healthy, and happy citizen. In his book *Scoutmastership* he gave an interesting definition of what Scouting is and is not.

WHAT SCOUTING IS

"It is a game in which elder brothers (or sisters) can give their younger brothers healthy environment and encourage them to healthy activities such as will help them to develop *citizenship.*

---

* See Girl Scout *Publications Catalog.*

[351]

Three Great Leaders

Lord Robert Baden-Powell, Founder and Chief Scout of World Scouting; Lady Baden-Powell, Chief Guide of the World Association of Girl Guides and Girl Scouts; and Mrs. Juliette Low, Founder of Girl Scouting in the United States of America. This picture was taken in the United States in 1919.

"Its strongest appeal is through Nature Study and Woodcraft. It deals with the individual, not with the Company. It raises the intellectual as well as purely physical or purely moral qualities.

"Happy citizenship developed through the impulse from within rather than through impression from without, individual efficiency encouraged and then harnessed for the good of the community—that is our scheme."

WHAT SCOUTING IS NOT

"It is not a charity organization for people in society to run for the benefit of the poor children.

[352]

"It is not a school having a definite curriculum and standards of examination.

"It is not a brigade of officers and privates for drilling manliness into boys and girls.

"It is not a messenger agency for the convenience of the public.

"It is not a show where surface results are gained through payment in merit badges, medals, and so forth.

"These all come from without, whereas the Scout training all comes from within."

GIRL SCOUTING IN THE UNITED STATES

Juliette Low, who spent many years in England, was a friend of Lord Baden-Powell and through him became acquainted with Scouting and Guiding. When she started her troop in Savannah, Georgia, she first used the handbook for Girl Guides. Juliette Low's adaptation of this book for American girls was published in 1913 and was called *How Girls Can Help Their Country*. The name "Guide" had been chosen for the British girls because of a famous corps of guides in India, distinguished for their handiness, resourcefulness, and courage. This name did not have the same significance for American girls for whom the word "scout" meant adventure, resourcefulness, and all the hardy virtues associated with our pioneer forebears. Therefore, in the United States, as in some other countries, it was decided that the term "Girl Scouts" was more appropriate than "Girl Guides."

From these early days Girl Scouting in this country has grown and flourished and been guided by women interested in developing the best possible program for American girls, based on the fundamental Scouting ideals. Other countries that are now members of the World Association of Girl Guides and Girl Scouts have also adapted and developed their own programs for girls, all based on the same ethical code.

A good chronological history of our development can be found in *Citizens in Action** and need not be repeated here. But there are certain aspects of our growth from the first troop in Savannah to over a

---

* See Girl Scout *Publications Catalog.*

million girls in every state, territory, and island belonging to the United States that would be of special interest to leaders.

In the United States, as in England, the times were right for movements such as Scouting. Much of the home activity that bound families together in cooperative enterprises had become a thing of the past. Frontier days were over. Girls no longer needed to learn skills such as spinning, weaving, or baking. The workshop was taken from the home into the community, and the factories, which took the men of the family to work all day, now made the necessities for family use. Moreover, families were concentrating in large industrial areas rather than in farming communities, and healthy exercise in the open air no longer was part of the day's work. Yet more than ever, in the increasing complexity of American life, youth needed pioneer courage and initiative and ability to work with others.

Encouraged by this transfer of industry from the home, women found new and wider outlets for their abilities. These opportunities demanded special training, and organizations particularly appropriate for girls of that day began to supplement home, church, and school.

Juliette Low and Lord Baden-Powell were colorful figures with a program capable of reaching an as yet unarticulated need. With her many friends all over the country, her enthusiasm, and her organizing power, Juliette Low was an ideal person to launch Girl Scouting in the United States. The idea spread from person to person as individuals became aware of a need for organized program for American girls and began to form troops in their own communities or to work with sponsoring groups.

The organization, incorporated as Girl Scouts in 1915, has had a rapidly increasing part to play in American life, since the last quarter century has intensified the conditions that furthered its growth. In the Articles of Incorporation there is a statement about our purpose and program that has guided us through the years.

The first meeting place of American Girl Scouts was the stable on the grounds of Mrs. Low's home in Savannah, Georgia. The Founder later willed this building to the Girl Scouts, and it now contains the Juliette Low Memorial Museum.

"The purpose of this organization is to help girls realize the ideals of womanhood as a preparation for their responsibilities in the home and as active citizens in the community and in the world. In the realization of this purpose, the corporation shall be the directing and coordinating head of the Girl Scout movement in the United States, its dependencies and possessions, and shall fix and maintain standards for the movement that will inspire girls with the highest ideals of character, conduct, and attainment.

"The program of the Girl Scout movement is open to all girls. It shall be built on educational lines, giving girls an experience in making and carrying out plans based on broad fields of interests. It shall encourage a love of outdoor life and a practical knowledge of health. The activities shall aim through comradeship to develop initiative, self-control, self-reliance, and unselfish service to others."

There has been development in the aims as well as the size of the organization. While changes in the program were made from time to time during the early days, it was felt that as the demand for Girl Scouting grew we had an obligation to analyze the effectiveness of our program as a means of character development. A program study, conducted by an impartial group of scientists and educators, was begun in 1935 and finished in 1936. The philosophy, the activities, methods, group relationships, and all other aspects of our organization were carefully analyzed in relation to the needs of modern girls and modern communities. The following words from the introduction of the study report were heartening—"To the members of the movement throughout the United States we are extremely grateful for the way in which they have cooperated with us. . . . We wish to go on record as saying that the movement is going in the right direction and is doing a really significant piece of work." Since the study substantiated the belief of the movement in the principles and philosophy of its Founder, the recommendations arising out of the study had to do in general with greater flexibility in the program and greater attention given to the present-day interests of girls.

In 1937 the new Brownie Scout program for girls seven to ten was launched. This same year saw our Silver Jubilee celebrating twenty-five years of Girl Scouting in the United States. In 1938 a revised rank and badge program, judged most suitable for girls ten to four-teen was published. This is now known as the Intermediate program and is to be found in the *Girl Scout Handbook*. The Senior Girl Scout program, developed especially for high school girls, was launched in this same year, which also saw our membership take a large annual growth and pass the half-million mark.

World War II found the organization ready and prepared to give service to the nation. Service Bureaus had been established all over the country prior to our entry into the war.

Girl Scouts of every age served on the home front and in the com-munity. Adults and girls became Volunteers for Victory, from the smallest Brownie doing her bit at home and in her troop to the many Girl Scout leaders whose service to youth took on an added significance.

Since the end of the war, we have felt more deeply than ever our responsibility for promoting international and intercultural understand-ing. We want young people from different racial, religious, and economic groups to know and appreciate one another. Joint activities within a community have brought together girls of different back-grounds. International camps, conferences, service projects, and letters have promoted world friendship.

Other important developments have been the use of girl planning boards in many communities and girls discussing with adults, both locally and nationally, affairs of common interest and concern. New ways of taking girls into partnership when planning local and national activities broaden our basic ideal that leaders and girls plan program together. This is part of training for citizenship.

A look into the future clearly indicates that our girls must be given more experience in working with many kinds of people on broader issues if they are to learn to think in terms of one interde-pendent world.

THE NATIONAL GIRL SCOUT ORGANIZATION

Undoubtedly Mrs. Low thought of Girl Scouting as a national or-ganization when she organized her first troop in 1912, and certainly when she established the first National Headquarters in Washington

[357]

in 1913. Legally, however, Girl Scouts came into being when incorporated in 1915 and the National Council held its first annual convention. Now every two years councils in different parts of the United States send their elected delegates to a convention. When these delegates and a few other persons elected by the National Council itself are assembled in meeting, they constitute what is known as the National Council of Girl Scouts of the United States of America. Important policies are made by the National Council at its convention, a Board of Directors is elected, and the general lines of emphasis to be followed in the two years between its meetings are decided upon.

Reasons for Having a National Organization

The existence of a national organization brings many benefits to local groups. Some benefits are tangible and easily recognized, others are intangible but nonetheless real. In the first place, a local group gains prestige and standing by being a part of a national organization whose reputation for high standards of work and quality in its program is well known. Local people are attracted to the Girl Scout organization because the value of its program is known throughout the country. The very words "Girl Scout" bring with them community confidence and good will, and the community accepts Girl Scouting because its name, its standards, and its prestige are well established on a nation-wide basis.

In the second place, every national organization is in a position to do for its local groups many things that they cannot do for themselves. Cumulative experience of countless Girl Scouts throughout the country is pooled by the national body, which can then evaluate, advise, and suggest solutions that local groups could reach only after years of trial and error.

Services to Local Groups

What are the national services about which one hears so much? Some of the more obvious ones come to mind immediately: the books

[358]

How the National Organization Carries Out Its Work

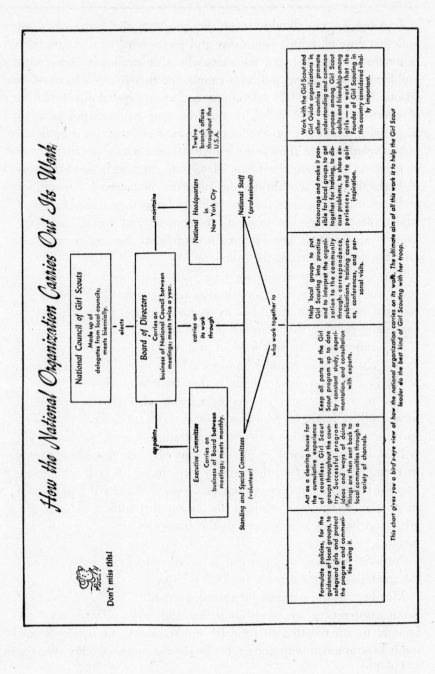

Don't miss this!

National Council of Girl Scouts
Made up of delegates from local councils; meets biennially.

elects

Board of Directors
Carries on business of National Council between meetings; meets twice a year.

appoints

maintains

National Headquarters in New York City

Twelve branch offices throughout the U.S.A.

Executive Committee
Carries on business of Board between meetings; meets monthly.

carries on its work through

Standing and Special Committees (volunteer)

National Staff (professional)

who work together to

Formulate policies, for the guidance of local groups, to safeguard girls and protect the program and communities using it.

Act as a clearing house for the cumulative experience of countless Girl Scout groups throughout the country. Successful program ideas and ways of doing things are then sent back to local communities through a variety of channels.

Keep all parts of the Girl Scout program up to date by constant study, experimentation, and consultation with experts.

Help local groups to put Girl Scouting into practice and to interpret the organization to the community through: correspondence, publications, training courses, conferences, and personal visits.

Encourage and make it possible for local groups to get together for training, to discuss problems, to share experiences, and to gain inspiration.

Work with the Girl Scout and Girl Guide organizations in other countries to promote understanding and common purpose among Girl Scout adults and friendship among girls — a work that the Founder of Girl Scouting in this country considered vitally important.

This chart gives you a bird's-eye view of how the national organization carries on its work. The ultimate aim of all this work is to help the Girl Scout leader do the best kind of Girl Scouting with her troop.

and pamphlets on all aspects of the program; the magazines and bulletins through which volunteers and professional workers are kept in touch; the national staff members who visit localities to help with problems, give training, and visit camps; the thousands of letters that go out from National Headquarters each year, answering questions of every variety; the publicity material and national publicity in magazines, syndicates, and radio that assist each local group to do its public relations job; the camping material and advice on all manner of camping problems; the financial services, to give help on matters of budgeting and accounting; the programs at national conventions and regional conferences that are planned for mutual stimulation and study; these are services generally recognized and appreciated. Not so well understood, yet even more important, are other and less tangible services, such as the following.

The Girl Scout program, for example, is kept up to date by constant study, research, and consultation with experts. In this way the national organization furnishes to its local groups a product that is capable of holding the attention of girls and of meeting their needs.

Experimentation in the field of training is constantly conducted so that national staff members and local councils will have the benefit of the best opinion and methods as they train adult leaders.

The national organization keeps in touch with other organizations in the allied fields of education, social work, and recreation. The specialists on its staff are active in organizations relating to their work.

In order that its local groups may have the benefit of new trends in thought and practice, the various ways in which councils administer Girl Scouting and meet their problems are analyzed and studied in relation to the best available theory on this subject. The results are given back to local groups in the form of standards and recommended procedures.

National policies are analyzed in relation to local situations and interpretations of them made for local groups.

Members of the national organization attend Girl Guide and Girl Scout conferences in other countries and older Girl Scouts are brought together with girls from foreign countries. Thus Girl Scouting is kept in touch with and profits by developments of other nations.

GIRL SCOUT REGIONS

The states included in the regional division are as follows:

NUMBER OF REGION	NAME	STATES INCLUDED
I	New England	Maine, Vermont, New Hampshire, Massachusetts, Connecticut, and Rhode Island
II	Hendrik Hudson	New York, New Jersey, Canal Zone, Puerto Rico, and Virgin Islands
III	Region III	Pennsylvania, Maryland, Delaware, Virginia, and District of Columbia
IV	Kenowva	Ohio, Kentucky, and West Virginia
V	Dixie	Tennessee, Arkansas, Mississippi, Alabama, and Louisiana
VI	Juliette Low	North Carolina, South Carolina, Georgia, and Florida
VII	Great Lakes	Wisconsin, Michigan, Illinois, and Indiana
VIII	Covered Wagon	Colorado, Iowa, Kansas, Missouri, Nebraska, and Wyoming
IX	Cactus	New Mexico, Oklahoma, and Texas
X	Hiawatha	North Dakota, South Dakota, and Minnesota
XI	Pacific Northwest	Montana, Idaho, Oregon, Washington, and Alaska
XII	Big Tree	California, Nevada, Arizona, Utah, Hawaii, and Guam

THE NATIONAL EQUIPMENT SERVICE

Uniforms, insignia, accessories, program materials, and books—all these and many more tempting articles are listed in the Girl Scout *Equipment Catalog* and *Publications Catalog*. The *Equipment Catalog* is sent free to every registered leader and Girl Scout. The Girl Scout *Publications Catalog* is free to every registered leader. The *Equipment Catalog* explains how to order, and just which items of official equipment may be purchased only by registered members of the organization. Books and miscellaneous equipment may be purchased without credentials. In addition to direct mail order service from the National Equipment Service in New York, and its branches in St. Louis and San Francisco, equipment may be purchased in authorized equipment agencies throughout the country. If there is a store in your city, by all means visit it—look over the books and equipment most useful to you.

HINTS FOR EFFICIENT SERVICE WHEN ORDERING BY MAIL

1. You order materials for your troop and yourself on the order forms provided with the *Equipment Catalog* and the *Publications Catalog*.

2. Official equipment—consisting of the uniforms, Girl Scout pins, badges and other insignia, and flags—may not be ordered until the troop is registered at National Headquarters. Printed matter may be ordered at any time.

3. A Girl Scout (troop scribe or any other member of the troop) may not order official equipment unless the order is approved in writing by the leader.

4. All orders sent to the National Equipment Service must be accompanied by check or money order (or stamps if the amount of the order is less than fifty cents). Coins should not be sent through the mail. The National Equipment Service cannot carry charge accounts or ship orders C.O.D., because of the large amount of capital as well as the additional clerical force this would involve.

The National Equipment Service will send a copy of the Girl Scout *Equipment Catalog* and the *Publications Catalog* upon request at any time.

The National Training Plan

One of the most important contributions that the Girl Scout organization has made to all social group work, as well as to the development of its own program, is that of training for the volunteer. Courses in leadership, in program planning, and in various special program activities, such as arts and crafts, camping, nature, music, folk dancing, and so on, are made available by both the local and national organizations. They are offered at conferences and institutes, in local communities, and in camps used as national training schools in every section of the country. You can obtain information about these courses, their content, length of time, location, and cost from your local office, if you have one, from the national branch office in your region, and from National Headquarters.

A Correspondence Course is conducted by National Headquarters for lone troop leaders and leaders who are under small councils without a professional worker.

The national training plan suggests many other forms of training that you will enjoy and find available locally. Conferences with other leaders, planned either by the leaders' club, the local office, or informally by a small group, settle many a problem. You can get good ideas and increased self-confidence by going to other troops, either as a temporary assistant, or for purposes of observation. You can visit school groups or play groups composed of girls approximately the same age as those in your troop and observe their interests and how the leaders or teachers develop programs and happy group relationships. Another source of help comes from having an experienced leader or professional worker visit your troop and talk with you after she has seen your girls in action. A wealth of opportunities for self-training exists in every community—lectures, radio programs, Girl Scout publications, books and magazines.

[363]

P.S.

Well, how did you like this book?

We know that you can learn far more from your girls themselves than you could gain from fifty books; still, we hope that this particular book will prove to be an acceptable guide, counselor, and friend.

As you work with your troop, you will be faced with all kinds of situations for which you will need guidance and information. Please use the Index that follows, for we believe that the majority of your questions are answered in this book. If you do not find the information that you need, write to Girl Scouts of the United States of America, 155 East 44th Street, New York 17, N. Y. We shall be glad to help you.

Index

Activity record, group, 160-163
Activities. *See also* Intermediate program
  appreciation, 193-195
  creative, 195-197
  problem-solving, 197
  skill, 197-200
Age groups, three Girl Scout, 9
Age range in Girl Scout troops, 27
Agriculture field, 92-96
American Flag, 61
American Girl, The, 62
American Red Cross, 348
Appreciation activities, 193-195
Arts and Crafts field, 97-101
  chart showing project in, 98
  creed for, 99
Association council, 342
  leaders' club in, 345

Baden-Powell, Lady, 352 (*ill.*)
Baden-Powell, Lord, 7, 352 (*ill.*), 355
  definition of Scouting, 351-353
  ideas on individual training, 297
  ideas on need for Girl Scouting, 351
Baden-Powell, Agnes, 351
Badges, 9, 65, 69-73
  charts showing plan for earning, 68, 70, 72, 74
  credit for work done in school, 71
  "Don'ts for Earning," 80 (*ill.*)
  guide for developing, 73
  for junior high school age, 71
  proficiency, as distinguished from rank, 65
  standards for, 71, 73
  time needed for earning, 71
Board of Directors, 358

Brownie Scout program launched, 356
Brownie Scouts, 9, 28-29

Camping responsibilities of Girl Scout council, 344
Ceremonies
  closing, 39-44, 47, 49-50
  Flag, 41
  investiture, 56-58
  troop birthday, 55
Character education, 296-321. *See also* Citizenship training
  leaders' records of, 306-321
  methods for, 299-303
  moral code, 303-306
  personality and ability of leader for, 297-299
Check lists, use in finding interests, 214-217
Churches and synagogues, 346-347
Citizens in Action, 353
Citizenship training, 10-13, 159. *See also* Character education
  Girl Scouting as an aid in, 7
  importance of, 3
Civic organizations, 348
Community cooperation, 20-22, 322-349
  churches and synagogues, 346-347
  civic organizations, 348
  in a democratic way, 325-326
  parents, 333-336
  program consultants, 336-342
  public libraries, 347-348
  schools, 346
  sponsoring groups, 332-333
  synagogues and churches, 346-347
  troop committees, 326-332

[365]

[367]

[368]